There are some losses in life that are so ɑ̲̲̲̲̲̲ ̲̲̲̲̲̲̲̲̲̲̲̲̲̲̲̲̲̲̲̲̲̲̲̲̲̲̲ ̲̲̲̲̲̲̲̲̲̲̲̲̲̲ that grief support and education are paramount. The death of a child is one of those. In 2002, my only child, Erika, died at the age of 32 from an extremely rare sinus cancer. As I looked around for the type of grief support I knew I desperately needed, I was stunned to find that it simply did not exist. That is when griefHaven was born. Today, the *griefHaven.org* website receives over a million visits a year from around the world and provides unique, loving, and educational grief support, which includes a focus on the science of the grieving brain.

Cynthia's journey took her to a similar place—a place out of her own desperation that led her to the world of research and education regarding the science of the afterlife. Cynthia needed to know whether or not she would ever see her daughter again. Her studies took her far and wide as she studied and stayed open to any credible information that might have evidence of life after death: From the origin of religion to quantum particles of energy; from consciousness to the power within us; from mediums to near-death experiences; from how the universe formed to the chemistry of our physical body. From her personal journey came the breathtaking and thought-provoking book *The Day My World Stopped*.

This is not just another grief book. This is an adventure that ties together two worlds: a mother's love, and science. In *The Day My World Stopped*, Cynthia Mitchell tells a story that will warm your heart, reminds you why every day is a gift, and presents you with a unique look into the world of science and of the afterlife. I highly recommend this book to all.

—**Susan Whitmore, BSBM, CGC**—
Founder and CEO / Integrative Grief Counselor
Professional Speaker: *https://griefhaven.org/inquire-about-speakers/*

"This remarkable autobiographical account is one of the most articulate descriptions of what it is like to lose a beloved daughter I've come across. It joins love, grief, and intellectual curiosity about consciousness and the operations of the universe in an amazing, synchronous way. This is a beautiful, powerful book. Do not deny yourself the opportunity of partaking in Cynthia Mitchell understanding."

—**Larry Dossey, MD**—
Author: One Mind: How Our Individual Mind Is Part of
a Greater Consciousness and Why It Matters

A MOTHER'S EXTRAORDINARY JOURNEY TO FIND PROOF OF

—— ETERNAL LIFE ——

THE DAY MY WORLD STOPPED

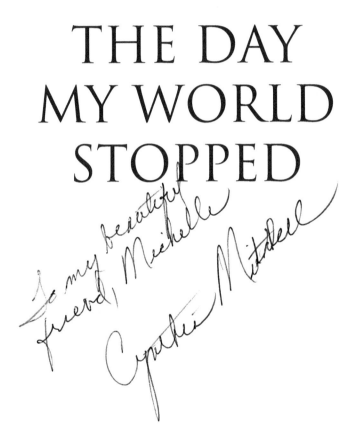

To my beautiful friend, Michelle

Cynthia Mitchell

CYNTHIA MITCHELL

ISBN: 978-1-78324-164-4 (paperback)
ISBN: 978-1-78324-165-1 (hardback)
ISBN: 978-1-78324-168-2 (ebook)

Library of Congress Control Number: 2020913337

Edited by Jo-Ann Langseth
Published and designed by Wordzworth Publishing
Cover concept by Rudi at 99design

Disclaimer:

This book is the result of reading authoritative books on various subjects along with many years of research. If you think you see yourself on these pages, rest assured there are other authors with similar interests and thoughts. It was those interlinking thoughts that caused me to form my own thoughts and put them into this book.

In memory of my amazing daughter, Breana and dedicated to her son, Owen, his adorable little sisters, Josephine and Samantha and to their dad, Ben.

CONTENTS

FOREWORD

I was so grateful for Cyndi's call, asking me if I would like to write the foreward for her new book, *The Day My World Stopped*. My world stopped on January 23, 2020, when my beloved mother passed. Mom suffered with COPD for over 20 years, but was blessed with a very peaceful passing. In fact, we were all blessed with the beauty and ease of her transition.

Cyndi did not know of my mother's passing before she called. As she and I began talking, we discovered that we had both been meditating for the previous three days. Interestingly, neither one of us had made meditation a priority in our everyday routine. Was it a coincidence that we picked the same time to make it a priority? Meditation can open a channel for intuitive thoughts to drop into your lap. On the third day, my body began to oddly tremble—sort of freaking me out. In Cyndi's meditation, *"Call Lorrie"* passed through her mind. I can't help thinking I was feeling that connection.

A few hours after her call, Cyndi was at my house and I was able to share with her the beautiful parting gifts my mother left behind: pictures of the colorful flowers she had grown, a long-lost family video, and many memories she captured in writing. Finding these hidden treasurers brought me comfort and I can't help thinking Mom unknowingly left them for that purpose. Cyndi experienced the same thing when she lost her daughter. At the most opportune times, she would discover a note her daughter had written for her, or a card or a photo. Most importantly, Cyndi found an "ear marked" book of her daughter's that started her journey to find the answers she so desperately needed.

How ironic that shortly after my mother's passing and our phone call the rest of the world would be stopped as well due to the COVID-19 virus. In some ways, I am grateful for this quarantine, as it allowed me the time to concentrate on writing this foreward and to reflect on what's happened to me since Mom's passing. I know Mom was set free and I believe she wanted that freedom for me, also. *Why?* While in my shattered state, I was driving my car when the sunlight blasted through my windshield and I heard these words: "flush the pills…my hopeful lungs…I can breathe again…step into a new day." *What?* I stopped the car and wrote down the name of the song, *Burn the Ships,* by For King and Country. I had never heard that song before, but I've heard it several times since. That song helped me face my fears and "step into a new day."

The pain of any loss can darken everything around us, stopping us in our tracks or propelling us into something we never thought possible. *The Day My World Stopped* is a testament for turning darkness around. In her search to find scientific evidence that would support proof of eternal life, Cyndi sheds light on the fears many have surrounding death, the mysterious quantum world, consciousness, and so much more. Our losses don't have to stop us, nor does fear have to stop us. Instead, let them take you in a different direction or lead you into a deeper awareness. Cyndi had no intention of writing a book. In fact, she felt she was stepping into another fearful unknown. It was Cyndi's desire to ease people's suffering that led her to overcome that fear and share her years of research and heartfelt writing with others.

I am ever an optimist and am happy to stay in my bubble, looking for all the good out there. I wake up each day and ask the universe what wonderful surprises am I going to receive today? Today, it was Cyndi and a copy of her new book fresh off my printer. Cyndi is one of those open souls who rediscovered faith, hope, and love. Her desire to bring faith, hope, and love to others will be realized as they read these pages.

Lorrie Larsen, Trusted friend and co-author of the chapter on "Coincidence"

PREFACE

We begin asking questions as children, and until we are old enough to reason things out for our self, we accept whatever answers we're given. However, as we reach the age of reason, we begin to question some of those answers. When I lost my only child, Breana, every unanswered question I had asked throughout the years came to the forefront. Where did she go? Do heaven and hell exist? If so, did she cross the "t"s and dot the "i"s required to pass through the "Pearly Gates" as outlined in the Bible? Is there any truth to these things? Is God even real? We are expected to accept, on faith, that these things are true. But for me, finding proof became my only option. Since no one had found proof, I expected to spend the rest of my life looking for it. Time didn't matter—nothing mattered except finding proof I would someday be with Breana again.

Unsure where to find the answers to my questions, I looked up and said, "Where is my Breana?" Knowing full well it was unlikely that anyone heard me, I wrapped myself in sorrow and fell asleep. The next morning, I awoke with the thought that I should drive to my and Breana's cabin on Mt. Baker. The cabin was our special place so I didn't want to go there, knowing she would never be coming with me. I ignored the urge to drive up to the cabin for as long as I could, but the thought wouldn't go away. I finally gave in and started the two-hour drive, crying as I drove. I foolishly envisioned her standing in the doorway to welcome me in.

Moving past my sadness that she wasn't there, I pushed the door open and began walking through the cabin, touching the things she had touched. I sadly thought, *Why am I here? This was all in my head!* I decided to look on the bookshelf, hoping one of them might bring me some degree of comfort. One by one, I pulled them off of the bookshelf but found nothing that could help me. I began to put them back when I noticed one I had not seen before. It had two markers in it—torn sticky notes, the kind Breana always used. One marker under the chapter CHILDREN and the other under LOSS! I could almost hear Breana say, "Wow, Mom, it took you long enough!" I knew that was the reason I was there.

The book was written by a medium. My religion taught me to shy away from mediums, but here I was holding this book. Who was leading me? God or Satan? *Don't be afraid, Cyndi. Just go with it for now…* I thought. It felt right; and I quickly wanted to know all about mediums. I began reading every book I could find on the topic. Those books led me to more questionable reading and, finally, into the world of energy and quantum mechanics. From there, the search for answers included delving into consciousness, the chemistry of our body, the workings of the universe, the power of thought, the origin of religions, who God is, and more. Without a doubt, I was led by a loving presence that knew where I would find my answers.

I am in awe at how this journey began and am grateful I acted on the urge to drive to the cabin. If I had chosen not to, would I have found another path or would I still be wrapped in uncertainty and sorrow? Because I acted on that urge, I found an abundance of scientific evidence that supports proof of eternal life. For me, I know with certainty we cannot die and I will be with Breana again. I was also grateful to discover there really is a loving presence which hears us, and learning to trust in the urges and little nudges it presents to us, will help guide us along the way.

My desire in writing this book is to help others remove the many fears they may have surrounding death, and to turn the *hope* of an everlasting life into a certainty.

CHAPTER 1

THE DAY MY
WORLD STOPPED

*"Death leaves a heartache no one can heal,
love leaves a memory no one can steal."*

— FROM AN IRISH HEADSTONE —

Without exception, everyone's life is dotted with highlights that bring joy and lowlights that bring sorrow or disappointment. Most of them are out of our control—they just happen. In fact, they never stop happening, and we are forced to respond to them. These happenings, as well as the people coming in and out of our lives, are what cause us to stop, refocus, and sometimes change the direction our life was going in. As children, we seldom question the purpose of happenings, but as time goes by, we begin to ask why.

My brightest highlight, and the day my life began anew, was the day my daughter, Breana (Bre), was born—May 25, 1976. The second brightest was when she gave birth to my grandson, Owen— Nov. 28, 2005. Bre brought me many warm and bright lights, and

I thought that would continue throughout my life. That didn't happen. The world I knew ended when she was taken from me, and the bright lights she created stopped. It was one month before we would celebrate her thirtieth birthday. I knew there would be no birthday celebration—no more of anything with my Bre.

I remember that day, and the circumstances around it, as though it were yesterday. My home had been demolished, and I was living in the little apartment in my friend Les's house. I was planning to remodel my home, but instead Les and I decided to tear it down and build one together. Bre was having a baby; in fact, everyone was having babies. We wanted a big home that would accommodate our families and extended families on special occasions. Everyone could be in one place. Bre thought I was crazy to tear the house down, but she loved large family gatherings. I was looking forward to her input during the construction. Suddenly, all joy was gone. Without Bre, I no longer wanted the big family home. I would sell the property and not finish the construction.

If it weren't for Bre's husband, Ben, that is what I would have done. He felt that even though it would not be the same home Bre grew up in, it would be where she grew up. He wanted to hold on to as many memories as he could for their son. I agreed that he was right. I was frozen and not mentally present during the construction, but the house was built using the blueprint, and we moved in eight months later. The home Bre and I shared together was gone, and she would never be in the new one. I had planned my future with Bre in it, and I couldn't see a different one.

The day Bre left I had friends from Arizona visiting for the weekend, so she let Owen spend the night with us. Of course, she called to check in on him and say hi to our friends. It was a brief call, and the last time I spoke with my daughter. After all this time that still makes my heart sink—you never think it is the last time. The next day was beautiful, and my friend's husband and Les were already on the golf course. My friend, Kate, and I were looking forward to some playtime with Owen. It was going to be a very fun day. Then, in an instant, the day became dark. We were sitting on the floor laughing and playing with Owen when the phone rang. It was the fire department abruptly telling me my daughter had died. How could anyone be so cruel? *Was this some kind of sick prank call?*

I screamed into the phone, "Who is this?"

He apologized and repeated that my daughter was gone.

He was wrong! We were looking forward to going to her cousin's wedding shower later that day. *As soon as I can open my eyes, this nightmare will end.* There was nothing on my radar warning me of this cataclysmic event. She was a part of me! I would feel something if anything ever happened to my Bre. *How did I not feel this?*

I frantically drove to her home and jumped out running. Ben's brother had arrived before me and was trying to console Ben. No one said anything, but there were men in uniform everywhere and more family was arriving. I looked around and saw everything she loved still in her home, right where she had put it; everyone she loved—still here. *She wouldn't leave us! This can't be true!* I don't know how many times I said that. Even when you know it is true, it takes years to actually accept it is true. I ran to her bedroom and saw my daughter lying on the floor where Ben had desperately tried to revive her. He knew it was too late, but, like me, he couldn't believe she wouldn't come back. Although they tried, no one could stop me from running to her side and begging her to wake up.

I cried, "Where are you? Please hear me, Bre!"

I couldn't accept that she wouldn't open her eyes and say, "I'm okay now, Mom. I came back."

I held her delicate cold hand as they took her away on that awful gurney and watched as they drove out of sight with my Bre. I would never hold my beautiful daughter again.

I walked slowly back into their home and grabbed a towel from her kitchen, as the tears would not stop flowing. I kept that towel, and still hold it, as though the essence of her is in it. That was the day my world stopped. The pain was unbearable, while the shock and disbelief literally froze everything in place. I remember thinking it was like any other day to the rest of the world. Cars were moving up and down the street, and children were walking to the nearby school. *Couldn't they feel something cataclysmic had happened?* She was my life, and now she was gone. I just wanted all of it to end when I knew we would never talk again. *Please, come back...* After that, everything was a blur.

The next thing I remember was sitting in my apartment, staring into the darkness. The day had gone and night had fallen, but I had no lights on. Ben's family had come to pick up Owen that morning, so even he was gone from me. My friends and Les were upstairs. I wanted to be alone in the apartment, and I felt I would always be alone without my Bre. Family was concerned and stopping by, flowers were being sent, and food was dropped off, but I couldn't respond. I was so engulfed in my own pain that I didn't recognize the loss others were suffering. Self-pity was a trap I easily fell into, but at the time I didn't care. I'm so sorry I couldn't have shown compassion to my wonderful friends and family. I'm grateful they understood and allowed me the time to move through the unbearable pain.

The days that followed seemed to move in slow motion. There was a dark cloud surrounding me that not even the sun could break through. My friends from Arizona extended their stay to help in any way they could, and we had a funeral to prepare for. I agonized over what Bre might have wanted and voiced that to Ben. He said he felt he knew, and ultimately it was his decision. I had been Bre's mom for twenty-nine years, but now she was Ben's wife. I had never thought about that before, but it was real to me now. He had lost his wife, the mother of his son and the love of his life. I was in second place. Ben chose to have a "family only" service and an open house at their home for all of her friends. He knew her well. She would never have wanted a big, sad funeral or to be the center of attention. And, she loved to gather all of her friends together whenever they were in town. In fact, that was a memory they shared with me that day. She was the glue that kept everyone connected.

I remember telling Ben I wanted flowers, lots of flowers—flowers everywhere. This was the last thing I would be able to do for my daughter, and I wanted her to have lots of flowers. When that day came, there were beautiful flowers. My friends who owned the Buzz Inn Restaurants catered all of the food, and Bre's friends made a poster board of her life. She had and has amazing friends. We all did, and they were all there. People shared personal memories they had of Bre. I knew I couldn't make new ones, so I loved hearing theirs. I wanted to disappear that day, but it was good to be with her friends and listen to the memories they had of my Bre.

I'd always viewed funerals as totally sad events, as I never knew what to say or do that would bring any comfort to the ones in despair. Now, I knew—I wanted people to feel comfortable talking about Bre. The stories I had never heard and the personal impact she made on their lives was like a bed of roses to rest on. In fact, I will always love hearing stories about my Bre. Recently, a friend found a picture of Bre and gave it to me. It was an old picture to her friend, but it was a new picture to me. I couldn't take new pictures of Bre, so an old picture I'd never seen felt like I had taken a new one. I loved taking pictures of her, and she would roll her eyes every time she heard my camera turn on. That memory makes me smile, and throughout this book I've scattered fun memories of Bre.

I didn't know if Bre had gone somewhere or ceased to exist. The Bible offered hope of eternal life, but I had many doubts in the credibility of the Bible. Those doubts had begun forming early in my life, and I explain how that happened as you read on.

CHAPTER 2

THE BIBLE OFFERED NO COMFORT FOR ME

*"Most people do not see their beliefs.
Instead, their beliefs tell them what to see."*

— MATT KAHN —

I was preceded by two brothers and followed by a sister. My first brother died at birth. My mother's religion taught that people were born sinful, and without baptism they wouldn't be allowed into Heaven—including her precious baby. Sadly, limbo and purgatory are not sanctified by all religions—a place, other than hell, for the unbaptized to spend eternity. In the following years, religions that once held the belief that all unbaptized were condemned changed their interpretation, and in the updated version, babies are excluded. For hundreds of years, people agonized over that old doctrine, and it made me wonder what else had been misunderstood.

Jesus said in Matthew 19:14, "Let the children come to me, and do not hinder them, for the kingdom of heaven belongs to such as these." My father believed that. He was raised Mormon (The Church of Jesus Christ of Latter-Day Saints), and they taught that babies were to be blessed and not held accountable for baptism until they were eight years old. Prior to that age, they would be incapable of committing sin. By age eight, they would know what sin was and be able to understand why baptism was necessary. It's understandable why my parents chose to raise their family in that religion.

I remember the day I was baptized. It was a really big day! I was dressed all in white, I was excited, and everyone was excited for me. I was magically saved when they cleansed my soul in the water—in the name of the Father, the Son, and the Holy Spirit. My sins were forgiven; the Holy Spirit was with me, Jesus was in my heart, and I would be with Him throughout eternity. Obviously, all that I understood about baptism was what my religion taught me in my Sunday school class.

The practice of the Mormon baptism was to be completely submerged in water, not just sprinkled. Only then would one be truly baptized. That was not true of other religions, but it was the ritual John the Baptist used, so Mormons believed baptism should be performed in that way. Tradition and ritual are important in most religions, just as they are important in any organized group. Wikipedia says, "Rituals create a unison of the mind, giving an inclusive strength to the forum." I became aware that different religions had their own set of rituals, but it seemed they should all be the same if God had anything to do with it. The Bible said God required baptism, but it appeared to me more like a ritual created by man to set their religion apart from other religions.

Joining the Mormon religion gave my mom the relief she needed. The baby she had lost was safe and saved. It was great to know we were all saved—until I heard that Mormons were pagans and not saved after all. The Bible teaches that infidels and pagans were to be converted or killed, so that wasn't a good label to hold. Converted to what, I wondered? I assumed my father knew everything, so I asked him. He said we were Christians, not pagans, so I thought perhaps they were the ones who had it wrong.

I was thirteen when we left the Mormon Church. Mom finally had enough of the hypocrisy. It seems no matter how devout a person believes he or she is, they can be selfish, judgmental, envious, greedy, and etc. It's hard to see the double-standard blind spots in ourselves when we feel righteous, forgiven, and saved. Mom wanted us to know God in other ways than from religion. She was never judgmental, nor held the least bit of prejudice toward others. That was the God she wanted us to know. I didn't give religion a lot of thought after that until I was older. Confusion and questions arose with each disappointment life threw at me.

I revisited religion when Bre's father and I divorced. I joined my brother's Bible study group hoping to find answers and a better understanding of "God's" Word. His wife, my best friend from high school, had been raised Lutheran, and he joined that church when they married. I found no comfort in that religion either, as my interpretations sometimes differed from those of the minister who led the Bible study group. He explained he was a "learned man," and the Bible said we should accept the teachings of learned men. It was hard to trust a "learned man" when there were so many learned men with different interpretations. I couldn't blindly accept his interpretation when I understood it differently. The Bible was written for all of mankind, so why did I need any learned man to tell me what it said? The minister told me I was seeing only what I wanted to see. That wasn't true, so again, I was filled with doubt in the learned man's understanding of the Bible. Might it be *he* who was seeing only what he wished to see?

I read the Bible three times, cover to cover, in an attempt to understand it for myself. The Old Testament said God required a blood sacrifice, so we killed an innocent animal to show our allegiance to Him—or even a child, if that's what He asked of us. Genesis 22:1 describes the test of faith God put Abraham through by asking him to sacrifice his son, Issac. At the last moment, Abraham and his son were spared that agony because by his willingness to kill Issac, Abraham passed the test before it was too late. No matter how many blessings He bestowed on Abraham afterwards, that God seemed cruel to me, even sadistic. I wondered why people ever pledged their allegiance to someone who could be so cruel.

Jesus was the Savior who'd paid the ultimate sacrifice to God, so no more sacrifices were required of us. I had a hard time accepting sacrifice of any kind, including the killing of so-called infidels, and all other forms of cruelty I found in the Bible. I felt the Bible held a chronicle of ancient events and prophetic messages that were believed to have come from God, but it was "learned men" who translated and interpreted those ancient writings.

Where were those prophets today? Did they disappear with the last word in the Bible? "Modern-day prophets" didn't inspire the same respect that the ancient prophets do, and did. I had read that God spoke only to the ancients to establish His church. Again, that struck me as odd, especially since there were so many religions professing to be His one and only church. I had been advised to pray and read the Bible because all the answers were in there. I did that, and found myself back to square one—the learned man's interpretations.

I felt God must be answering prayer for those in every religion, and not just one, or there would be nothing to base their religion on. I was told Satan was always on the lookout to cause pain and confusion, and was therefore sneakily answering prayers for the members of other religions. Wow! So, when I prayed to God, I couldn't trust God was answering me? If the One to whom I prayed was my Father in Heaven, surely He would be happy I was talking to Him and not allow Satan to intercept our communication. I felt

God would have absolute power—including over Satan. Life was complicated enough without worrying that He would hang me out to dry with Satan and not protect my conversation with Him.

The final break from the Lutheran Church, came when the minister's sermon had to do with which religions were pagan. He said that if the followers of those religions didn't change what they believed, they would be condemned to everlasting torment in hell. I guess that's better than killing them, which had been the custom in earlier times. That sermon was probably directed at me, since we had discussed the Mormon religion. It occurred to me that turning religion against religion was turning people against people. I knew people from many of the "pagan" religions and traditions he had spoken against, and I liked them. Was God so self-centered and cruel that He would condemn those caring people to the agonizing flames of hell for all eternity because their interpretation was different? I got up and left that day and never went back. Mom was right: if God existed, I would not find Him through religion. I also concluded that the Bible had more ideas of "learned men" in it than of God's.

Above all, Jesus emphasized love and forgiveness. Punishment was not central to His teachings, as was the tradition, but rather mercy and forgiveness. He wanted us to know how fully and unconditionally God loves everyone, regardless of their status, religion, or nationality. Jesus was a Hebrew who practiced the Jewish faith. He did not create the Christian religion; man did that many years after His death. Jesus dissolved the imaginary walls between God and man, showing that we do not need an intercessor or a clergyman to know, love, and *speak with Him*. He taught us we could speak directly to Him ourselves, and He to us.

Jesus was a teacher, and like many Jewish boys, most likely educated in a synagogue on the temple grounds. It seemed He was able to read and write, but no one knows for certain. His thoughts were important, so I often wondered why He didn't write them down. Do you suppose He did, and they were lost or destroyed? After all, because His radical teachings threatened the very existence of the "learned men" of that day, Jesus became a condemned criminal. It was believed He was a descendant of King David, so was He really a peasant? His body was put in a rich man's tomb instead of the criminal's graveyard, which was the custom. And who was Joseph of Arimathea, the rich man who risked his life to petition Pilate for the body of the criminal, Jesus, and then put Him in his coveted family tomb? Was he a follower or a family member? Most followers were in hiding. So much is simply not known about Jesus, and the things Jesus taught were written as recalled and interpreted by other men.

I needed proof of eternal life and that I would see Bre again, but I didn't know where else to look for that answer. I was concerned that turning my back on religion was the wrong path, but I found no comfort there. It was as though I was staring into a dark alley that I was afraid to enter, but I had no choice. If there was any chance of finding answers, I would need to find them in the things that jumped out at me from inside that dark alley.

CHAPTER 3

ENTRANCE TO MY DARK ALLEY

"Ask and it will be given to you. Seek and you will find. Knock, and the door will be opened for you. For everyone who asks receives."

— MATTHEW 7:7-8 —

That is a beautiful passage, and I now believe it is the truth. God was a mystery to me, yet when all hope was gone, I always turned to prayer. I pleaded with God, "Where is my Bre?" When my father passed, I accepted his death and chose to believe he was with God and I would see him again. I couldn't accept Bre's death, so such assurances were no longer enough.

Sadly, the fear of hell had been ingrained into my mind as a child, causing me concern. I hoped Bre had crossed all her "t"s and dotted all her "i"s, so that she could now be with God. If for some unknown reason she was in hell, I would never leave her all alone. Wherever she had gone was where I wanted to be, and I voiced this in prayer just in case there was a God and everything I learned as a child were true.

Bre knew how I felt about religion and the doubts I had about God, but more importantly, so did God. As shocking as it seemed, I believed I was being led down a forbidden path (according to the Bible) to find answers. This was the entrance to my dark alley:

I awoke one morning with an overwhelming sense that I should drive to our cabin. I will explain the significance of the cabin in a later chapter. I didn't think I could ever go there again. The pain of knowing Bre would never be there was more than I could handle. It was our place, and it was the last place she and Ben had taken Owen. She called it their first "mini-family vacation." Yet, here I was, feeling compelled to drive up there. *What did that mean?* I foolishly hoped she might be there. I had to go!

I arrived, opened the door, and was hit with an overwhelming sense of loss. *She's not here. Why am I here?* I felt there had to be a reason. There were a few thought-provoking books there, and I wondered if that might perhaps be the reason. I pulled some of them off the bookshelf and began to read. *No, this isn't it. Why had I felt the need to come here? That sense of urgency was all in my head.* I needed to leave! I walked back to the bookshelf and began to put them back when I noticed a book by Sylvia Browne, *The Other Side and Back.* Sylvia was a well-known psychic and medium. I had never read, nor had I seen that book before. I wondered where it had come from. I noticed two markers in it—the kind Bre always used (a torn sticky note). One was in the chapter, CHILDREN and the other under LOSS. Overwhelmed, I couldn't understand how those markers had made it onto those pages. I was convinced that finding *The Other Side and Back* was the reason I felt compelled to drive to our cabin.

I didn't believe that the book had magically appeared, so I began to investigate where it might have come from. As it turned out, Wendy Goosman, whom Bre lovingly referred to as her "other mom," had given her a stack of books and believed that book was in it. It was possible Bre was looking for answers after she had her miscarriage. I explained that her baby was probably not well, and it wasn't meant to be. I didn't realize how cold that must have sounded to her. After I lost her, I revisited that conversation. I had no concept of the pain she surely felt, and wasn't there for her in the way she needed me to be. In her eyes, her unborn baby was her precious baby, and she was suffering great loss. Those two chapters must have given her comfort, when I could not. Was it unrealistic to believe she led me to it, in the hope it would help me as well? It did make me wonder—in fact, more than wonder.

It didn't feel accidental, so I brought the book home with me and began to read. If I was being divinely led, I wondered why it was to a book written by a medium? I was taught their messages were deceitful, even demonic, and that it was a sin to seek their counsel instead of God's. I felt genuine comfort from reading *The Other Side and Back*. Browne's words gave me hope in eternal life and in an infinite power that loves us and whom some refer to as God. I needed more information about mediums before I would pass judgment. *The Other Side and Back* was only an intro to the many things that jumped out at me while making my way down that dark alley. However, before we go deeper into the alley, you may want a little history of my and Breana's life.

CHAPTER 4

MOTHERHOOD

"A mother holds her child's hand for a short time, but holds their hearts forever."

— WISE QUOTES —

I was married in 1970 to a friend I knew from high school. While dating, we both decided to become hairdressers. He left college and I quit my job at Boeing. A year later we were working in his parents' salon, and six years after that, Breana was born. Like most couples, we had many dreams for our future. Instead, we were divorced after seven years, which of course was never in that dream. In many ways a divorce can feel like a death. There is heartache and pain for all people involved, and your once secure future is gone.

Our baby, Breana (Bre), was six months old at the time of the divorce. Afraid and alone, I knew I had to take care of myself and my daughter. When I was young, Mom advised me to choose a career so I would always be able to rely on myself. I had no idea how valuable that advice would be. Bre became my highest priority. With the support of family who pitched in to help watch her,

I was able to extend my hours at the salon. I was always worried about having enough money. What if she wanted to go to college? Would I be able to make that happen? What about private schools, medical and dental, extracurricular activities, and clothes? And what about maintaining a house with a yard for her to play in? All of those things were very important to me.

I discovered Bre's priorities were different from mine. I was feeling exhausted after working all day, and she sat down beside me and said, "You should go on welfare and not work so hard!" I'm not sure where she heard that, or how that notion got into her head. I know she was concerned for me, and I think she thought that would be the solution.

Did I make my little girl feel like a responsibility instead of a pleasure? That's hard for me to say with any certainty. As an adult, she understood and was proud of my work ethic and what it taught her. However, if I could do it over, I would focus more on "quality time." It takes only a moment to make someone feel special. Time seemed to be in short supply. I would hurry home from work to get things done: mow the lawn, pick things up, do the laundry, make dinner, give her a bath, and put her to bed—sometimes too tired for a bedtime story. Poor baby, what a stressed-out mother she had. It would be wonderful to live life with no regrets. But life doesn't work that way, and I often wonder if we learn anything without regret.

For me, divorce was a dirty word in the 1970s, and my religious teachings were at the cause of that. In fact, the minister told me it was a sin for me to remarry. I finally found help in another book outside of the Bible: *Your Erroneous Zones*, by Dr. Wayne Dyer. He helped me understand that I had power over how I chose to feel or respond to anything in life. What a concept! I didn't have to be a victim led by uncontrolled emotion, much less a despairing sinner. I accepted my true identity as a single mom and not a sinful divorcee. I finally let myself move forward without guilt.

Finding it hard to work with my husband after the divorce, I moved to another salon in a different city. I knew that to secure the future, I would need to own a salon one day. Aware of the commitment involved, it was something I actually never wanted to do. I had always envisioned myself as a mom like my mom, supported by her husband and raising their children together—so much for that vision. Seeing no other option, I began planning for my future as a single parent and becoming the sole provider.

My first step toward that goal was to form a partnership with the man I was working for. In truth, that was his and his wife's idea when I told them of my future plans. That worked well for a few years, but life changed again. Now, he and his wife were divorcing, putting me in the middle of a not-so-friendly battle. I loved both of them and wouldn't choose a side. We had two salons at the time. I offered to buy the one I was working in, and just like that, I was on my own. His wife, who was once my partner, was now a hairdresser working for me. She also became my landlord after the divorce settlement left the building to her.

She was now a single mother with two children of her own, and she had the same concerns I did as a single mother. The building was not in the best location for a salon. We knew we would have to move it one day when she felt more solid in her new circumstances. It took three years for that time to come around. There is no retirement in this business, so I knew I would have to invest my money wisely. Real estate, I believed, was the best place to put it. Knowing that, I began looking for a location to purchase and relocate the salon.

Of course, I needed a loan to purchase the 3500-square-foot building I had found, so off to the banks I went. Armed with a surveyed list of clients saying they would follow us to the new location, and a projection done by my accountant (a study of probable growth), the banks trusted me enough to take the risk. Plus, it helped that I owned my own home. Collateral is always a good thing. I had Mom and Dad to thank for that since my ex-husband and I had purchased it from them years earlier at a very good price.

The building I found needed extensive work, basically to be gutted and fitted with all new everything. That was quite a learning experience in itself. My daughter was twelve by this time and wasn't sure about my decision.

I can still hear her say, "Mom, no one is going to come to you there."

The yard was a jungle, the green paint was chipping off, and moss covered the roof. I certainly had to agree with her on that one. I assured her I would hire someone to fix it up.

"I hope so," she said.

If you knew Bre, you would have heard the sarcasm in those words, and it still makes me smile. It's interesting what time does. I can remember the sound of her voice, but I can't hear the actual sound. I loved her laugh. Oh, how I miss the sound of her.

Gene Goosman, the contractor I hired, was a client of the salon. The building needed new wiring, plumbing, and pretty much everything imaginable. He assured me I could go on vacation and trust that the job would be done. I didn't go on vacation, but he was true to his word. He redesigned the plans a salon designer had drawn for me and made them work. Bre and I became very good friends with him and his family during that time.

It was during that time also that I met my second husband. Oh my, how blind love can be! It's curious that we often see only the parts we want to see. That marriage lasted three years, as I struggled to hold on. I finally accepted that things would not change, and that it was I who had to make some changes. Most of my time and energy went into building my business and working on a doomed marriage, when I could have been spending it with my daughter in her high school years. These are the kinds of things I look back on and feel such sorrow. However, it's interesting how people come together. His sister became my best friend, and her husband was a building designer. Our friendship has lasted all of these years. Together we enlarged and remodeled the salon, adding a boutique and an espresso bar for her to manage. Gene was the contractor through all of it.

Bre was graduating from high school as that marriage was ending. I was never able to give her the family life I grew up with. I had two loving parents, an older brother, and younger sister to play with throughout my childhood. I felt sad that Bre didn't have that, and now it was too late.

When I shared this with her, she said, "Mom, we are our own family. We don't need anyone else."

She was so right, and I cherish that day. After all, it was all she knew, and she was fine with it. I was the one who wanted more for her.

Bre and I spent many weekends with Gene and Wendy at their cabin on Mt. Baker, skiing and just being with them. They will never know what a comfort it was to be with such a healthy and loving family. Their son and Bre had become best friends and, as I said, Wendy was her second mom. We often wondered if our children would get together, but Bre encouraged him to date a girl she thought would be perfect for him. Since they are now married with two boys of their own, I guess she was right.

In conversation one day at the Goosmans' cabin, the idea came up that we should buy our own cabin. Of course, that was Bre's idea. I was opposed—one more responsibility. I owned a house and a salon, as well as the property they were on that I needed to maintain. Why would I take on anything more? She had the solution: she would take care of the cabin and had saved enough money for the down payment. That made it hard to say no. She was nineteen years old.

Some might wonder how a young person could have saved that much money. I was always very careful with money, but Bre took it to a new level. When she was young, I gave her an old checkbook. I had Oprah to thank for that, as she had a program outlining the idea. In the checkbook, Bre would track the money she earned from her allowance and any monetary gift she received. I was the actual guardian of the money. When she wanted something, we would look in her checkbook to see if there was enough. She would then write me a check and deduct it from her check register.

As she got older and had a job in an espresso bar, she took it up a notch by putting the money into categories. I was no longer the guardian of her money. She divided it into a house fund, a car fund, and entertainment. I felt education was my responsibility. She wasn't interested in college, but I convinced her to take a few classes. She said it was just to humor me. She was a good sport that way. She never bought things she didn't need, and wouldn't dream of charging anything. She loved things that had already been used. She just couldn't see spending money on something new when secondhand would do. Bre thought everything should be recycled.

Well, we bought that cabin in the mountains, and in memory of my dad (who entertained us with his guitar and yodeling), I bought a guitar to place by the fireplace in hopes that someone would play it. That happened when Bre had friends over after skiing, one of whom entertained us by playing that guitar—what a fun memory to have of my daughter and Dad. It was an amazing place where worries just seemed to melt away. She told me I was a different person at the cabin, and she was right. I didn't feel the stress of the business or anything else, only the joy of hanging out with my daughter.

We spent holidays there and made our own Christmas decorations—paper chains and strings of popcorn. We enjoyed fun meals around a picnic table that we made into our dining room table. We upholstered cushions on the benches with our trusty staple gun, and it was transformed. We became so confident with that staple gun that we upholstered all the old furniture that was left there. I must say, I wasn't as confident about that as Bre was, but she was right—it turned out great. It was amazing what we could do together with very little money, a bit of work, and some imagination.

When New Year's Eve rolled around, Bre and a few of her friends decided they would celebrate up there. I warned her, the forecast was for snow—and did it ever! They were snowed in and lost power. The gas fireplace was not installed yet, so they could only burn wood. It was freezing inside the cabin; even the toilets were frozen. With nothing to do, they decided it would be fun to jump off the second-story deck to the snow below. She couldn't resist telling me about it, even knowing I wasn't going to see the same humor in it that she and her friends had.

Bre was always telling on herself. I once told her, when she was very young, that her eyes would turn green if she ever lied to me (I wonder if my eyes turned green). Bre knew if she told me the truth she wouldn't get in trouble, but if she lied, she would. Here's a cute memory:

She was playing with my expensive conditioner in the bathtub. I asked her if that was what I saw floating everywhere in the water. She quickly looked down and shook her head no. I asked her to look at me, and as she did, there were tears in her eyes and she was shaking her head yes. I can still see that whole scene in my mind, and it warms my heart. I thanked her for telling me the truth, and she never played with my conditioner again.

She knew she didn't have to lie to me; she could talk with me about anything without reprimand or judgment. Anyway, we had many great talks and wonderful walks in the fresh air and memories I will cherish forever—and all because of the cabin that I didn't want to purchase. I reimbursed her every penny of the down payment!

It wasn't long after that I met my best friend, Les. He seemed to like the cabin as much as we did. Bre and I had done some remodeling, like moving cupboards around, but Les helped take it to the next level. He showed Bre how to use a nail gun, and she was off. Together we were able to finish the basement, completing the half-plumbed bathroom and adding cedar to the cement walls and ceiling. We converted that ugly basement into a very cozy place where our friends could stay. Les jokingly said he thought the cabin was a place we came to for rest. He seemed to really enjoy any project we could dream up, but mostly I noticed how much he enjoyed my daughter. That spoke volumes to me.

Meeting Les was accidental. Some friends were going to Lake Havasu for a long weekend and invited me to come along. Their friends owned a vacation home there, and Les was one of the owners. The plan was to lie around the pool and drive to Laughlin for a little casino time while the guys played golf. Sounded fun to me, so off we went.

The first thing we did was walk through the house to the pool. I noticed a man sitting in a deck chair, sporting a red bathing suit. He had a dark tan, black horn-rimmed glasses, silver hair, and a cigar in his hand. He looked very serious. What would you think if you saw that? I wondered if he was the Godfather himself. But no, this was Les, and much to my relief, not a godfather—in fact, very much the opposite.

The weekend went as planned, with the girls doing their thing and the guys playing golf. As we were getting ready to leave for the airport, I made a comment about wearing my same old dirty jeans while making a gesture of brushing the dirt off. You know the routine—you bring a suitcase full of clothes and end up wearing the same thing.

Bre believed if it didn't fit in a backpack, you didn't need it. I never mastered packing the way she did. Then again, she had traveled to Europe and made road trips to California and Georgia. She joined a travel group in Africa where a silverback gorilla charged her, and a bird swooped in to steal her lunch. In Indonesia, she rode an elephant through a torrential downpour, and a monkey jumped on her back to slap her. I have the picture that captures the shock on her face. This was a trip Les had taken Bre and me on to celebrate his birthday. It was a wonderful memory and an awesome gift—especially to us. The world, with all of its people and animals, was very important to her. She wanted to see it all. Bre had learned to travel on a shoestring, and always with her trusty backpack. Ben, Bre's husband, told me he still has that trusty backpack.

After we returned home, my friend called and asked me to meet her and her husband for dinner. A bit later, Les walked in carrying a Nordstrom box. I was completely shocked when he handed it to me. We'd barely had a conversation all weekend, and here he was giving me a gift?!

He said, "It was your birthday, wasn't it?"

"Yes, but what's this for?"

"Open it," he said. It was a new pair of jeans! He even chose the right size and style.

I started laughing as he said, "I thought everyone should have at least two pair of jeans." That was how I met Les. I was forty-nine years old.

I was very happy with my life when I met Les, so I wasn't interested. He was persistent though, and the friendship that developed between him and my daughter finally gave him the green light. He was truly a friend to both my daughter and me. She was always invited, even on vacations. He was there for Bre whenever she called, and he was there for me through my darkest hour. Relationships can be good, but I had taken my daughter through some bad ones. You think you are protecting them from your experiences, but they go through each heartache with you. I was happy she finally saw a good one with Les.

Bre and Les developed their close friendship when they planned my fiftieth birthday party. Bre and I shared the same birthday. What an incredible gift she was! The nurse brought me a cup of ice cream with a candle on it to celebrate her birth with mine. Now, she was planning my fiftieth with more than ice cream.

Les told me that when he suggested it would be fun to celebrate the day on a harbor cruise line, she looked shocked and said, "I can't afford that!"

"Let me help you," Les said. That was all it took, and they were off and running!

He said when he saw her sit down in the middle of the store, surrounded by various colors of paper plates, trying to decide which colors I might like, he knew he was going to have fun—and they did!

By the way, Les surprised her with her own birthday cake and a huge poster of herself for everyone to sign. She was twenty-two. He truly was a good friend to Bre, and I am forever grateful for that.

Without my being aware of it, my child became an adult. My role as her parent had changed, and the advice she would seek from me was different. That hit me hard when she said it was time to move out and wanted my advice as to whether she should buy a house or rent an apartment. Moving out into the little house she purchased was a shock, but not as shocking as when she asked, "Mom, do you think Ben and I should get married?"

Ben was in the military and becoming a ranger. In order to receive any information about your enlisted loved one, you needed to be married. I didn't want Bre to make the mistakes I had and advised her to live with him first, but she didn't want to risk not knowing what was happening to him. She and Ben had gone together in high school and reunited as adults, so she believed she had found the right man—that sounded familiar. I agreed it was a serious decision that shouldn't be taken lightly.

I can still see the surprise on her face when I said, "Well, if you think you have the right ingredients to bake the cake, then bake the cake. However, if you find an ingredient is missing after you put it into the oven to bake, then I believe in divorce."

I just wanted her to know that a failed marriage wouldn't mean she was a failure. Life doesn't have to be this big complicated thing like I thought it was—trying to make every decision the right one. Some decisions are going to seem wrong, but seeming "failures" are simply experiences we learn from.

Bre had been my first great gift, and their marriage gave me my second greatest gift on Nov. 28, 2005. She and Ben invited me into the birthing room as she gave birth to my beautiful grandson, Owen, her own little miracle. Because I'd been given strict instructions to be very quiet, I watched with my hands over my mouth as she brought Owen into this world. I am still overwhelmed by their generosity in sharing that moment with me.

Owen was in distress when he was born, turning grayer by the second. Everyone rushed off with him, leaving my daughter alone and afraid. I was torn; I didn't want to leave my daughter.

I asked, "Where do you want me, Bre?"

She looked at me in disbelief and said, "Go, Mom, go!"

Earlier in her pregnancy she'd said, "What if I'm not a good mom?"

I said, "Are you kidding? Look how you are with Max, Molly, and Liberty (their rescued pets). Your baby couldn't ask for a better mom."

I knew she would always put her baby first. Little did I know we would lose her five months later, and Owen would never know the incredible person she was and the love she had for him. Originally,

I started writing because of Owen. I wanted to give him a glimpse of the person his mom was, and to share with him the evidence that proves my knowing that he will meet her one day. It's interesting that if Bre hadn't given us Owen, I would never have written any books.

CHAPTER 5

MEDIUMS

"Being skeptical is a good thing, but being blind to evidence, believing it could only be fraudulent because it's not yet an explainable phenomenon, is ignorance."

— THE AFTERLIFE EXPERIMENTS, —
BY GARY E. SCHWARTZ, PH.D.

My brother, a beautiful Christian man, was worried where this journey might be taking me. Leviticus 19:31 in the New Living Bible says, "Do not defile yourselves by turning to mediums or to those who consult with the dead. I am the Lord your God." I remember being lost in a dark cloud that had no color or light in it, so nothing mattered to me—I was already in hell. There was only finding my Bre. He understood the doubts I had about the Bible from previous conversations throughout the years. His fear of hell, and the possibility I might end up there, was of great concern to him.

Sorry that he was worried, I explained, "I asked God to help me find proof I would be with Bre again, and that wherever she was,

I wanted to be there with her. If hell is my destiny because Bre is there, I would never leave her alone in it. We were taught to trust in the power of prayer. Please don't worry. Just pray for me and trust that God will answer your prayers. That will be the greatest gift you can give me."

I know he prays for me still, and I am grateful for his love and concern. Had I let fear stop me, I would never have found any answers.

Mediums speak with the spirit of people who have passed; so I will jump ahead of myself in order to help you understand who, what, and where spirit is. We created fear around spirit by calling them dead people, and some were evil spirits, demons, and ghosts. I don't like the word spirit because it refers to us and them—when there is only us. When we leave the physical realm we return to the spiritual realm, known by some as the other side, or heaven. A gifted medium has the ability to communicate between these two realms. This communication would seem natural, had we not dreamed up ghosts and demons and evil spirits around it.

I had been reading a lot about mediums, and knew that the only way to make informed judgments, was to expose myself to these gifted people. What I found was very enlightening. On my most recent visit, my friend, Dede, wanted validation from her son and husband and invited a medium to her home. She asked five people to join her, including me, my sister, and Les—the skeptic. Boy, was he surprised when his mom came through! She was *very* excited to talk with him. She told him that she would send him butterflies, so he would know that she was with him. It was winter, and that seemed impossible. The next day a car stopped in front of us, and there it was, a big decal of flying butterflies.

Although we were there to support Dede, our loved ones will come through uninvited when they are not intruding on anyone else. My dad was an unexpected pop-in, but he knew my sister and

I were there. He wanted us to tell our family how involved he was in our lives and how much he loved us. The medium said Dad was having a lot of fun over there, and he had a big smile on his face while relating Dad's information to us. I knew Dad had an impish, lighthearted side to him, but he put himself through college and worked very hard while raising us, so we seldom got to see that side. Dad knew I was wearing their wedding ring, and he described my grandson's grade-school graduation party that he had attended. He knew Mom was depressed because of her dementia and wanted her to know that he, and all of her friends, were there waiting for her. Even my grandmother jumped in to tell us she would stay by Mom's side, and would hold her, until she was ready to leave.

It was wonderful to hear from my grandmother and Dad, but Bre didn't come through until Dede invited her. Bre knew that I didn't need validation any longer, so she held back until she was invited. I didn't know what impressions Bre was giving the medium, but he looked inquisitive and asked, "Did you write a book? I ask because she's holding a book and telling me you should continue spreading the word."

When I said yes, he said, "It doesn't appear to be the usual book."

I wanted to ask more questions of Bre, but I knew the medium was very tired because there were six people in our group, and he had already made contact with many people. The concentration it takes to remain in contact can be exhausting. I knew I could talk with Bre on another day. I thanked her for coming through, and let her go back to whatever interesting thing she had been doing.

Love is what keeps these connections alive, and that doesn't change. When Bre left, I could feel her around me, but I didn't feel my dad. I wondered why and discovered the answer while studying mediums. Dad knew I would be okay because I was prepared for his passing. He remained aware of what I was doing, but didn't feel the urgency to be present in my life in the same way Bre did because she had left so abruptly.

These fields can have charlatans in them, much like those found in politics, business, religion, etc. Their goal is personal gain. Any arena in which people can be led opens the door to greed and the opportunists who profit from people's trust and innocence. Give me your money and I will ease your pain and make your life better! When I was young, I called a psychic hotline. She asked me to wait on the line while she made contact with her spirit guides, and you paid by the minute. I waited for over twenty minutes before I realized I had been duped. I don't remember what it cost me, but I sure learned a valuable lesson. You cannot feel diminished because you've been fooled. When you are an honest person, it's hard to put yourself in the mind of a deceitful person. Shake it off and don't give any unnecessary energy to the anger you feel. Next time, gather more information about the organization or person you give your money or allegiance to. Bob Olson is a known expert of the afterlife. He has a list of reputable mediums on his website, so that's one place to start when searching for a medium. Nothing like that was available when I was young, but we have access to all sorts of information today. We learn from experience, and that's a good thing. So say thank you for the lesson and move on.

Mediums are everyday people like you and me, who also have an extraordinary gift—the ability to see, feel, and/or hear people from the other side. It is beautiful that a connection to this world exists, and it's normal, not paranormal. Like the rest of us, they do not have the same level of awareness or abilities, and their personalities are diverse. Some are extroverts who can handle criticism and have no problem speaking before large groups of people. Others prefer to work in private, staying out of the public eye. Many were warned that their abilities are of Satan, freightening them so much as to block their visions and messages. Feeling it an intrusion upon their personal life, some simply ignore their talent. Those who regard it as a gift believe it is their duty to help people who are suffering, and use it for that purpose. Many religions drape fear and loathing around it. Is that because they want to be in control of all information concerning the other side? Skeptics debunk it because, chained to conventional science, they don't believe there is another side, so all psychic mediums are scammers. Many communications are undeniable, but a skeptic will not budge—there is always a scam, even if they can't find it.

Mediums appear to be psychic because they hear of or are shown things that happen in the future. A psychic does not communicate directly with spirit. They have visions, impressions, or dreams of future events. A person can be both a medium and a psychic. In fact, they can have any number of seemingly paranormal abilities.

An intuitive is a person who has a heightened sense of intuition, and are sometimes highly sensative to vibrations in energy fields as well. Since the sensative can absorb other peoples' feelings, they must learn how to turn their sensitivity down. Intuitives receive impressions from energy fields—usually in the form of premonitions. Everyone is born with the gift of intuition, which is a sudden knowing without any reasoning behind it. Most of us aren't that open to this inner knowing, so we often ignore it. This ability can be painful at times, because frightening premonitions can come from the blue, and the receiver often doesn't know who the vision is for or how to prevent it from happening. You can understand why some don't regard this ability as a gift.

A friend told me that when she was young, she was known as a crybaby. She didn't know she was just absorbing other peoples' pain. If you have a child who is a sensitive, don't deny or be afraid of their abilities; teach them how to release the pain or take them to someone who can.

What is a trance medium, or channeler? This type of medium allows spirit to use the medium's voice to communicate with. The communication is more clear; but, oftentimes, the medium is in a deep trance while it's happening. Since the medium is often not aware of what's being said, a translator or an audience is required to witness the message. I must say, I was taken a little aback when I first heard a channeler speak. My first impression was one of paranormal weirdness, and I felt uncomfortable. However, the more information I gathered, the less weird things seemed to be, and I finally had to admit that my fear was unfounded.

You may have heard of Edgar Cayce (1877-1945), a trance medium who offered medical advice and prophecies through a channeled spirit, or team of spirits. He was given the nickname, "Sleeping Prophet," and, while unaware of what he was saying, his secretary, Gladys Davis, served as transcriptionist. Because one can never be absolutely sure of the channeled spirit's level of enlightenment or knowledge, there is always room to question the information. Cayce was often startlingly right; his medical readings were especially impressive. The Edgar Cayce Institute for Intuitive Studies was established for further research into these anomalies. You can imagine the impact that people like Cayce would have had on our ancient ancestors. It's understandable how some might have been deemed prophets, especially those purporting to receive messages from the Divine. On the other hand, many were considered witches, who received messages from Satan. How sad is that!

Have you ever heard of remote writing? These people can put a pen in their hand and begin writing or drawing a picture. Sometimes they can hear the words or see the picture, and sometimes they are in a trance and aren't aware of what they are writing or drawing. *Seeking Jordan,* by Matthew McKay, Ph.D., was a New York best-selling book. Dr. McKay wanted to have conversations with his son, just as they did when his son was alive. He developed his ability for remote writing, and has had those conversations with his son. In fact, it was Jordan who supplied his father with the outline for the book. We all have the capacity to develop any of these abilities; we just have to be open to it and not let fear stop us from learning how to use them.

I also learned of cases where a near-death experience (NDE) could soften the barrier between here and there. One such person is a friend of mine. When I lost my daughter, he told me of his near-death experience. He was a young boy when he was electrocuted, and for an unmeasurable moment in or outside of time, he found himself somewhere he wanted to stay forever. The kind of love he felt was like nothing he could explain or has ever felt since—it wasn't of this Earth. Because of that penetrating love, he knew with absolute certainty that the experience was real and nothing he could have imagined. Years later, he was able to see his parents after they had passed. In fact, they sat next to him while he was driving in his car. He knew this other world existed, so it wasn't startling as you might expect. It was a peaceful and loving communication. They wanted him to know how much they loved him and how happy they were. He shared his story with me to help ease my sorrow. He knew where Bre was, and of the love that surrounded her. I will be forever grateful for the abundance of love that people showed me during my darkest hour.

Over the centuries, we let an integral part of who we are atrophy. But it's no wonder we built barriers, when stonings and other tortures could be your fate for having otherworldly insights—Joan of Arc comes to mind. Thankfully, that is not a big worry today. Whatever abilities we may have can be enhanced through disciplines such as meditation and visualization. For instance, there is one fun exercise that I especially like to do. My nephew, Aaron, taught it to me. Besides being a great masseur, he is a licensed psychotherapist—and a shaman.

Here is the exercise: He stands at the entrance of a trailhead and imagines what it will look like (the moss on the trees, the rock formations, a fallen tree, water, etc.). Then he walks down the trail. For many tries, nothing happened. Then, miraculously, one day it was all there, just as he had envisioned. Now, it seems he knows what he'll see before he walks down any trail. I asked him how that could happen, and he explained that his spirit walks the trail ahead of him. I didn't understand that then, but I do today. I imagine he will teach his son to envision the trail they are about to walk down. What a gift! I try this exercise whenever I'm going somewhere I've never been, even just to visit a friend's new home. I am not devoted to these exercises in the same way my nephew is, but this one is fun and easy to do.

I was afraid of meditation because I was taught it was a sin to rely on myself and not soley on God for guidance. Marie Curie had said, "Nothing in life is to be feared. It is only to be understood." That is absolutely true. Meditation clears the mind of jumbled thoughts that are spinning out of control. If anything, we are closer to God when we meditate. Perhaps the interpretation of prayer was incorrect, and meditation with intention was the correct interpretation. Since religious leaders were the ones who told us what God wanted, I believe it was their power they were afraid of losing because people would no longer rely on only them for guidance. The fear of sinning and its horrible afterlife consequences kept us in their fold. That same fear stopped me from investigating meditation for myself.

One evening in the early 70s, I was sitting with a group of medical researchers having dinner. One of them had muscular dystrophy so severely that his wife had to help him eat. He said he practiced Transcendental Meditation (TM) to help him navigate his difficult life. He was an amazing and intelligent man, but I was hesitant to speak with him further about TM. Think of what he could have taught me had I not been crippled with fear.

Bre had a very curious mind, and this was something she wanted to learn. She asked me to attend a meditation class with her. In the back of my mind I still held that fear and didn't want her to go alone. Bre was able to achieve a deep meditation while I was more interested in what she was experiencing. She looked frighteningly gone to me, so I disturbed her, which disrupted the whole class. The peaceful state everyone was in was gone because of me. Fear stopped me from sharing this moment with her. Had that not happened, we would have continued to share a prayerful and meditative life together. Knowing what I know now, that would have been amazing.

I don't consider the way I think today is a "New Age" way of thinking. It's all very old. I'm just looking through a lens without any particular settings or restrictions in it. Paranormal abilities are not sinful or abnormal; it is completely normal for us to have them. As Pierre Teilhard de Chardin, a Jesuit priest, famously said, "We are not human beings having a spiritual experience. We are spiritual beings having a human experience." It's time we get to know who we are.

It isn't easy being a medium, or for them to openly share any of their gifts, as they are open to a lot of scathing criticism and accusations. If they were born with their abilities, mediums initially think everyone sees, feels, and hears the same things they do. When they realize others don't, it is confusing. As a child, they may be shamed and told not to tell people what they saw because it came from an evil place. How scary! As an adult they might question their own sanity. *Am I psychotic, or is this what schizophrenia looks like?* As research continues in all areas of the paranormal, more evidence is collected and skepticism lessens.

Why don't they get their impressions and predictions right every time? They are ordinary people trying very hard to interpret the messages they are receiving using whatever abilities they have:

clairaudience (hearing the inaudible), clairvoyance (seeing beyond sensory contact, or into the future), clairsentience (sensing or feeling subtle energies). The more they practice, the stronger each ability becomes; and the more abilities they have, the more clear the message is. Here are a few reasons why mistakes can be made:

- We vibrate at a higher level on the other side, so voices can sometimes sound like a record on fast-forward. Because of this, the medium can miss something or completely misunderstand it.

- A medium can be influenced by his or her personal beliefs and filter messages through them. They try to tune them out, but that's not easy.

- People on the other side will often use an object or project a vision to get their message across, which can be seen as something different from what it was intended to be.

- Sometimes spirit will use a sort of universal symbol, and the medium has to learn what that symbol represents. It takes patience and practice to learn these symbols, and each medium may have an additional set of symbols that have meaning only to them. It takes dedication to become a strong medium.

- Predictions are not cast in stone. They can go in any number of other directions, depending on the choices we make surrounding them. I found that amazing, and it demonstrates that we have more power than we know!

Because mistakes can be made, mediums advise us to develop our own abilities and have written how-to books on the subject. Medium, James Van Prague is one of many teachers, but a good place to start. When the message is for you, your own interpretation will be more accurate.

Mediums bring comfort and are often correct in their interpretations, but I don't make hasty decisions about my life based solely on the advice of seers, regardless of how gifted they may be.

Here's an example of not seeing the full picture: I asked a medium if she could tell me something personal that Bre and I might have shared. She said, "I see her bedroom, and it is full of flowers. All the walls are covered in flowers."

That certainly wasn't Bre's bedroom. She liked flowers and had a picture of one, but her walls were not covered with them. It could have been about the many flowers I wanted at her funeral, and she was showing me she had lots of flowers. It's also possible it wasn't about her bedroom walls at all. Had the medium looked further, she might have seen a cat curled up on the bed. Our cat, Flower, was special to Bre and me. When Flower had two kittens, Bre named them Petal and Blossom. Had I seen that vision myself, I would have known for certain what Bre wanted me to see.

It was comforting either way, so I let it go and asked another question. "Does Bre see my dad, and are they together?"

She said, "Yes, and an uncle."

Bre's son, Owen, was named after her father's brother who was killed in Vietnam. She always wished she had known him. It could have also been my brother— the baby my mother lost at birth. I should not have been surprised by that reply, but I wasn't thinking about an uncle and didn't expect it.

Was this medium speaking with Bre? Yes! She used expressions only Bre would use. In fact, it made me smile to hear her direct replies to some of the questions I asked. Even the medium laughed at Bre's to-the-point answers and said, "Wow, I really like her." That was Bre when she was here, and that is Bre over there because she is the same person but with a higher awareness. After we cross over, this is true of all of us

Bre told me, "You're reading too much and you need to chill." She was always giving me advice, and I was glad to hear her talk to me in the way she had talked to me when she was here. It made me laugh. I didn't see myself as reading too much, so I denied it. Bre insisted I was and repeated, "You need to chill, Mom!"

Of course, she was right. I was devouring books, and I haven't stopped reading. I knew that wasn't what Bre's message meant. I had become disconnected, and she wanted to remind me that there were people who still relied on me. She also wanted me to know she was aware of what was happening in my life and the lives of the people she loved.

This medium was one that Ben had asked me to see. Bre had a lot of friends, and Ben was now dating one of them, her friend, Rosey. Another friend worked in a holistic clinic with an acupuncturist/medium and asked her how Bre felt about this.

Her reply was, "Bre is okay with it and even encourages it."

Ben was rattled by information coming from any medium and knew I had been studying them. He called to ask what I thought about it. I told him I would need to know what abilities this medium had, and what sort of person she was. I agreed to meet her. He was relieved I would, as he was uncomfortable going himself—like many people are. It struck me then how sad it is that we've been taught to fear these blessedly gifted people. The comfort they bring us is a blessing, not a curse.

People from the other side want us to move forward in our lives, and Bre wanted that for Ben. However, there is only so much information they can give us, as they will not interfere with our purpose and what we came here to accomplish. Ben and Rosey's "on-again and off-again" relationship ended in friendship, but they had two beautiful little girls together, sisters for Owen to grow up with. Their names are Josephine and Samantha. It's interesting Bre felt it was important for Owen to have a sibling to grow up with, and now he has two—and their mother was Bre's friend.

Tragically, eight years from Bre passing, Rosey passed. Ben was alone with three children to raise. Now, Rosey's mother was asking the same questions I had. *"Why?"* I believe our lives weave together, and understand how the people coming in and out of them have a purpose. We don't know what the big picture is and can only see what's a few steps in front of us. Don't let it paralyze you, as it can so easily do. Slowly take a step, and then another, just as Ben has done through his tour in Iraq, losing Bre, and now losing Rosey. Through his pain, or what he learned because of his pain, he has been able to make his children feel safe, secure, and loved. He continues to amaze me moving forward with his children one step at a time.

I know that was an emotional and shocking story. Knowing we are eternal beings and cannot die, will help buffer some of the pain we endure in life. We, and the people we love, continue forever; the fact that they have the ability to communicate with us offers an abundance of evidence to support that.

Gifted people have been with us long before they had a label. In time, they became known as shamans, wise men, mediums, oracles, prophets, etc., and some of the less fortunate ones were called witches or false prophets. Deuteronomy 18:9-22 defines a false prophet as one who tells of things that don't come to pass. A person could be a prophet one day and a witch the next. They were just people with a range of abilities, and they made mistakes. It makes you wonder why anyone would divulge what they thought was a divine message, when the risk was death.

It was uncomfortable to realize that the beliefs I had about God were the result of an ancient people who believed they had a direct pipeline to the heavens. The messages received through gifted people were judged to be coming from either Satan or the Divine—and a man made that decision. When I first asked for help in finding Bre, I half expected to be led back into religion; but, in fact, I was being led farther away from it. If hell was at the end of the dark alley, and if God sent my beautiful daughter to hell, I would never want to be with Him anyway. I was committed to this journey, wherever it took me.

CHAPTER 6

NEAR-DEATH EXPERIENCES

*"Science cannot solve the ultimate mystery of nature.
And that is because, in the last analysis, we ourselves
are a part of the mystery that we are trying to solve."*

— MAX PLANCK —

Although my search for Bre started with a book written by a medium—and a quest to understand what they are—I quickly and simultaneously moved into near-death experiences. Those who have experienced a near-death experience (NDE) have firsthand experience knowledge of another world. Most of us have heard or read or watched YouTube about NDEs, but we haven't experienced one, so we're left with doubt. I drew hope from the possibility, and wanted to see if there was any research that supported them. I ignored the stares of people passing by as I sat on the floor at the bookstore surrounded with books off the shelf. I planned to read all of them. My friends thought they had lost me, and in many ways, they had. I was a desperate mother on a mission to find my Bre.

One reason we know so little about near-death experiences is that we fear there may actually be a life after death. As long as we believe that death is the end, we are impervious to religious rhetoric. Then science discovered the world of energy, and realized that our bodies are made of that energy which would never cease to exist. To keep the shield up against notions of personal survival, they said the energy of our body was simply absorbed back into the matrix of energy, where it would be recycled to grow a tree or another human. If the NDE were scientifically proven, it would validate the phenomenon of individual life-after-death, so I could understand why some people would rather disprove NDEs than prove them.

Dr. Eben Alexander believed that most NDEs happened when the heart stopped, and the neocortex of the brain was temporarily inactive. Whereas science explained the NDE phenomenon as the result of a primitive brain-stem program, a hallucination brought on by an anesthetic, or just the wild dream of a dying brain. Dr. Alexander personally experienced otherwise. Strictly material functions may explain some NDEs, but not all of them. Some are satisfied with conventional explanations while others, like myself, want to understand what the "but not all" is about.

In his bestselling book *Proof of Heaven*, Alexander, a Harvard neurosurgeon, describes his NDE and the journey he took on the other side. The neocortex of his brain was not just inactive; it had been reduced to mush by bacterial meningitis. His out-of-body experience left Dr. Alexander with an absolute certainty that the astonishingly beautiful and life-transforming experience he had was real. After a period in the dark "lower realms" (which I'll talk about later), he was guided upward by a beautiful person who filled his mind with amazing scientific knowledge.

He didn't recognize the beautiful person who was guiding him and wondered why. The patients who subsequently spoke with him of their NDEs had said that they knew the people who had met them. As it turned out, Alexander's guide was a biological sister whom Eben, an adoptee, had never met. He learned about her only when shown a picture, months later. I hope he doesn't mind my sharing that bit of "spoiler" information with you, but there is a lot more to his astounding journey. He hadn't believed in his patients' NDEs before his own experience. Now he wanted to fully validate them, and wasn't worried about the criticism that would inevitably follow. He knew his experience was real, and that it was important to share the details of his journey with others.

Near-death experiences became more tangible to me when I studied the quantum world. The biological matter we appear to be composed of is made of atoms, and atoms are constructed from quantum particles of energy. We are energy-beings. Einstein said, "Energy can neither be created nor destroyed; it can only be transferred or changed from one form to another." The mysteries found in NDEs coincide with the mysteries of the quantum world. States such as "nonlocality," in which near-death experiences feel they can be here and over there in a nanosecond, or in no time at all, along with the sense of intregal connection to all-that-is (everything and everyone), was common to their experience. The world they describe is intriguingly like the interplay of energy in the quantum world.

Some NDE'ers have reported they heard a popping or swoosh-ing sound as they left their body. Was that the energy being released from their body? In any case, they found themselves floating above their body, or on an indescribable journey when that happened. As they looked down at their physical self, it appeared to be an empty shell. Clearly, the body requires energy to be alive, but energy does not require a body to be alive. They were conscious and aware of their body, but no longer felt physically or emotionally attached to it. Consciousness does not seem to be separate from the energy of the body, but rather the informing aspect of it. When our body can't sustain itself any longer, our energy leaves, and consciousness goes with it.

Religion makes frequent reference to the soul within. Could that be the ancients' translation for energy infused with consciousness? I felt science and religion were swimming in the same water but looking through a different pair of lenses. It dawned on me that consciousness may be the same thing as our soul—different words to say the same thing. Religion and science, swimming in and as the same water, was an intriguing thought for me. Had the ancients been privy to the language of science when interpreting their folklore and divine messages, we would have fewer mysteries to solve today.

One reason I read so many books on NDEs was because of the differences I saw in individual experiences. If "the other side" is the same place, why the differences? I began to look for similarities rather than differences, and hoped to find an answer through going in that direction. The first obvious similarity was that the experience left a profound and permanent impression of being loved far beyond anything the experiencer had ever felt before.

It was said to be a wholly peaceful place, where they felt completely accepted and lovingly connected to everything and everyone they saw. They heard beautiful music that permeated their whole being, which they often interpreted as "the angels singing." Everything seemed alive and connected to them with a beauty they could not explain. Even water seemed to be alive and emitting love. If we felt that same love from, and for, the water here, we would take greater steps to protect it. In fact, if we understood connection the way NDE'ers do, we would take better care of all things, including one another.

It seems many things trigger a memory of Bre, and her love of water came through here. She carried a water bottle with her everywhere filled with fresh spring water, never purified. She said purified water was like drinking nothing. She learned to scuba dive and was surprised not to feel claustrophobic. Instead, she felt like she was in another world that was open and full of life. She loved the water and would have loved the idea that water could love her back. I love the visual of her sitting on the edge of a beautiful blue lake with her feet dangling in, soaking up all of that love.

Having seen and felt the connection between all things, self-importance and ego concerns suddenly take a back seat for NDE'ers, while their sense of true self-worth increases. Self-worth is knowing you have great value, and admits of no insecurities. The self that considers itself more important and valuable than others doesn't know its true worth, and responds to that insecurity with arrogance. All judgments fall away when the experiencers suddenly see that everyone is on a journey, and that each journey has a purpose. Absent understanding of another's journey, it cannot be judged. "Thou shalt not judge," takes on a whole new meaning for them.

There is also a shift in values wherein material possessions, personal achievements, and status lose all importance. That there is a far greater reason for their existence becomes apparent. Now living more consciously, and with reverence for all living things, the NDE experiencer is radically transformed. I'm not saying that those who have this experience give away all of their worldly possessions. Rather, they appreciate all facets of life more fully, feeling grateful and humble about any worldly possessions they may enjoy.

The different lengths of time that people spend "there" (which may have no location) may vary from days to seconds. Obviously, the longer they are there, the more comprehensive the information is that they receive. Even seconds may offer a flash of insight and the feeling of a penetrating love. Near-death experiences do not seem to diminish traditional belief systems; they enhance them. Christians, for example, generally have experiences within the framework of their tradition, meeting God, Jesus, angels, or others. They may even experience hell. Atheists and agnostics may be infused with great volumes of information that answer any or all of their questions, thus imparting the loving confidence that believers see as faith. Many, believers and nonbelivers alike, see an intense light with love emanating from it. Others, engulfed in warmth that penetrates to the core, find themselves wondering if *that* was God; regardless, they love it. Nothing is forced on them. All NDE'ers become more spiritually aware, no matter what their experience was.

To me, the most compelling cases are when people, blind from birth, see for the first time. Needless to say, the beauty is overwhelming. Imagine having never seen color before, just how beautiful everything would be. It seems that perfect health is restored to everyone within this dimension. Then again, we don't take our physical body with us. Our energy body is and always has been perfect.

Some pass through a dark tunnel or walked down a path toward an irresistibly loving light, while others feel themselves instantly there. There may be a sense of floating or flying, even if they are walking on the ground. Many are met by friends or family members, while others are warmly received by a loving guide or religious figure who takes them on a tour of this amazing place. Although it can happen to people who aren't there for long, I never came across an NDE in which no one came to greet them. It may be upon arrival or take some time, but they always come. Even their loving pets have bounded forward to greet them. I'm looking forward to that as I have many pets I want to see, and I know Bre is with them and is loving it.

An energy body does not feel pain in the way that the physical body does. People speak of going into the light or seeing a light so bright it would hurt the human eye, but in this state we are energy, and there is no discomfort. As a colorist, it seemed impossible to me, but some see colors they hadn't seen before. Could it be that there are colors of another spectrum that are nothing like our primary reds, yellows, and blues? The visible light we see has spectra of light we don't see within it. Ultraviolet and infrared light are invisible to us, yet they exist. Dogs cannot see the same colors we see. It is possible we cannot see the full spectrum of color with our physical eye. Perhaps this is why people who have had NDEs can't discribe some of their experiences while in that state. How can you explain something that doesn't exist here? We enter a world that is foreign to our physical one, and we don't have the vocabulary for it.

Dr. Alexander wrote, "I was able to instantly and effortlessly understand concepts that would have taken me years to fully grasp in my earthly life. Words weren't spoken, they were instantaneously absorbed. In the physical world words come out one at a time and take years of study." Imagine a complicated question being instantly understood, or seeing your life play out in a moment. We are no longer held back by a physical brain, body, time, or space. The greatest of profundities may be absorbed in an instant.

Knowing that we never die, it would follow that another plane of existence would have to exist. If we could accept that, we would want to know all that we could about this plane, rather than fearing and denying its existence. Death is addressed by religion and science, many of their conclusions and conjectures causing great fear. Death became less foreboding to me after reading so many accounts of the NDE. It is a part of our life's cycle; it does not end life, because our life never ends. If the information from NDEs were acknowledged by all, we would have better funding for research. Fortunately, many people do have an interest, and a number of non-profit organizations are studying NDEs and other paranormal phenomena. IANDS (International Association for Near-Death Studies) and Rhine Research Center are just two of them.

"Back" from an NDE, the experiencer brings the knowing that "all is well." They know there is nothing to fear, that life is eternal, and that unconditional love awaits them. What a wonderful gift! Wouldn't you love to have the assurance that "all is well" while living this difficult life? It is clear to them that all is as it should be, and the good and bad experiences of life no longer holding power over them as they had before their NDE.

Space and time have no reality or significance there. Many say they are illusions, created to serve as coordinates for our physical world. We need a form of measurement here, but it is irrelevant in a world of energy where space and time hold no meaning. Of course, such an unimaginal state exceeds our grasp. For all their intelligence and erudition, scientists are equally baffled. Time and space are a mystery to them as well. NDE'ers report traveling great distances in less than an instant—in "no time at all"—again, because time and space don't exist there. They are comfortable with and accept this reality while they are there; it's as if they've always known it—and perhaps they have.

Some are shown the Big Bang, and many Big Bangs. Is that the same universe starting over, or is it to demonstrate several different universes in an infinite space? In any event, there is the sense of being part of one living system. Some report traveling to other planets. This kind of mind-blowing information is hard to explain or accept, which makes it easy to dismiss as a fantasy or delusion. Most of us respond this way to many things we can't explain.

Some are involved in a life review in which they can empathetically see and feel the effects of their actions on others during their life—both good and bad. One popular but facile explanation for this phenomenon is that a dying brain could somehow cause the sum of one's life to flash before them, but this whole experience appears to be very different: it comes with previously unknown information, loving guidance, and restoration. It all seems to happen in an instant, yet is played out like watching a movie. While painful to watch at times, there is no overlord poised to dole out punishments—only guidance to help them learn from the discordant things they thought, said, and did. In truth, that is what all loving parents aspire to do for their children.

I was taught that God is my "Father in heaven." He has and will always love me, but only if I comply with certain standards of behavior. Otherwise, I could face His eternal punishment. Today, I know that punishment is not what makes a good parent or a good child. Then it hit me: the traditional description of who and what the creator is had to be wrong. There was no one singular deity ruling over us from the heavens. Rather, it seemed to be an infinite and loving energy that permeated everything as the essential aspect of all things. That explained the connection NDE'ers felt with the things they encountered—everything was an expression of the all-inclusive loving energy.

Dr. Alexander clarified that "Everything was distinct, yet everything was also a part of everything else."

In the movie "Phenomenon," John Travolta's character tells of the largest-known organism. It is acres of aspen trees in Colorado. They look like individual trees, but they are connected to one root ball. Also appearing as individuals, I believe we too are all intregral parts of one living system. Just as the subatomic world shows everything to be part of one energy system, so too are NDE'ers fully aware of their connection with all-that-is. That understanding has a profound effect on their life and stays with them ever after.

As I continued my research, the correlations between what NDE'ers shared and what science had discovered became increasingly apparent. Even my Sunday school teacher had taught that "We were all one family." However, within that family one could almost feel the divisions and boundaries built-in by human ego and the punitive God who would one day tear that family apart, sending the good ones to heaven and the "bad" ones to everlasting hell.

In ancient texts there was no standard symbol for the creator, so I can see how representations were translated as a masculine and mighty god. That was all they knew. The state of the NDE'er is similarly foreign—clearly a barrier when trying to describe some of the mind-boggling nuance. Absent the vocabulary to explain something we don't know, we try to explain it with words we do know. Some recall understanding everything while they were there, but assume they'd forgotten the technicalities of it when they returned. Did they forget, or was there no vocabulary for it?

Mark Twain said, "The two most important days in your life are the day you were born and the day you find out why." I'm looking forward to finding out why I came, and to visiting cosmic libraries (which some refer to as the Akashic Records) where I will find the answer to every question. I have all of eternity to do that in, so I think I'll follow my fun-loving dad's lead for a time and just have fun. I want to dangle my feet in the water with Bre, hang out in her garden, and play with all of the animals that I know will be with her. I would enjoy doing that for a very long time. I hope that it doesn't sound like I'm in a hurry to get there, because I'm not. I know my time here is valuable, just as it is for all of us. Life becomes an adventure when you know nothing that happens here is permanent—it is just an experience.

I can't leave this chapter without recognizing the negative NDE experiences some people have. They are rare, but it does happen to some. They think they've been to hell because they believe there is a hell. I don't personally believe in hell, at least not in the biblical sense. I believe we create negative energy in the physical world because of fear. *Without fear, we would be living in heaven.* Negative energy is tangible. As the saying goes, "It feels so thick you can cut it with a knife." So from a spiritual level, it is possible we would actually be able to see this dark energy and all of the ugliness in it. That may have been what Eben Alexander was seeing before he was pulled out of it by his sister.

It seems this dark place could be somewhere between here and the place of light, as some pass through a velvety darkness without stopping, while others never get through it. It seems likely that the people who resided there chose to be there. What stopped them from going to the light? Did they believe they were sinful and would face judgment, so it was fear that kept them from moving forward? Had they lived a dark and cruel life, and now, repulsed by the beauty and love of the light, were choosing to stay in that place? Were they confused about where they were and what just happened to them, so they didn't know they could keep going forward? Whatever the reason, many believe that this state must be hell. I am grateful to the people who shared their negative experience, alerting us to this possibility upon arrival. The choices we make here, as well as what we've been taught to believe, could result in the place we *choose* to occupy there.

My nephew told me that when he heard Bre had passed, he went to find her. She was in a dark place. He told me that some people don't know they have died. Bre understood what had happened, but she was confused. She was afraid that if she continued to move further, she would be too far away from Owen. My nephew was able to help her understand that if she went forward, she would be closer to Owen. As I said earlier, Aaron is a shaman who often uses his spiritual connections to help people move through the darkness. When we go to the light we are met by someone, but they have to come and find us when we stay in the dark. Even if you don't believe any of this, just remember one thing as you leave this plane—move forward and look for the light!

Most who had a negative experience report that their lives subsequently changed, dramatically for the better, in much the same way as for those who had a positive experience. However, some are left with the fear of hell, which can lead to depression upon returning. Some go back to church, hoping to be saved from returning to that place. It's a dark and loveless place where the residents and/or phenomena have a repulsiveness about them, so I can understand their fear. I wonder if this is why small children are afraid of the dark. Do they have a deep memory of this dark place?

I didn't find much information about it, perhaps because not many people experience this. It may be the hell the Bible speaks of, but the descriptions vary depending on the nature of the experiences and how they interpret them. I've read that there is always hope for people in the dark. Higher beings from the light continue to visit, trying to help those who are resistant to acknowledge the light. Now I know that embodied human beings like Aaron help as well. I remembered thinking how strange it was that all of this weirdness was beginning to be less weird to me.

It surprised me that people who had positive experiences could also feel depressed when they returned. For some, it was a place they didn't want to believe existed, so they tried to forget it had ever happened. Others felt they had been home and longed to stay there. Utterly confused by the experience, they didn't know what to do with their life and all of the emotions they felt while on that journey. Though it seemed that they did choose to come back, sometimes it was to a painful and perplexing life, which was distressing. The upside was that they no longer had the same fears about death, and believed there was a purpose for coming back. They just wanted to know what it was and get it done—now!

This is something else that could cause experiences to differ. In *The Afterlife Interviews* by medium Jeffrey Marks, interviews with people on the other side, revealed our mind can invent situations and things that aren't really there. That made sense to me because I know how powerful our thoughts are in the physical world, and when we express as pure energy beings, they are probably even more powerful. An NDE'er can be creating visions of things they expect to see without knowing they're doing it, and their companions on the other side may also accept those visions with no effort to change them. They know we will come to understand everything at some point, but it will be in our own time and in our own way. Wherever we are on our journey of life serves a purpose, so our visions will vary from person to person.

So much of this journey has caused me to revisit the things I had assumed were true and see them differently. My goal was to find proof of eternal life and record memories of Breana to share with Owen one day. His little book has continued to grow into something much larger as the journey takes me into other areas I could not have foreseen.

CHAPTER 7

THE MYSTERIOUS QUANTUM WORLD

"Although we perceive science as an ultimate truth, science is finally just a story, told in installments."

— LYNNE MCTAGGART *THE FIELD* —

"The enormity of it all boggles the mind, challenges religion, and excites scientists."

— BRIAN THOMAS SWIMME & MARY EVELYN TUCKER, —
JOURNEY OF THE UNIVERSE

In the beginning, man believed in worshiping gods, the stars, the moon, and the sun, believing they held the answers. From there, religions evolved and told us they had the answers. We assumed the Earth was in the center of empty space, with shiny things sitting all around it. Then science came along and proved the Earth was not at the center and space was not empty, it was full of stars and other planets. The universe was continually expanding, stars were exploding, galaxies forming, and everything was made of—and permeated by—particles of energy.

Things began to fall into place when I discovered some of the mysteries of this energy world. When I first asked for help in finding Bre, I wasn't sure if I was talking to anyone. Now, I knew something or someone was guiding me because I never expected to be led into such a difficult and comprehensive field. I'm a hairdresser, who might more credibly be writing a book about the business I have loved for over forty years. Suddenly, I was no longer a hairdresser. I was a mom on a desperate quest to find proof I would see my daughter again. I began to read every book I could find that might hold an answer; if there was proof, I would find it. The earlier books I read had quotes from physicists and made references to the quantum world—the world of energy. I knew I had to stay focused and be patient with myself as I tried to understand something that was completely foreign to me.

Some might wonder, *Why should I care about understanding the quantum world? That's for scientists to figure out.* At least that's what I used to think. The reasons people may have will of course vary. Mine was to find proof of eternal life. Aerospace giants want to understand how to tap into this field of energy as fuel for future space travel, perhaps in the form of nuclear fusion, as I'll attempt to explain later. Can you see the enormity of fully understanding that? It would be a clean and never-ending source of energy. Goodbye dams, windmills, coal, and oil. Environmentalists are interested in finding a way to dissolve toxic waste and other polutants that threaten our environment. We know that energy has been used for the destruction of life, as in the atomic bomb. Perhaps we will find a way to neutralize that destruction before it escalates into total destruction. Our own health is another reason, as we are made of energy. Imagine the significance of that. We could alter defects in DNA before birth or stop disease before it affects us.

Of the many discoveries and technologies that have come from understanding the invisible world, the most important is the computer. Because of the computer we have the ability to unwind mysteries at a much more rapid speed. I think the second-most important was the discovery of DNA, the blueprint for how the human body is put together. To understand the invisible world of energy is to understand creation itself. No wonder so much time and money has been spent by many factions trying to unlock its secrets.

I recently had a conversation with Owen's little sister, Josephine. She said her grandmother liked to tell her how things were when she was young, and Josephine wondered how things would change when she grew up.

I smiled and said, "Well, when I was young there were phone booths and telephone wires running everywhere. Now, we have wireless cell phones. When you grow up, you'll tell your grandchildren that when you were little, there were gas stations and roads running everywhere. Now, we fly home in our solar-driven, computerized, floating cars."

She laughed as she imagined that possibility. I so love my conversations with Josephine, Owen, and Samantha.

That made me think of how far we've come in my lifetime. The first computer, ENIAC, was completed in 1946—two years before I was born. It was 1,800 square feet and weighed more than thirty tons. The computer my dad used in his workplace occupied an entire room. By the early 1980s, desktop computers were becoming common, and now I have a portable laptop that can travel with me. You probably have one as small as a watch that does far more than the big one my dad used. My grandfather had a horse; I have a car with a computerized dash. My cell phone is a camera, a video camera, and a mini computer with all of the information I want at my fingertips. Goodbye to the encyclopedias I used in high school—I have search engines that continually update and can answer any question. In 2006, I had a wall of bookshelves built into my home to hold all of my books; now I can store a whole library on my little reader or my phone. Jets that zip through the air replaced prop planes, and rockets have taken people to the moon. We can grow tissue from our own cells. Imagine growing a heart or a kidney out of our own tissue. What will Owen, Josephine, and Samantha see in their lifetime? The impossible no longer seems impossible, and discoveries are coming ever faster since discovering the invisible world of energy—the quantum world.

Twenty years ago I couldn't see the need for a cell phone. Wow, I can't believe I said that! Thankfully, Bre thought I needed one and gave me one for Christmas.

She said, "I can never reach you when I want to, so you need this."

I agreed she was right and said, "Well, I guess I need one then."

It's funny, but that sounds like something you would say to your child and not the child to the parent. That was my Bre; I only wish there was cell service in the home she is living in now. I so miss our conversations. Although she knows what is happening here, I don't know what is happening there. I wish I could give her an interdimensional cell phone for Christmas.

For many years I wouldn't upgrade that old cell phone. The only recording of Bre's voice was a greeting she made for me on my old cell phone. I was told it wouldn't transfer over because my phone had old technology. I had a copy of her greeting on a computer disc, but was reluctant to delete the old phone. Finally, in 2016, I made that difficult decision because there were many things the old phone was not capable of doing. For instance, I wasn't receiving the pictures Ben sent of the children. The phone company knew of my concern and tried their best, but failed. Sadly, I knew I would have to set up a new voicemail. I decided to use the default voice on the phone and not replace her voice with my own.

Because I didn't want to hear any other voice than Breana's, Les said, "I'll call your phone and see how the message sounds."

Miraculously, it was not the default voice but her sea-song voice that answered, "You have reached Cyndi's cell phone. Leave a message."

Was it a fluke in the technology, or was it something else? Since I had been on this journey for several years by then, I knew it was something else.

Issaac Newton (1643-1727) nudged an opening into the invisible world of energy when he proposed a force called gravity. That force was holding the universe together—not God. It was blasphemy to say such a thing. God was all-powerful and was "up there" ruling over everything and holding it together. In time, Newton's theories were proven mathematically to be correct, and he was finally redeemed. Now, science had to figure out how to calculate in that very strange and invisible world they never knew existed.

Most school teachers didn't know much about the quantum world (the world of energy) in the 1960s, but they taught us that everything is made of atoms. I had learned that my body is composed of biological matter, but in truth, it is made of atoms. The atom, in turn, is made of particles of energy, which means that all matter is fundamentally energy, including my Bre. Learning that energy cannot be destroyed was an earth-shattering "aha" moment for me.

I will describe the quantum world in three different ways, and I apologize for any repetition. The first one is: The quantum world is the world of energy. It is not a separate world from the physical world like we thought—*it is what the physical world is made of*. What a shock it was, to discover all matter (which includes us) is made of energy. Solid matter eventually disintegrates, but the energy it is made of never does. That was music to my ears. Even though we look and feel solid, we are energy that has bonded together. Think of ice. It looks and feels solid, but it is water that has bonded together through cold temperatures. Einstein said that "matter is an illusion," when it was discovered to be a different form of energy. Ice is an illusion because it is actually a different form of water. The reality we know is all one big illusion. For some, that might be all they need to know about the quantum world, and they would be right. But for those who want more information, I will continue.

While studying the world of energy, many terms confused me, and I don't want them to confuse you. Quanta is the plural of quantum particle, and a subatomic particle is the same thing as a quantum particle of energy. The quantum world was believed to consist of waves of energy (I'll explain waves later) and particles of matter. Now, we know it's all energy. The science community needs to name, measure, and understand what each quantum particle does. Atoms are not fundamental because they can be broken down further into electrons, neutrons, and protons. Is a proton fundamental? No, it's not. If we crash protons together, as we did in the Large Hadron Collider, something smaller comes out. Upon discovering that quantum particles of energy mysteriously bond together to form seemingly solid masses like the planets and us, science began searching for answers to solve this mystery.

Next, is a visual description of the quantum world. I think Bre would have liked this, so here it is:

Visualize the universe as a ball. Now, hand the ball to a very bright and curious child, instructing her to take it apart to see what is inside and what it is made of. She easily sees the planets, stars, and life forms; but as she takes them apart, she finally finds the atom, which is impossible to visibly see. Soon she discovers that the atom can be broken down into even smaller things. She calls these smaller things quantum particles of energy, or quanta. She then notices that everything in and around the atom is also bursting with particles of energy. That body of energy is known as the quantum world. There is no empty space, and nothing is actually solid, but rather comprised of energy. The entire ball had been nothing but energy right along.

The larger objects are held in place by gravity, making them easy to find and measure. Gravity has no affect on the tiny quantum particles, so they are spinning around every which way. Determined to find, measure, and name every little particle, along with the laws that governed them, the little genius developes a special kind of math to help her study these invisible particles. She calls this math quantum mechanics. Each calculation starts with a quantum theory, which is tested by experiments and either proven or disproven. When a theory is disproven, a new theory is introduced until a calculation proves it to be correct. While all of this testing and experimentation is time-consuming, that curious child is in the mind of every scientist, who just won't quit.

This a more scientific way of viewing the quantum world: In 1911, a mere hundred years ago, Max Planck proved that empty space is not empty at all but bursting with energy. In Latin, the definition for quantum is *one's share or portion*. Planck used the word quantum to describe the invisible world of energy. He surmised that this world of energy can be broken down into independent particles. He called these particles quanta. It was soon learned that some of these particles could change into different forms of the same particle, which were called flavors or colors. So, you can have one particle that can become two or more different things. Can you imagine the confusion? Many of these quantum particles have the ability to change from a wave to a particle and vice versa. This was one more thing I attempted to understand. A wave was considered energy and a particle was thought to be matter because it was still assumed that energy and matter were two separate things. The ability to flip from wave to particle and back again led Einstein to believe that energy and matter are interchangeable; they are different forms of the same thing. His well-known and now proven equation for that is E=mc2 (Energy = mass times the speed of light squared).

When early physicists realized that the general laws of physics do not apply to a world that has no gravity, they acknowledged that a new way of calculating would need to be developed. That came in 1927, when Heisenberg introduced the uncertainty principle, which is the concept that *the more precisely the position of a subatomic particle is determined, the less precisely the momentum is known.* That was clear as mud to me, but I will make an attempt to explain it this way: Since there was no gravity to determine the position and momentum of these tiny particles, it was impossible to predict their movement. Calculations went from absolutes to probabilities. With each calculation they added a theory and said, "If this theory is correct, it will probably do this." If it didn't do that, they would attach another theory until one was proven and clicked into place. This is where the term "quantum theory" comes from. All I can say is, Wow! You would think a physicist would throw his hands in the air and choose another career path! But no, they love the challenge.

Physics has many branches, and each branch has its own field of inquiry. Quantum mechanics is the branch that studies subatomic particles. All scientists must have an understanding of quantum mechanics because all things are made of subatomic particles. The uncertainty principle or "probability" theory used in quantum mechanics has thus far proven to work, and science has come a long way in proving each theory, one calculation at a time. However, with each proven calculation more questions arise, and there are still innumerable theories yet to be thought of. As much as we understand and have proven, the world of energy is still very much a mystery.

The earlier assumption that a particle is matter and a wave is energy seemed obvious—afterall, solid matter is visible and tangible, the stuff of everyday lives. It has to come from somewhere. Then science discovered that human *consciousness has an effect on quanta!* A wave could become a particle, or visa versa, because of an observation. For me, and many others, that means the quantum world is made of "waves of possibility," and all things develop from thought. I had heard about the power of thought before, but I didn't expect to find the explanation for it through my study of the quantum world.

That consciousness can affect those tiny particles inspired some to consider the possibility of a higher power, or God. That was more music to my ears. Something was controling energy before man had his first thought, and that was uncomfortable for those who believed there was no God. But because consciousness cannot be measured in the same way as a particle can, mainstream science feels justified in ignoring it for now. Nothing is provable without a measurement. In an episode of "Scorpion" this statement was made: "We can't measure love. So, does that mean love isn't real?" Some real things may be immeasurable. Thankfully, researchers love a puzzle and continue to look for impossible measurements. It's just as Richard Feynman said, "Once I get on a puzzle I can't get off." It was through the perseverance of researchers like Dr. Feynman, and the books they wrote, that I began to find pieces to my own puzzle.

Centuries ago, a division between religion and science was necessary to protect people of science from persecution. It was assumed that everything down here (in the visible world) was man's world, and scientists could investigate that. Everything out there (the cosmos) was God's world, and only religious leaders could address that. At the time, they didn't know it was the same world, and inadvertently accepted two separate worlds when there was only one. Einstein spent his life looking for a mathematical formula that would show how these two worlds connect, which is known as the unified theory. What do they share? Consciousness governs both worlds. A picture began to form in my mind—the creator as a conscious energy-system and not a powerful god. I could see how that dovetails with the mystical knowing, "We are all one with God," and Jesus' statement in the Gospel of Thomas, "The kingdom of God is inside of you, and it is outside of you." Did the Bible hold the answer to the unified theory, but was explicated through mysticism and superstitions?

I met a man while on a cruise recently. He told me his son was a physicist but had completely changed profession when he began to see the probability of an intelligence outside of us. He didn't like where that was leading him, so he completely changed careers. After all these centuries, there is still trepidation when it comes to anything that might suggest there is a higher power beyond our own, governing the laws of the universe.

Religion and science ask the same question: "Where did we come from?" I wondered where we would be today had religious leaders and scientists been able to safely work together. I believe consciousness unites both worlds, and many others agree with that observation. Mainstream science cannot be fully engaged in the study of consciousness until the past conflicts with religion have been put aside. Consciousness is to close to admitting that there is something out there that resembles a god. Consequently, we don't have the complementary findings of science behind religious teachings. What a conundrum!

Max Planck, the father of quantum theory said, "All matter originates and exists only by virtue of force. We must assume behind this force the existence of a conscious and intelligent Mind. This Mind is the matrix of all matter."

Einstein said, "Everyone who is seriously involved in the pursuit of science becomes convinced that a spirit is manifest in the laws of the Universe—a spirit vastly superior to that of man," and, "I see a pattern but my imagination cannot picture the maker of the pattern…we all dance to a mysterious tune, intoned in the distance by an invisible piper."

In the past I thought the quantum world was a world that had nothing to do with me. Now, I know it has everything to do with me—and my daughter. We are connected through one energy. I just can't say that enough. Even though the introduction of consciousness into the world of energy complicates things for some people, it was music to my ears, and I was hearing a lot of music. I needed evidence to prove there is a higher power out there that heard my plea and was holding my daughter. Luckily, I don't require a measurement to know that consciousness is real.

In an effort to find a mathmatical equation to solve the puzzle of the unified theory, string theory and M-theory arose. I realized there were other theories to explain our beginnings, but I put my energy into investigating quantum theory. I read a little on string theory and found *The Fabric of Reality* by physicist David Deutsch easy to understand. It didn't change my views much, but if you have an interest in another theory, you might like his book.

With a few exceptions, a particle can become a wave. They pop in and out of existence as they reverse roles, allowing them to be over here and over there instantaneously or even simultaneously. Einstein called this phenomenon "Spooky action at a distance." Obviously, time and space don't mean anything in the world of energy, just as NDE travelers observed while on their journey. If time and space don't exist in the world of energy, do they exist at all? Are they illusions created for the physical world, as NDE'ers claim?

Time kept coming up, and I wondered, *Why is this journey causing me to consider such impossible things?* I had to laugh at myself as it occurred to me that everything I was learning seemed impossible—so why not add time to the equation? In March of 2008, Joel Achenbach wrote an article for *National Geographic*, "At the Heart of All Matter." In it he said, "Our existence, our entire universe, emerged from things that happened at the smallest imaginable scale. The Big Bang theory tells us that the known universe at one time had no dimensions at all—no up or down, no left or right, no passage of time, and no laws of physics beyond our vision." What a wonderment the concepts of time and space must be for physicists. They certainly are for me!

So, what is a wave? Technically, that's a complicated question to answer because they vary in many ways. Clearly, this is not a scientific explanation but it's how I understand them to be. Visualize a calm ocean with gentle waves moving up and down until there is a disturbance, like the wind blowing or the Earth moving. Waves suddenly take action and change, forming whitecaps, waves crashing into each other, and tidal waves popping up. Now, visualize the world of energy, its waves peacefully vibrating until there is a disturbance, such as a conscious thought. The waves take action and change, banging into each other and connecting to one another to form many different things. As the saying goes, "The universe is made of waves of possibility." You think it, and the energy of the universe creates it. This is a simple interpretation, but it's how I summed up the complicated science books I was reading.

Another strange reality is that particles know and respond to what the others are doing no matter how far apart they happen to be. How is this possible without a connection of some kind? There *is* connection! Everything is made of and connected through one inifinite – and conscious – energy field that started all of creation from one tiny dot of energy—"Once connected, always connected." Knowing and sensing this, connection took on a whole new meaning for me. Everything and everyone has been energetically and consciously connected since the beginning of time.

In relation to connection, *The Secret Life of Plants*, by Peter Tompkins and Christopher Bird, is a book that explores the Backster Effect. This is the surprising result of polygraph tests performed on plants to see if they might respond when the scientist burned one of their leaves, or even the leaf of one of the tested plant's "friends." According to Cleve Backster, they do. He also recorded similarly strong responses to the mere thought of harming a plant, or any of its associates. Many see this as the telepathic expression of pan-psychism, the view that *consciousness is the fundamental feature of reality*. These tests demonstrate the connection between all living things through an energy that is conscious, right on down to our feelings of empathy for one another.

My sister had a similar experience with one of her favorite plants: she heard it *scream* while cleaning a leaf with a cloth she had been using to scrub the bathroom with. Not believing what she had heard, she cleaned another leaf. It screamed again. She is such a credible person it is hard to tease her about the vocal cords her plant must have. The next day those leaves were brown, and she was left feeling amazed and a little guilty. Now I feel differently about the plants in my care—and fully accept my sister's story. To take this further, I understand the plant's cry would have been heard telepathically, which is something else we don't have much knowledge of.

I inherited most of Bre's plants, though what I wanted most and didn't get to care for was her corn plant. She carried that plant with her when she joined Ben in Georgia, where he was stationed, and she carried it back with her when he left for Iraq. Even though I didn't think about it at the time, it must have held special mean-ing for her. Max the cat made its pot his personal litter box when Bre left this plane, and it was too late when Ben asked me if I was any good with plants. I'd like to think she has it with her now. In any case, her other plants seem to like me, as they are all doing fine—although Les tried to help once by fertilizing them. One died, and we were heartsick. I couldn't throw it out. Instead, I cut it back and told it how sorry we felt. That sort of makes me smile, and we were redeemed when that hardy little plant grew back again.

Bre is made of energy that cannot be destroyed, so she reverted back to the energy she had always been. I just had to move through this journey one "aha" moment at a time. When I lost Bre I felt like my life had stopped, unaware that I was actually moving forward toward an eventual conclusion and to my Bre. Reality wasn't what I thought it was, and I was beginning to understand how and why the physical world was not actually real. All of the things I thought I knew were changing, and nothing seemed impossible for consideration.

Most believe in the Big Bang theory where what became the universe was compressed into a dot smaller than a pea, burning at 18 billion, million, million, million degrees—give or take a degree. Then boom! That dot filled the universe allowing matter to form— atoms, stars, galaxies, and us. Nothing would exist without that one singularity: a dot the size of a pea. Maybe not…

Others theorize that space was an ocean of energy (a gooey soup) that had always been, and the galaxies formed within it. Big Bang or soup—it didn't matter to me. Everything was still connected through one energy field. The Bible describes God as having no beginning and no end. Maybe there is truth in that. What or who is that ocean of energy, and where did it come from? Did energy exist as an eternal gooey soup, did energy explode out of a dot, or had it existed outside of both? No matter which theory is correct, it doesn't close the door to an intelligence that stands outside of what we perceive to be space and time.

I felt I should try to understand how the universe was physically put together, according to the Big Bang theory. One book I found interesting was *Journey of the Universe*, by Mary Tucker and Brian Swimme. When that little proton exploded, it filled the universe with quarks which crashed into one another forming other little particles. Those particles began connecting in a variety of ways, forming the different atoms. When atoms combine, they formed elements. Elements are made of one specific type of atom that groups together, forming solid masses like rocks of copper, iron, lead, etc. Or, they can be gas atoms that group together to form clouds of gas, like hydrogen, oxygen, helium, etc. When elements group together they form compounds. Some of these Big Bang couplings were violent, but it was those bombardments and explosions that gave birth to stars, and it was the explosion of stars that filled the universe with the necessary elements for life.

If you're wondering about the nature of these little particles that make up the different atoms, here is the basic recipe: As the universe became a cosmic soup of energy, for some reason protons and neutrons liked hanging out together, forming the nucleus of the atom. Electrons, which were also floating around out there, had a negative charge, protons, a positive charge. And for no apparent reason, protons and electrons were attracted to each other. Maybe that's where the saying, "Opposites attract," comes from. It was this attraction that caused the electrons to encircle the nuclei (protons and neutrons), forming the first atoms. The variations in the numbers of each particle within the atom cause atoms to differ from one another. "This miraculous and sometimes violent dance was performed perfectly a gazillion times when so many things could have gone wrong," *Journey of the Universe*.

Even though the atom has never been seen with the naked eye, it was proven mathematically in 1913. It had a measurement of 10-30 (ten to the minus thirty) meters wide—that's a 1 with 29 zeros in front of it, less than two billionths of an inch, or a million times smaller than the diameter of a single human hair. The diagram I memorized in school of the atom was only a guess, and they may not look like that at all.

Atoms can bond together only on Earth and can never collide or merge. That requires a lot of heat and only happens on the sun or other hot stars. If the nuclei of two atoms merge, it forms a more massive nuclei and a type of energy called nuclear fusion. This is not to be confused with nuclear fission, which splits the nuclei of the atom into two or more smaller fragments, and is how the atomic bomb was created. We have not been successful at duplicating fusion in laboratories because of the tremendous heat it requires. Science is trying to do this, as it is an inexhaustible and clean source of energy for future generations. You can understand why environmentalists and aerospace giants are interested in this. It is clean, and it is everywhere. The need to access more fuel while traveling through the universe would be eliminated, and we would no longer view oil as the best source of energy.

So, how are we put together? As atoms bond together in a variety of configurations, the physical world begins to take shape. Your hand and your body would simply pass right through the wall, or your seat, were it not for the energy bonds that hold atoms together. Atoms make elements; elements make compounds. Compounds become molecules, and molecules make cells. Cells make tissue, and tissue makes organs. DNA is made of molecules and tells every cell where it belongs in the body. Everything started with itty-bitty particles of energy. Yet, here we are looking very solid; but, in reality, our bodies are superglued together. In fact, all matter is superglued together. Einstein was right, "Reality is merely an illusion, albeit a very persistent one."

It seemed the only thing about me that isn't superglued together is my consciousness. My illusive body has kept me safe while on this journey just as Bre's beautiful body had kept her safe. I didn't expect to find an "aha" moment while studying chemistry, but I found a big one. Our physical body is made of bonded-together atoms mysteriously infused with consciousness. I realized that we

72

are unimaginably more than I thought we were—further evidence of a higher power inside and outside of our reality.

I have forgotten if science was a fun subject for Bre, and wondered what she knew about the atom. I do know she would have liked some of the books I was reading. *The Disappearing Spoon*, by Sam Kean, made studying chemistry fun for me. I remember her telling me how important it was for her to make the honor role. This had been a stress she put on herself. I always told her the effort was all that mattered. High grades hadn't come easily for her, and she worked hard to maintain that position. She couldn't understand how her friends could go out in the evening and still ace their tests the next day. It's been too many years, and I can't remember her favorite subjects. Even though I know it doesn't matter anymore, for me to know which subjects were her favorites, I wish I could remember more. I didn't know then how important every memory about her would be.

I hope my journey through science isn't too boring for you, but I just couldn't believe that a mystical God would will all of this into existence without having any knowledge of science. I felt God would know everything there is to know about how to do everything He needed to do. *In fact, the Creator would be the ultimate scientist that invented all of the science.* It was essential for me to learn at least the rudiments of how this universe works and how we came into being through what science had discovered, and not what I learned in my Sunday school class.

Elements are made purely of one type of atom and are listed on the periodic table. They have three different forms:

- Approximately 11 gases, such as hydrogen, oxygen, helium, etc.
- At least 76 solids, such as copper, zinc, iron, etc.
- There are 4 liquids, such as mercury, cesium, francium, and bromine.

In case you're wondering, water is not an element. It is a compound of both hydrogen and oxygen, which I'll talk more about in a minute.

The numbers on the periodic table change as more elements are discovered or created by man. Yes, we have that capability. I was surprised to learn we could create something so fundamental. These are known as synthetic elements, but they are elements just the same. They generally aren't very stable but help with research. Fifty years ago, scientists had found 90 elements in nature. Today we are at 118, of which 94 are found naturally and approximately 24 are synthetic.

As discussed, when atoms bond together they form elements. That bonding happens when, for instance, there are one too many electrons in an atom and it goes searching for another with one less to hang out with. Remember, elements are made of like-atoms, and those atoms need a certain number of electrons, protons, and neutrons, so they find friends to hang with to obtain those numbers. That is an elementary form of the many complicated forms of bonding. I wasn't interested in learning other ways of bonding, especially for the formation of compounds. I just wanted a basic understanding of the superglue I referred to earlier.

A molecule can be a compound with two or more different elements in it, or it can have only one type of element in it. A molecule is just bigger than an element because there is generally more than one element in it. Our cells are made of molecules. The "recipes" that cause cells to differentiate into the various types of cells (skin, lung, heart, etc.) are vast. It really is astounding how any of this could have happened, especially by accident. Everything started from one tiny quantum particle, and then began the bonding process until there was one large planet, one large tree, and one large human.

One of the more extraordinary compound-molecules is water. Water is made of two different types of atoms. When one oxygen bonds with two hydrogen it creates a compound water molecule known as H2O. There is an intermolecular attraction (another type of superglue) that brings water molecules together—hence you get running water. Something powerful happened while the solar system was forming that caused two gas elements to combine and create a liquid water molecule, when it should have created another gas molecule. In fact, it would more likely have been a really big combustible molecule, as both hydrogen and oxygen are highly combustible gases. It remains a mystery still as to how this life-giving miracle could have come into being.

When I learned that the water on Earth is all of the water that has ever been here, and through the centuries we have recycled the same water over and over, I understood the concern about the rate at which we are polluting it. Imagine drinking the same water that Jesus or Aristotle drank!

Although we know how to make water today, we do not have the technology to manufacture water in large quantity because of the huge explosion it would create. As I said, I learned way more on this journey than I expected. The love and respect I feel for this planet and all things on it, have grown immensely. It is truly miraculous how perfectly everything works together. In her own way, Bre already knew this, as she was an advocate for animals and the environment. She was wise beyond her years, but I was unable to see then what I see now. In fact, Bre's concern for Mother Earth was sometimes annoying. She even made me turn the water off while brushing my teeth, because you need it only at the beginning and at the end. She was right, of course. Don't dismiss the wisdom of your children as I sometimes did.

I was surprised at what I was beginning to understand when I thought it would be an impossible task. My mind had barely touched the surface, but it felt saturated. Yet science gave me hope and continued to urge me forward, because it was moving me toward Bre. The more I learned, the more it seemed unthinkable to imagine that there is not an intelligence behind the absolute perfection that creates an environment that can sustain life. It wasn't created by a magic wand or happenstance. Everything came into being through a chain reaction of events that was well thought-out. All we have left to do is take care of each other and what was given to us.

Physicist Freeman Dyson said, "The more I examine the universe and study the details of its architecture, the more evidence I find that the universe in some sense must have known we were coming."

CHAPTER 8

A Little Deeper into Science

"I learned very early the difference between knowing the name of something and knowing something."

— RICHARD FEYNMAN —

I was caught up in the excitement of science because it was leading me to Bre. It was like a virus that kept spreading, and I wanted to learn more. I'm including this chapter for those who caught the same virus.

Relativity was used to calculate the movement of planets in the universe. I had never understood that, so I wanted to research it for myself. Einstein knew that the electromagnetic field has forces within it that are invisible. Gravity is also invisible, but what is the force within it that holds things in place? His first realization was that gravity holds no forces—it is space itself. Space is made of something, so it has a texture! When something heavy is placed on it, space will bend, as though it were a piece of fabric onto which you set a ball, creating a dent. This causes objects to move toward each other and roll around each other. With the right amount of tug from the mysterious dark energy, and the right pull from gravity, you get solar systems like our own Milky Way.

Everything moves relative to something else. Now I know where "It's all relative" got its origin. With this knowledge, science had the tools to accurately calculate the behavior of planets. It was even possible to measure the changing distance between celestial bodies going back in time, toward the Big Bang. Then, using the same formula, scientists could move forward into the future, allowing them to know the rate of expansion in the universe. Since I hadn't given science much attention before losing Bre, I had certainly never thought of an unimaginably large universe, continuously expanding. As I've said before, creation is a chain reaction that continues growing all by itself. Evolution of the outer physical world, as well as our ineffable inner world, has no limits.

That Einstein didn't get the Nobel Prize for relativity was a mystery to many. Some thought it was because he proposed the theory of general relativity in 1915, but it was not proven until 1950, so too much time had passed. It's sad to think it could have been a political decision, but that was a possibility as well. It's hard to imagine he did not receive a Nobel, no matter how much time had elapsed or whose ego had been bruised. It is disturbing that politics, ego, and/or greed can block acknowledgments or possibly new discoveries, when they go against the Establishment or someone's purse strings. However, he did receive a Nobel in 1921 for his work in theoretical physics and especially for his discovery of the law of the photoelectric effect (Light shining on matter releases electrons, or other free carriers). That is what caused him to conclude that particles and waves are interchangeable, which he later proved.

Gravity works differently on Earth but is still relative. We are held on Earth because our mass is small compared to Earth's mass, so we are pulled toward it, with very little tug away from it. There is always something with mass pulling on every other thing with mass. It is like a big tug of war, and it's that tug of war that holds things in place.

The dictionary defines zero gravity as, *The state or condition in which there is no apparent force of gravity acting on a body, either because the force is locally weak, or because both the body and its surroundings are freely and equally accelerating under the force.* A physicist might tell you there is no such thing as zero gravity. It's a form of free fall. An astronaut is moving at the same rate he is speeding through space. The way we understood gravity and what holds things in place was changed through what we learned from relativity. It seems impossible that some believe the universe, and all of its intricacies, is a haphazard accident. The science to make this happen is too well planned, and I believe there is an Ultimate Scientist behind creation who informs and expresses all of the science we are just beginning to understand.

Relativity also applies to light which curves relative to objects it must go around, and does not follow a straight line through objects. Fascinatingly, from the curvature of light, Einstein surmised that time must also change relative to something else. Time moves relative to space and velocity. So would we be older or younger when we return from our space vacation? We would be younger than the people we left behind. That was demonstrated in the science-fiction movie, *Interstellar*—one of my favorites. Science fiction isn't all fiction today because much of how our universe works appears to be in sync with many of sci-fi's earliest conceptions.

Another strange thing about time is that when two people watch the same clock, they will see it running at different rates if they are moving relative to each other. It seems there are different universal laws that exist outside of our reality, and one day science will have some of the answers. I can't imagine time not existing, but then again, I can't imagine it changing either. It should be constant. The older I get, the faster time moves. Does time move relative to age as well? It sure seems that way. There is so much we don't understand! But we do know that everything moves relative to something else, and that includes time. As I've said before, time kept coming up while on this journey. Obviously it's important, but it's not for me to figure out.

A physicist wants to find and understand the strange laws governing the subatomic world. They don't wish or expect to recognize a creator of those laws, and they are obliged to find a mathematical formula to prove anything. While a creator seems evident to me, some of our scientific friends can ignore that possibility and continue looking for an equation that probably doesn't exist. It is said that with Newton's laws, along with Einstein's theory of relativity and Planck's quantum theory, they have *almost* everything needed to understand and calculate the physical world of the senses, as well as the invisible world of quantum particles.

One measurement that is missing in their illuminating theories is dark energy, and, as for consciousness, that measurement is missing as well. Science knows dark energy or dark matter must exist because the universe would have remained stagnant without it. It does not reflect light or give off detectable radiation, so until it's found, no measurement can be taken. Perhaps that is an ever-illusive (or ever-elusive) measurement as well. Maybe you or one of your children will find and somehow nail down dark energy. I thought it might be especially fun if it were my grandson. He loves math and science, along with video games and of course superheroes, so it's possible.

Of all the black stuff, black holes are the only ones that have been detected because of their gravitational pull. A black hole results when a star burns up the core of its matter and implodes, bending space to such a degree it creates a hole of enormous gravity. Researchers can find black holes because they can see the things being sucked into them, including whole galaxies. Imagine the enormity of such a galaxy-gobbler! That would be something to consider when flying around in space. A black hole is not to be confused with a supernova, which does the opposite: that star has too much condensed matter and then explodes. It seems a lot of things in creation have an opposite in order to maintain a balance. As I said, pursuing these subjects was like a virus because the more I understood the more convinced I became that there is an intelligence outside of us that has a plan—and that plan is for the physical world to evolve.

Stephen Hawking said, "Because there is a law such as gravity, the universe can and will create itself from nothing." It's true that the pull and tug of gravity causes a chain reaction, but to our knowledge, there was nothing including gravity before the Big Bang. Some want to believe Stephen Hawking's theory because it argues the need for a creator, but others know that only nothing can come from nothing. Something must have been out there before the Big Bang that started the chain of events.

In the 1930s, physicists assumed a particle must exist that sweeps away the radioactive decay expelled from the atom, or life could not exist. It's interesting that they didn't need a measurement to know of its existence. It had no electrical charge and almost never interacted with other particles, so they couldn't find it. They simply passed through everything like little vacuum cleaners. The superglue that holds us together is porous because they are continuously passing through us every second. In 2015, a Nobel was awarded to physicists Takaaki Kajita and Arthur B. McDonald for discovering this elusive subatomic particle. They could finally measure it. It was named the neutrino and translates in Italian as *small neutral one.* Clearly, there were many behind-the-scene activities going on that allowed for the existence of physical life.

Fred Alan Wolf, Ph.D. said, "There is no empty space. When we go down-down-down there is vibration, stuff popping—invisible connections—entanglement." Space is full of activity, and its made of something which brings me back to the same question, "What was here before space existed?"

Another big discovery was announced in 2015, proving one more theory. Einstein, while developing relativity, theorized gravitational waves were rippling through space and time, marking a cataclysmic event. Since space has texture, those waves would be like seeing ripples in the ocean after an explosion. The ocean represents the continuum (space and time), and following the ripples back, you would find where the explosion occurred and be able to establish a timeline. The ability to do this can help us form a timeline of events that happened in the universe.

Bre was my universe, and I made a timeline of her life. I recorded important events that happened on the continuum of her life so that I could present it to Owen one day. Did her life continuum fluctuate every time a big event happened, such as graduation or buying a house? If you could see gravitational waves, you would have seen ripples on her continuum and been able to trace them up to the date her son was born. That event was so big, I felt the Earth move.

The timeline was something Ben asked me to do during that first year. He was afraid I would forget if I didn't write everything down, and he wanted the events of Bre's life recorded for Owen to have. I realized he was right. You think you will never forget, but somehow memories slip into the depths of your mind. Writing this book has helped me recover some of them. Many are buried too deep, but I will always have the memories I record in this book and the ones I posted on her timeline. It was sad for me that Owen never knew his mom, and I'm glad he doesn't feel that same sadness. It was hard for him to grasp the idea that he had a different mom other than the one who raised him during his first few years. I hope he will catch a glimpse of Bre through her timeline and reading this book—when he is ready.

Owen's little sister, Josephine was only seven years old when her mother left to join Bre, and she wanted to learn how to cook for the family. Her grandmother had given her a cookbook for Christmas—what a special gift. When I came to visit, she offered me a cupcake she had baked. Ben didn't have paper cups for them, so she apologized for how funny they looked. I thought they were wonderful, and now her daddy has lots of paper cups for her. Little Samantha was two when her mommy passed and won't have many memories of her, but she has Owen, Josephine, and Ben to answer her questions. These three beautiful children have lived a lifetime already. I am so grateful they have each other, and their father to help guide them, and that I have them in my life. They are forming their own timelines, and I try to record the moments when their continuum fluctuates.

What follows is how they found the elusive gravitational wave: Some 1.3 billion light-years (one light-year is approximately 5.88 trillion miles) from Earth, and a million years ago, two black holes merged. Knowing what a black hole is, you can imagine the enormity of that collision. When that happened, a sound wave was emitted, producing gravitational waves—ripples. It was mind-boggling for me to imagine something so far away, and so long ago, still fluxing its way through time and space.

Science began looking for gravitational waves/ripples when Einstein first suggested they were there. With new technology, special equipment was built at the Laser Interferometer Gravitational-Wave Observatory to register any change on the spacetime continuum. The continuum has a rhythm, and a flux was finally registered in September of 2015. Scientists followed the wave back to one million years ago, when those two black holes merged a gazillion miles away. After 100 years, Einstein's gravitational waves had finally been observed. How fun it would be to hear his comments about this discovery since he believed they would be impossible to detect. It is amazing we have this technology today, and with the development of new technologies, we will be able to find and measure more impossible things. Hopefully, consciousness will be among them. We live in exciting times.

Bre had an open and very curious mind. She would ask the questions, lots of questions, and loved the debates that followed. I've come to believe she is sharing this journey with me and is loving it, but I am sad that I cannot hear and see her reactions. I can almost see her throw her head back and laugh, but at the same time feel proud of me. Anyone who knew Bre would understand why I sometimes felt like the child and she the parent. It's funny, but it makes me happy knowing she might be proud of me.

CHAPTER 9

WE ARE A PRODUCT OF OUR ENVIRONMENT

*"The chance that higher life forms might have
emerged randomly is comparable to the chance
that a tornado sweeping through a junkyard might
assemble a Boeing 747 from the materials therein."*

— SIR FRED HOYLE, ASTROPHYSICIST —

There are six million parts in a 747 and three billion genetic letters in human DNA. To believe we were an accident seemed impossible to astrophysicist, Sir Fred Hoyle. A human being took six million parts and used a blueprint to build the 747. We, on the other hand, evolved from a universe made of countless quantum particles of energy. We are made of 65% oxygen, 18% carbon, 9.5% hydrogen, 3.2% nitrogen, 1.5% calcium, 1.2% phosphorus, and traces of several other minerals. Nature took those elements and combined them in different recipes which created the three billion genetic letters in our DNA. DNA is like a blueprint that shows where all of the genetic letters need to be in the body.

Physical life seems impossible without intention. However, if you believe we were put together bit by bit through trial and error, it doesn't change anything for me. My physical form doesn't have as much to do with who I am, as does what's inside my physical form. Where did the consciousness inside of me come from? Our physical form evolved out of its environment, and there could be different physical forms scattered throughout the universe that evolved out of the environment of their planet; but the energy they are made of and their consciousness inside of them and us, is what makes us aware—and also what connects us.

Beyond the atom I learned about in my grade-school science class and what my religion taught me, I hadn't given much thought as to how I came to physically exist until I lost Bre. It was in the first three years of my research, when I read *The Biology of Belief*, by developmental biologist Dr. Bruce Lipton. Finding Bre meant I needed to know if there is a governing force beyond us. Dr. Lipton believes life is not an accident, but is, rather, well planned. His book gave me hope and new meaning as to our interconnection to everything, and insight into the miraculous little cell. I learned that cells have a nervous, digestive, circulatory, reproductive, and an immune system of sorts, and even a form of communication. "The cell, in so many ways, was already like us."

The environment of Earth was toxic at first. As more elements were added through the bombardment of supernova explosions, our atmosphere changed and cells began forming. Three billion years ago, single-celled organisms had developed and were thriving. In order to survive, these smart little guys began to combine with one another, evolving into various plants and animals. That demonstrates intelligence at the cellular level, but instead of recognizing intelligence, scientists called it instinct—"the instinct to survive." If we were a hit-or-miss conglomerate of atoms, even the "instinct to survive" would have been a very strange hit-or-miss accident.

In time, we became aware of our human superiority and believed we were created separately, by a god. Yet, we were made of atoms and had the same instinct to survive as everything else. I believe all life is of intelligent design, and the instinct to survive is part of that design.

Each of the estimated 37.2 trillion cells it takes to make a human body holds 23 pairs of chromosomes containing our DNA, the blueprint for life. That would be 37.2 trillion times 23 pairs, equaling a staggering number of little blueprints directing cells to where each belongs in the body. Cells need to know if they are going to be a brain cell, lung cell, heart cell, etc. Good thing we have a well thought-out blueprint. However, the nutrients our cells are receiving from their environment can affect that process. Because Bre was an advocate for the environment, there are a lot of memories of her in this chapter.

Genes are found inside our DNA, and each person has between 20,000 – 25,000 of them. They are like markers passed down through generations and play a role in human development. The genes of each body are 99.9% identical to every other body, which leaves 0.1% to make us look and seem to be different from one another. It is that 0.1% that all prejudices are based upon. We put way too much emphasis on that 0.1% of what and who we are—it's irrelevant, so stop it!

Bre had friends from all walks of life and in all different colors. She didn't see the differences, she only saw if they were a kind person or not. She especially liked old people and loved to talk with them about their life. One instance was when we were in Germany, and she saw an old man sitting on a bench inside the Dachau con-centration camp. He looked sad and lonely, so she walked over to him and began to talk. Most of us wouldn't have an interest, or might think we were bothering him, but not Bre. She learned he had been a boy in the camp, and came every day to talk with people about his experience. There was a movement (that continues to this day) to erase what the Nazis had done, and he didn't want that history forgotten. Bre had a genuine interest in people, and thought he needed company. Anyway, we learned something we would not have known had she not felt this connection with others.

This reminds me of a tattoo she designed for her lower back. It was a world encircled by all different people and animals holding hands and paws. There was a dolphin jumping from the sea and a bird flying above it. Her fascination with tattoos began when she was very young. She liked watching *National Geographic* and thought indigenous people were beautiful with their tattoos and piercings. It wasn't long before she asked me for her own tattoo. I told her to wait until she was older and could afford to pay for it herself. She had a happy little blue fish on her foot, a small diamond in her nose, and her unified world on her back. These symbols describe my beautiful Bre and say a lot about the person she was.

When Bre left, I wanted to have her little fish tattoo on my foot. However, the designer had drawn a bigger blue fish with beautiful orange fins. Three of her friends had come with me for support, and together we decided it was the mama to Bre's little blue one, so I should have the bigger one instead. I was told it was a fifties fish. Bre loved the fifties and had decorated her home in that style, so I felt she was telling me she was there to support me as well.

Genes are passed down to us through our parents, which inclines many to believe they are victims of their genetic endowment. But that's not true, and Dr. Lipton is at the forefront of this research. We now know much about what's in the foods we eat. That and our environment affect our body's ability to communicate. What we eat and drink, think and feel, along with the sleep we get, and the air we breathe are all part of that environment. As an example: We know cancer loves sugar. So, even if your family is genetically predisposed to cancer, changing your diet and lifestyle can change your body's environment and override genetics, preventing cancer from manifesting. "We are what we eat" is more accurate than previously known. Give a plant water and fertilizer and watch it grow; give it polluted water that confuses its signals, and watch it die. We need a healthy environment for communication to be clear.

Many diets out there can ward off disease. I love my computer for any search of this nature. (By the way, I didn't know much about computers or how to use "search" before I took this journey. And I never cease to be amazed that all information is available to us at our fingertips.) We actually do have some control over our health once we understand the importance of the environment our cells swim in. *It is always better to prevent something from happening than it is to fix it once it has happened.* That was a concept I developed through owning a business, and one that can be applied in all walks of life.

Bre once told me I needed to eat more organic fruits and vegetables that were alive and bursting with enzymes. Anything that was heavily processed or came in a box was like eating "dead food." She loved to garden and was a vegetarian, so I imagine her son, Owen, would look like the Jolly Green Giant by now had she been here to feed him. I keep telling Owen, Josephine, Samantha, and their dad that they need to learn to like vegetables, but without much success. "They're just sticks with moss on them," as Josephine would say. Owen just moves food around on his plate and would rather eat cake. Surprisingly, Samantha likes vegetables, although it's really the "dipping sauce" she likes. They make me laugh, and I love that.

It was the impact of meteors and exploding stars which were filled with life-giving minerals that changed our atmosphere, creating a swampy, nutrient-rich environment—the perfect primordial "soup" in which life could begin. We really are made of earth after all. Is this another truth in the Bible that was buried inside of distorted interpretations? Since cells communicate via the environment they sit in, we should listen, moment by moment, to what our body tells us. When a big green salad sounds especially good, or if we just feel like crying, or stretching like a cat, it could be just what our cellular environment needs. If we get out of its way and pay attention to its signals, our body seems to know how to take care of itself. I'm not sure where or if I heard this somewhere, but it's stuck in my mind, so I'm passing it on to you. *If we could keep laughter in a bottle and take it in pill form, there would be no depression.* Laughter triggers the production and release of endorphins, and endorphins give a sense of well-being. It also strengthens the immune system and reduces pain and the damaging effects of stress. That's something to consider while warding off the Corona virus and other diseases. The body is slow to recognize the various pharmaceuticals we take to release endorphins, but it immediately recognizes laughter because our body came already equipped with that Rx,—a clean and fast-acting medicine, with no side effects.

Bre's wisdom fills my mind as I write this chapter. She strongly believed eating organic foods and juicing, along with exercise, helped with her depression. She was right, of course, and I smile when I think of the concoctions she came up with. I tasted some and thought *yuck* but she thought they were yummy. Bre didn't go halfway on things. When she and Ben rescued Liberty, she bought books on dog behavior. When she got pregnant, she purchased books on pregnancy and being a good parent. She had books on eating as a vegetarian and vegan. Giving up dairy products proved too rigid and difficult, so she made sure her dairy came from "happy animals"—free range and organically fed. She told me if I was going to have turkey for Thanksgiving, it needed to be a "happy turkey." Although she wouldn't eat it, she wanted to know it lived a happy life before I ate it. It's funny to think how over the top I thought she was, but now I know she was *on* the top.

Before the microscope, we didn't know about germs and bacteria. Absent any knowledge of what caused disease and infection, we lived in fear of falling victim to them. Even God was fair game for blame, as many believed illness and abnormalities were punishment for sin. I have come to know there is no punishment administered by a god. Illness has nothing to do with sin and everything to do with the messages our body-mind is not receiving, due to the filth and misperceptions that have infiltrated and deranged it. Through advancements in science, antiseptics and antibiotics were developed. However, in our ignorance we overused and misused our wonder drugs, enabling those smart little guys to adapt and become drug-resistant superbugs. The "instinct to survive" extended further than we thought, so we didn't give bacteria the attention they deserved. Since I believe there is a form of intelligence or consciousness in all living things, their ingeniousness came as no surprise. We could have anticipated and avoided this problem by understanding the intelligence of bacteria, then limiting and monitoring our use of antibiotics.

Today we know microorganisms are not inert but very much alive and can communicate at some level, mutate, and evolve in relation to their environment. So, before we tinker with nature by altering the genetic code of the atoms in the foods we eat, we need to be aware of the lasting effects our experimentation could have on us. Our bodies were designed to defend themselves, given proper nutrition, rest, and cleanliness. I'm not sure our bodies recognize genetically engineered foods, preservatives, and additives. Also, let's not forget the toxins we spray on our crops, and coat our beautiful green lawns with, and the chemicals we feed to our animals. Even our irreplaceable water supply has become infused with insecticides, herbicides, and other toxins. We know our digestive system has a harder time breaking down some of these foreign foods, and that many other inputs are toxic, but what else are these man-made intruders telling our cells to do or not to do? Regrettably, that knowledge will come only by using them. Many mysterious illnesses have been cropping up within recent years, and I've never known a time when so many people were suffering from food allergies. Where is this coming from?

It's a catch-22. How do we feed the growing population without being able to produce bigger and hardier crops? How do we preserve our food and kill harmful organisms without additives? Factory-farmed livestock are given antibiotics and growth hormones to increase production, and we, in turn, consume them. Ever wondered why our children are maturing quicker? Maybe it's the hormones they're consuming. It is possible we may have to go back to the basics one day but, hopefully, not at the expense of our children's health and development.

I love this (anonymous) little joke that Dr. Victor Bloom shares in *A Short History of Medicine*:

"Doctor, I have an earache."
2000 BC "Here, eat this root."
1000 BC "That root is heathen! Here, say this prayer."
1850 AD "That prayer is superstition! Here, drink this potion."
1940 AD "That potion is snake oil! Here, swallow this pill."
1985 AD "That pill is ineffective! Here, take this antibiotic."
2000 AD "That antibiotic is poison! Here, eat this root!"

Bre would have posted this poem on her wall, as at one time in her life she wanted to be a naturopath. Hoping a visit to Bastyr University would encourage her to go to college, we went on a tour. Although she loved the tour, it was not enough to make her want to go to college. I didn't give up. I asked her to attend Johnson O'Conner aptitude testing. She humored me and agreed to go. Thinking this was a waste of time, she jokingly told them she wanted to be an attorney. After three days of testing, she was told she would love the litigation but hate the research. Boy, was that true! It was humorous to listen to some of the debates she got into with her friends. Instead, her scores were off the chart in excellence for musical engineering, but she was told she would not like playing the instruments.

When Bre was young, she and I liked listening to "Hooked on Classics." She would pick out the different instruments being played. I didn't know she even knew what the various instruments were, let alone hear the distinction between them. I made her take piano lessons, which she was good at but never liked. Having an aptitude for music doesn't automatically mean you would like playing an instrument. College was something I dreamed of for her, but it wasn't her dream. So, I will dedicate all of the environmental issues in this book to her. Her love of the natural world, its flora and fauna, awakened something in me that wasn't there before. She didn't have to go to college to make a difference in people's lives, but it might have opened other doors that were closed to her.

As you know, we cannot manufacture water in quantity. When it's gone, it's gone. We buy our water in little plastic bottles because we don't like the chemicals in tap water, and then we throw those little bottles into the garbage. I hope you recycle. We wear synthetic fabrics, and when we wash them, tiny synthetic fibers spill into our oceans. We are aware of pollution and global climate changes. But despite our awareness of these life-or-death problems, greed or being inconvenienced causes many of us to turn a blind eye. We alone are responsible for the welfare of this planet, and everything on it. It is my believe we will evolve into a more compassionate people who will understand our interconnections, and rectify the damage we are doing before it's too late.

A healthy environment allows our organs, and especially the immune system, to work at full capacity. Trees filter pollutants from the air and release oxygen, so we need a lot of trees. We should be planting them everywhere. Instead we are cutting seventy-eight million acres of rainforest every year. That's 31,000 square miles. As Joni Mitchell sang, "They've paved paradise and put up a parking lot." We know that fresh fruits and vegetables hold oxygen and other life-giving nutrients necessary for our bodies—all we have to do is eat them. Nothing can live without oxygen, even fish take oxygen from the water, just as we take oxygen from the air we breathe and the foods we eat. The cleaner the oxygen and our foods are, the cleaner our internal bodies are, and the clearer their messages. I find it interesting that oxygen both gives and decays life, and that water is made from two explosive gas molecules. The two most essential necessities for life should be impossible. I didn't know what to think of that, other than the doings of an intelligence above our own—the ultimate scientist, who set these things into play.

The body will completely rebuild itself every seven years. We shed 500 million cells a day, and new cells replace them. It doesn't take a rocket scientist to imagine the success of that when bodies are receiving the right information from their environment. There was a commercial out that said something like, if I could do one sit-up to have a stronger heart, if I could eat one piece of broccoli to improve…Maybe you've heard it. Anyway, I laughed each time I saw it, but that one step could lead to two and three, and ultimately to a healthier me. I just have to take that step, but I'm not very good at remaining dilligent—I like pizza and apple fritters too much.

For years, environmentalists and other informed humans had expressed their concerns. Sadly, they were often painted as being troublemakers or extremists. When they didn't have big money to launch a public campaign, they would use whatever means they could to protect mankind and this planet. Remember the endangered spotted owl and all the trouble it caused the forest industry? Even I considered them extremists, when it affected so many people's jobs. Then, I learned the story behind it. I went on a hike with friends and one of them was an environmentalist, collecting evidence for the presence of the spotted owl. She told me that protecting them was the only way to protect the old-growth forests they lived in. Our planet is held together by interlocking root systems of vegetation that hold the soil in place, and old-growth forests are important to that system.

The runoff of soil affects our rivers and oceans. Fish are losing their habitat, our oceans are warming, and in places the air is unbreathable. It's clear we will not be able to turn a blind eye forever. The clear-cutting of oxygen-producing trees and the pollution of our water, air, and soil are evident to us today. We are all one living, breathing organism, and all things work together as one. Most environmentalists are not extremists, and one day they will be viewed as saviors of the planet and not troublemakers.

A large campaign was launched to tell us it would be expensive to label our foods with "genetically modified food," and they knew we wouldn't want to pay more for our food. So, of course, we voted no on that initiative. The companies that produced the seeds or raised genetically modified crops were the only ones I could think of who would have a reason to launch such a campaign. The true profession for all companies is to know how to stay in business. If it was perfectly safe and all tests had been done, why were they afraid to list it? Genetic modification is a process that alters the genetic code of the atom—the very thing we are made of. That is why the body doesn't always recognize those foods. I wonder how expensive it would have been to list that in with the ingredients. Anyway, they more or less won, and we don't always know when we are eating genetically modified foods.

To be fair, science tells us GMOs are safe for us and the environment. The seeds can be modified to make them resistant to the insects that like eating a particular crop. That eliminates the use of blanketed insecticides that kill all insects, and certain insects are necessary for the health of the soil. That would be a good reason for GMOs, although I do wonder why the bug won't eat them. Thirty-eight countries have banned GMOs, yet most still import the food. That is confusing, but they believe GMOs can hurt their economy and the small farmers. Many of our farmers have been seriously affected, so that concern is real. It is despairing we may not have an answer to this controversy, until a generation or more have passed.

Because of advancements in social media, more is brought to our attention and people are speaking up. Nations are finally paying attention to concerned people, environmentalists, and scientists, taking steps to reduce the huge footprint we are making. When we are led by greed and convenience, it is hard for us to change. Mother Nature is the one on top of the food chain, and we will be forced to nurture her whether we choose to or not. I love this green planet, with its sparkling blue water, so I take whatever steps I can to keep it that way for my grandson, his little sisters, and their children to come. Like so many others, I myself don't like to be inconvenienced, so I am guilty of not taking all of the steps. It's one step at a time, and every step helps.

One person can turn into millions. Look what happened with recycling; we now have bins for that in most homes and businesses. The universal symbol for recycling is recognized by most people on this planet. Companies are advertising they are green and environmentally conscious. Stores offer aisles and sections of organic products because they're what customers want. Manufacturers have moved away from the cruelty of animal-testing for their products because they heard the outcry. None of this was an issue when I was young, so I know we are moving in the right direction.

We tend to blame big oil companies for destroying our environment, and indeed they have. If there were no market for what they sold, there would be no drilling and fracking for gas and oil.

We have to take some responsibility for the destruction ourselves. We love the comforts and conveniences oil companies provide us. Stop throwing stones and look for other sources of energy for those conveniences. *Companies stay in business because they have a customer. When you stop being a customer, you will have the right to throw stones.* I have a gas-driven car, heat my house with gas, and love my gas fireplace. In clear conscience I cannot throw that stone. As other sources of energy become easy and affordable to obtain, we will all make this change. Buy stock in those companies and not in the polluters' companies. Money will allow more research, and this is one step I have taken.

Imagine if you stopped using herbicides and then millions followed. Again, if there were no market for the products they sold, the companies manufacturing toxic killers would look at producing something we would buy. Everything on the ground gets into our water and into our bodies. Little by little, companies are hearing the demand and removing some of the chemicals from their products. Check out Thrive Market, an online venue for affordable organic foods. Offering reasonably priced organic fruits and vegetables from local farmers, Thrive delivers right to your door. When you do a search on your computer you'll find many options. People are becoming aware, and it's making a difference.

We might be led to believe (or hope) that the pesticides, herbicides, or fungicides that a company sells are not harmful to us or our environment. But what the manufacturer doesn't tell us is that their new product kills the bees and other pollinators essential to the foods we eat. Plants can't reproduce unless they are pollinated. Did you know that the rusty patched bumble bee is on the endangered species list? As a child, I remember being fascinated by this cute, fat bumble bee who wasn't interested in stinging me. My nephew was raising bee colonies as a hobby and letting us taste the honey. For three years in a row, they all died in the spring. Why? Could insecticides and weed killers have been the cause, or did they become infected with a mysterious disease? In either case, without bees we have no food. On a small scale, vinegar mixed with dish soap kills weeds. I know some dish soap can be toxic, so look for biodegradable. If we could see the beauty in weeds, we wouldn't have to kill them. Les and I are not quite there, so we use soap and vinegar. High-acid vinegar is also available on the internet and works well without soap.

Because the public is informed through online media, it is often used as a tool for disinformation from both sides. You've heard the saying, "You can't believe everything you read." Even our friends on Facebook are being hacked, so you can never be sure who is doing the posting. I find it a big job to investigate everything, but I try not to repost anything without first researching it. Living in an ideal world, posting a lie to further your cause or damage another would be unthinkable. We don't live in such a world. If you read something that triggers a reaction, look for the source of the information before you react to it.

Our body literally glows with light that we can't see, but we can measure it. Light photons were lost in cancer patients, while in MS patients, the opposite occurred. There were too many photons, causing chaos in the natural rhythms of the body. When we become ill, our body's vibrations are out of sync, and the light emanating from it is altered. Every cell has a unique vibrational frequency, and finding corresponding frequencies will help balance our body's rhythms. When pharmaceutical companies find a way to profit from these technologies, and put their money into that research, things will move more quickly. A more recent discovery is that sound vibration can extinguish fire. This made national news. Imagine the implications! With the necessary funding, wonderful technologies will come from the study of light and vibration. Again, we can help by supporting this research through donations, or buying stock in the companies using these technologies.

Our thoughts also affect our bodies' environment. At the fundamental level, our bodies are made of particles of energy, and we know energy is affected by thought. Thoughts carry emotional vibrations, and our bodies respond to those vibrations. Negative thoughts disrupt the flow of energy moving through us, whereas positive thoughts keep things moving smoothly and naturally. Pay attention next time you are sad or angry, and then notice how your body reacts to it. When you are happy, your body releases chemicals that energize you, you can think more clearly, and physical pain is minimized. Negative thoughts stop the energizing flow, opening the door to pain, disease, and mental anguish. Feelings are important! Pay attention to the way things make you feel—and change the things that make you feel bad, or change your view of the things you cannot change.

Your subconscious feeds your body with negative and/or positive thoughts all the time. In fact, it is said that we have some 60,000 to 80,000 thoughts per day, and most of them we are not even aware of. Bruce Lipton wrote that for the first six years of life, we're not actually engaged in consciousness. We're just downloading experiences and behaviors. The things we hear and see as children become facts because we don't have the ability to consciously reason out what is true and what is not. Consequently, many deep-rooted thoughts and feelings come from our childhood—both good and bad.

We can be side railed throughout life because of toxic relationships. When you're in a belittling or abusive relationship, you begin to believe that because you incite such aggression and anger from your abuser, there must surely be something wrong with you. You have been broken down in such a manner as to believe you are insignificant, don't deserve better, or have no value. You can't see that it is really their own feelings of inferiority being projected onto you. A truly "together" person doesn't need to make someone else feel insignificant in order to make themselves feel significant. You need to move away from that environment as soon as possible, or at the very least, don't believe them. Take your power back; don't give it to them because that's what they crave, and your power belongs to you. An abuser is like a mosquito that drains your life force, but it can never be entirely depleted—your life force is simply awaiting your direction to swat that mosquito away. A world of meaning and joy awaits those who recognize and regenerate their own power.

Charged memories and interpretations of life experiences become the way you view the world. Now that you're aware of that, it is time to change the negative thoughts you may have formed. *Entering Your Own Heart* by Carole J. Morton, and *Healing Your Life with Water* by Diana E. Ruiz, are especially helpful in this type of healing, but there are many others. States like depression, loneliness, anger, and panic attacks are born of subconscious thoughts you're not aware of. "Your life will change when you clean house," says Ruiz. Her book includes exercises in the back that will enable you to isolate and expel the untruths. Bre and I would have had a lot of fun with that book at the cabin.

Consciously examine the things going through your head and ask yourself if they are true or not. If they are true, they will feel good. If they feel bad, they are not true. I believe our feelings act as a guiding system—a gift we were born with. Maybe it is time we trust our feelings and learn how to use them. Our subconscious may be telling us that we are dumb, ugly, or just unlucky in life, or it could be telling us that we are loved, lucky, smart, beautiful, handsome, etc. It could also be clinging to the idea that we are weak and sickly, or strong and healthy. There are other ways you can be strong and healthy that have nothing to do with the physical body. Never stay in a place of despair and hopelessness; step out of that and see the glorious unlimited person you are. Tune into your feelings, and you will know which thoughts are true and which ones are not. All you have to do is keep the truths you were born with and throw out the non-truths you've been taught. Simple, right? There would not be so many books on this subject, were it not important for us to remember the truths and stop believing the untruths. We are made of vibrating energy, and our thoughts profoundly affect that energy. Change your thoughts and you change you, because you changed your internal environment.

One of the first books Bre and I took to our cabin was, *You Can Heal Your Life* by Louise Hay. It had a list of physical ailments along with the mental patterns that created them. We had a good time with it, and our friends joined in the fun when they visited. We laughed at some, but there were many that rang true. At the time, around 1996, I had no knowledge of positive and negative vibrational energy or the quantum world. We were going to be around for a very long time, so none of that was on my radar. When I went to the cabin, hoping Bre would be there, I began to reflect on the books we had collected. Clearly, she had led me on a journey that went beyond finding proof of where she was. It led me to better understand the things that were important to her, and to a loving consciousness that stands both outside and inside of us.

CHAPTER 10

CONSCIOUSNESS

"Everything in the physical world is made
out of atoms. Atoms are made out of energy.
And energy is made out of consciousness."

— JOHN ASSARAF, *THE ANSWER* —

B
efore I lost Bre, I didn't feel the need to dig deep into the difficult questions I asked throughout my life. It would be far too much work to make the effort and probably prove inconclusive. I would just live my life—and at the end of it, I would either receive the answers or not exist at all. I no longer had that option because Bre's life had already ended. I had to find her, and as I walked down the alley, the impossible puzzle began to form a probable picture.

Even though there were no hard cold facts telling me what consciousness is, things began to fall into place when I began to study it. I couldn't come to terms with the biblical description of the creator, but I'd always felt there was something out there. Consciousness seems to have come from nowhere, as though it had always been here—was that a better discription of the creator? Consciousness has an effect on energy. Why would that be, if consciousness were not a necessary part of creation? It seemed it was both inside and outside of us.

The Bible teaches that God created the heavens, the Earth, and all its hosts in six days, and then He rested on the seventh day. That was accepted as the literal truth until science discovered that it took *much* longer. To defend their position, it was explained that no one knew how many hours were in God's day. How many other mistakes were made? The Bible said God created man because of His love for us. That means we have always existed, for He could not have loved us without knowing us. We were given the freedom to choose. That was interpreted to mean we were given the choice to choose the "one God Himself," over all other gods. To me, the freedom to choose means more than that. We expand our awareness and learn from the choices we make throughout life, and that is the purpose of life. In scripture, He used the power of thought to create the universe. "Let there be light, and it was so." His thoughts became reality just as our own thoughts become reality. Genesis 1:26 says, "Let us make mankind in our image, in our likeness, so that they may rule over the fish of the sea and the birds in the sky, over livestock and all wild animals, and over all creatures that move along the ground." It is consciousness that gives us that ability. So, is it our physical form or consciousness that is in the image and likeness of God? That was uncharted territory, but this whole journey had been uncharted for me.

Assuming that various degrees of consciousness permeate everything, I wondered if all of creation might have come from one superconsciousness. That "he knows our thoughts" would not seem mystical if we understood that we are part of—not separate—from the one consciousness that is common to all. That was another "aha" moment for me. Ages-old superstitions and the lack of scientific knowledge would of course scramble and distort the revelations of ancient shamans, prophets, mediums, and seers. Afterall, they knew nothing about energy, consciousness, or interconnections and only saw separation. Their messages passed through time via oral stories and ancient texts. They were rewritten again and again, employing words and beliefs that people could understand for the time they were living in. Efforts are being made to reexamine ancient texts through a scientific eye. Gregg Braden is a leading researcher of ancient texts, and there are others. That wouldn't happen if they didn't believe there could be hidden messages in them.

Many describe consciousness as something that is everywhere, or nonlocal, and permeating the field of energy. The quantum world consists of vibrating waves of potential, until a thought is introduced. Would those waves randomly vibrate without a conscious thought to direct them? We affect the energy of the quantum world through our conscious thought, and I believe our consciousness is part of an endless, timeless continuum of pure consciousness that "knows our every thought," and "has numbered even the very hairs on your head." (Luke 12:7)

Sadly, some scientists are still adhering to an ancient rule that no longer exists, that they study only that which is measurable. Consciousness may never have a means of measurement, but science can't ignore it indefinitely. Many experiments, using plants or people, have clearly demonstrated connection through consciousness. This should have been accepted long ago and shouted from the highest hill! Had they not pushed the study of consciousness and our interconnections aside, we would perhaps be more compassionate toward one another today. Knowing what a super-consciousness might be and where it comes from, we would have more trust in the power of our thoughts. We would treat disease and mental illness differently, using fewer drugs and trusting in the power within us and outside of us instead. As a united people, we would send thoughts of loving intentions into the world, thus minimizing conflict. Consciousness is the one dynamic that affects both the physical and energy worlds. It is the missing link, and it solves the mystery of creation. Until we recognize what consciousness is, we can only imagine the implications of having that kind of power inside of us.

Thus far, a unified theory has not been found, and nothing about consciousness or our genesis has been proven mathematically, either. It is all speculation. A conscious energy that was here before the advent of the physical world seems obvious to me and others, with or without a measurement. Am I seeing only what I want to see? No! The evidence is overwhelming. It's disappointing that the full force of money and research that's poured into "mainstream" science is not available to those in the "off-stream," who study the unmeasurable. When our view of consciousness is no longer feared to be a link to a god that stands outside of us, funding for consciousness research will increase dramatically.

The HeartMath Institute is actively researching vibrational energy produced by the heart and how our emotions are tied to that vibration. Emotional energy generated by thought is measurable, and that may lead the way to measuring consciousness. We know more today, and we're not as superstitious as we once were. We will learn to trust our intuition and the feelings generated by conscious thoughts, when we know it is coming from the greater consciousness inside and outside of us. I acknowledge the signs and/or coincidences I am presented with and no longer brush them off as odd or insignificant. It was like an awakening for me, but until you recognize this for yourself, it's just my words. Perhaps we're not ready to use that kind of power, and the mystery will solve itself in its own time as we grow in awareness and compassion for others.

Conscience—as in "Let your conscience be your guide"—is not the same as consciousness. Your mind is filled with learned ideas.

106

Consciousness is our state of inner and outer awareness, and communicates through physical sensations, feelings, intuition, and coincidence. It is not prejudiced or judgmental. It will never guide you to harm another, nor will it hold self-righteous pridefulness within it. Unskilled at hearing it, we tend to filter everything through the preconceived ideas of our conscience. I am ever mindful of my amazing consciousness both inside and outside that informs me, and will continue to hone my abilities to hear its *loving* guidance throughout my life.

As defined in the dictionary, consciousness is *the state of being awake and aware of one's surroundings.* I see it *as an awareness inside of us that has the ability to express itself,* and I believe the consciousness in each of us is helping us to become aware of our connection to it. Consciousness is as integral to us as our biology. Throughout this book, connection, consciousness, and vibrational energy permeate the pages because that's where the evidence kept taking me. *I see the creator as an infinite and conscious energy-system that creates from its thoughts, while science would rather see no creator at all. I see the universe, and us, as an integral part of one infinite energy-system that is conscious. Science sees a separate field of energy that is strangely affected by consciousness.* Science took us apart and found we were made of that energy, but consciousness was separate and mysteriously came out of nowhere. Things were becoming very weird in the world of science after the mysteries of the quantum world were (partially) unveiled, and consciousness is a big one. Nothing was what they thought it was supposed to be, and consciousness will prove to be more important than what they believed possible—perhaps the ultimate.

British psychologist Max Velmans said, "How many years will it take before 'the matrix of energy' is discovered to be consciousness, giving rise to a whole new world?"

Why were we born with consciousness, and the self-awareness and imagination it makes possible? They're not necessary for physical life. We could still function through instinct, but what would we learn without a conscious examination of the experiences we had? Without consciousness we would be living in a void without empathy or compassion, where our only thoughts would be our next meal and sexual release. However, why would sexual release be necessary if procreation was not an essential part of the plan? With every day, month, and year that went by, I became more and more convinced that we were planned, have a purpose, and nothing about creation is an accident.

I didn't see how anything could exist without energy and consciousness. *E+C=R (Energy + Consciousness = Reality)* is my formula for all of creation, and I can't see a different one. We have been evolving since the universe exhaled, and in time we will know the creative power of our conscious thoughts. *I have come to know that the energy of the universe is neutral and never judges—it simply responds to whatever thoughts we send into it. The universe is part of creation, but it is not the creator. The creator fills infinity and exists inside and outside of the universe.* No wonder the ancients described the creator as a godlike king; they couldn't conceive of anything greater than that. It also explains why most NDE'ers didn't see an actual "God" but felt connected to a loving and immense presence.

Today, researchers are open to the study of mysterious, intangible phenomena and are receiving less ridicule. Phenomena such as telepathy, remote viewing, remote healing, and so on may be explained through connection, consciousness, and the field of energy that is filled with waves of all possibilities. Mediums are thought to tap into the spirit of departed loved ones. We are conscious, energy beings that never cease to exist, and that is what makes mediumship possible. The paranormal will be explained through the study of conciousness and the quantum world—there is no paranormal, just a lack of knowledge. Old superstitions and fear bog down legitimate investigation. Let's move through this and get to the answers.

We can't break consciousness down through biology because it is not of the physical realm, and that is beyond our sense of reality. The Bible refers to the soul or the spirit within. What is the spirit within or soul if not the living consciousness inside of us? For some, it seems preposterous to think of themselves as anything other than the human body they look at in the mirror every morning. The evidence I found proved to me that I am more than what I can see, and so is Bre. As science continues to evolve, it takes us closer to recognizing the truly amazing and eternal beings we actually are.

Psychiatrist and psychoanalyst Carl Jung (1875-1961) was a pioneer in the study of consciousness. He collected enough evidence to convince himself that consciousness does not die with the body or the brain. He saw it as "the invisible, intangible manifestation of the soul." He didn't see humans as small or unworthy or in need of forgiveness, but as "the radiant Godhead itself."

CHAPTER 11

THE ORIGIN OF RELIGION

*"People take different roads seeking fulfillment
and happiness. Just because they're not on your
road doesn't mean they've gotten lost."*

— DALAI LAMA —

"Beliefs are what divide people. Doubt unites them."

— PETER USTINOV —

I had studied the Bible, but I had never studied the origin of
it or of religions. I knew it was important for me to do that.

A short time before Bre left, she told me she had been going
to a Bible study class at her cousin's house and had accepted Jesus
into my heart. Bre understood my wishy-washy stance on religion.
She may have thought I wasn't interested because of my neutral
response to her announcement. I wish I could have been more jubi-
lant, or at least told her I appreciated her independence in choosing

what she thought was right for herself. Bre was searching for answers, and that is always good. I didn't give it the attention Bre thought I should have, and I regret that. At one time in my life I had been on the same journey. It was easy to be caught up in the wonder of the Bible and what Jesus taught. My brother and his family could help her with that better than I. As long as religion doesn't cause you to pass judgment, disconnecting from family and friends, then it is a good thing. I didn't want to discourage her from something that could be right for her, so I simply closed that door without much discussion.

Life would be easier if everyone believed in the same things, but it wouldn't be interesting. *The beauty of life is that we think differently. The ugliness of life is that we want everyone to think the way we do.* Religion is no exception. "All religions are true but none are literal," said Professor Joseph Campbell. The truth and value of one's religion cannot be proven with fact, so it shouldn't be controversial. If we could accept that, life would be much more peaceful. We make things controversial by choosing sides and forcing our individual beliefs on everyone else. We feel the need to judge one another, setting ourselves above others. Anger, sadness, and separation are the results of that mindset. There is no justification for tearing families, communities, and countries apart when the Bible clearly says, "Thou shalt not judge." We tend to ignore this teaching when we're passing out judgments. Religion, in general, was meant to explain why we are here, where we come from, and what happens when we die. If you believe yours has it right, put your attention there and not on the others—then let everyone else do the same. I believe we have always been connected through one consciousness that favors no particular religion. There is no need to force my beliefs on you because we think differently. The separation between us is only the separation we create in our own mind.

Inside every religion there are beautiful beliefs and wonderful, loving people. It is radical beliefs that vent cruelty and fearful people that give religion a bad name. I hear people say religious beliefs cause war; and since people equate God with religion, He also gets the blame. Religion or God may be used as an excuse for war, but man is the cause. Do you suppose that if God and religion had never been devised by man, that war would never have happened? I imagine we would find another venue to show our superiority and seize more land and/or resources. We even fight with each other over things that don't really matter. Is this just human nature, or will the future look back on this time and call us a primitive people? Until we evolve beyond the weaknesses that drive us (greed, envy, power), we will find an excuse for war.

God has been the scapegoat long enough. The creator allowed for man's existence and gave them the freewill and power to choose between good and evil. Good thought and action feel good, and evil feels bad—pay attention to how things feel in your heart. We are here to learn from the choices we make, and it has nothing to do with choosing the one true religion. Feeling superior or more righteous than another because of your choice of religion or belief creates separation. That would never be the intention of a creator who created the universe and everything in it through connections. Tolerance, unity, and compassion strengthen connection.

The Council of Nicaea was established in the fourth century by Roman Emperor Constantine. People had different views of Jesus' teachings which caused division and fighting. One disagreement was in their interpretation that God, Jesus, and the Holy Spirit are all one entity—not separate as some believed. This is known as the Trinity. They were close. Now, we know that everything is a part of one energy which was way out of their ability to comprehend. Constantine wanted to establish order. He chose scholars and leaders from the many different belief systems to decide which documents would make the cut. Many documents were modified or considered duplicates, and others were thought to be pagan and deleted. Through this process one book and one unified Christian religion was established. The Roman Catholic Church was the result, and all people were forced to follow it. The Greek translation for catholic is *unified*. As well-meaning and sincere as they were, I doubt that God had much input. The Bible was written by men with their own agendas. Constantine should have insisted on tolerance for all beliefs. The world might be different today had he made that the law.

This explains how the Christian faith became one unified religion, but where did all of the ancient texts and philosophies come from that brought about the confusion and division? It seems that cavemen practiced a burial ceremony of sorts, so maybe some were expressions of ancient beliefs. Otherworldly experiences occurred throughout time, and all over the globe. And through the centuries, those stories were passed down via the oral tradition. No matter what part of the globe you were living in, these were superstitious, pre-science times. It's easy to understand how a powerful god or another otherworldly entity would have been created to address their helplessness and relieve their fears. Of course, these mystical entities had demands, and they were interpreted in various ways: through kings, prophets, shamans, wise men, and etc. Rituals were established, and brutal punishments were meted out to enforce the rules. That could explain how so many different philosophies and religions evolved all around the globe and became so strong.

When a person of impressive authority declared he had a direct line to the divine, and articulated those communications, the people listened. And the more charismatic the seemingly enlightened ones were, the more followers they would attract, and just like that, another religion was born, complete with a set of god-given demands. It was a man, or sometimes a woman, believing they were a prophet, who created religion—not God. I believe the creator is nothing like a physical being and is far above needing anything from us. The only desire and injunction was for us to love one another and the world that was created for us. We are still clinging to many of the old stories and beliefs, but in time science will show us another story.

People of religion believed their prophet served as an intermediary between them and God, which is similar to a medium who is an intermediary between the physical and the spirit world. Other than their word, there was no way to know for certain who or what had spoken to them, or if their vision was divine. In any case, the Bible condemns mediumship because one is seeking comfort and advice from the dead and not from God. Its authors and editors did not understand that the world of the "dead" is the living spirit world, and that is our world, and the world of the creator. There are no dead people. The Bible was transcribed by men who believed being dead was a bad thing, unaware that "dead people" are us. As I've said before, it was never easy for me to accept on faith what a "learned man" was telling me. Subjective experience and objective knowledge would be the only way to find the answers I was seeking, so I ventured into subjects that were considered forbidden territory for many of us.

After 9/11, prominent atheist and evolutionary biologist Richard Dawkins said, "Revealed faith is not harmless nonsense, it can be lethally dangerous nonsense. Dangerous because it gives people unshakable confidence in their own righteousness."

It's wise to question everything that's exterior to oneself—religious dogma, gurus, politicians, commercials, psychics, friends, teachers, family members, etc. Doubt makes us think, as it did for me, and that is not a sin. Clergy and followers of many religions defensively feared our asking questions they couldn't answer, befriending people of other faiths, and especially marrying outside of their religion. Some even condemned these actions as sinful, handing out severe punishments and forecasting excruciating outcomes in hell. The Bible says God justifies these horrendous punishments, but it sounds more like they were written by men who wanted to hold people inside their "one true religion." It has always been the case that the more followers, the more money and power a religion could wield, so I can understand the fear of losing followers. In my opinion, the creator would have no fear of losing followers because he knows he will never lose any of us, so he would have no need for any kind of rules.

As Socrates pointed out, "The highest form of human excellence is to question oneself and others."

Not long ago, the Catholic Church considered it a sin to so much as enter a non-Catholic house of worship. I don't mean to single them out, because this is true of several other religions as well. And it can be even worse. The instruction from the Muslim prophet, Muhammad, was for all nonbelievers to be put to death, subjugated, or converted. That's not out of line with the Bible, which has verses mandating death for anyone worshipping other gods. Deuteronomy 13 and Numbers 31 are barbaric when it comes to dealing with nonbelievers. This was not only the idol worshippers of the day who didn't worship their "one God," but also about people of other philosophies.

What is known about the people who wrote this stuff, and why is it still believed to be divinely inspired? Holding the threat of damnation or death over your head, if you didn't believe what your parents and pastor ordered you to believe, would be a persuasive way of keeping people scared and in line. Almost as compelling (possibly more so) is the prospect of ostracism. From the very beginning, the god of religion was given human weaknesses and anthropomorphic qualities of all kinds—even jealousy! It seems obvious that an intelligence with the power to create heaven and Earth would be far from insecure; one who uses force and fear to make you do his bidding is hardly an almighty God. I found something I didn't expect to find when I investigated the so-called forbidden things—a truly loving energy who wasn't afraid of any-thing, including what I might find.

The First Commandment states, "You shall have no other gods before me." Many religions have different ideas of who that god is and what He wants, so which god is it? When I was young, I put my faith in what my religion told me He was, and what He wanted. I now put my trust in a loving energy far greater than anything I had known before. This energy doesn't need or want anything from me because it has, and is, everything already. It doesn't require my worship to feel powerful because it already has all of the power, nor does it care if I attend a weekly service. This loving energy is in all religions, just as it is in every person. In fact, it's inspiring to attend different religious services. All of them have something good to offer. This may be a time when your conscience seems to be telling you not to do this, but that is learned behavior. The God I know did not create through division, He created through connections—and the natural world proves this.

In tribal societies, nature (wind, water, fire, the earth, the air/sky, plants, and creatures) was known to be infused with Divine Spirit. From the beginning, mankind has continued to receive the same kind of messages and to experience mysterious events, but understood them differently. They developed their own stories and interpretations to explain them. For many tribal societies, any vio-lence against, exploitation of, and waste of nature was seen as a transgression against the Spirit. No one owned the land or anything on it because it belonged to everyone. Imagine their shock and sadness at the aggression of the new people coming to their land and viciously ripping it apart. It's sad the values of their spiritual wisdom was not incorporated into biblical teachings, and the many spiritual texts that followed and predated it.

They saw men killing buffalo for sport from a moving train. The newcomers showed no respect for the land or for the animal and what it had to offer in the way of food, clothing, and beauty. (Bre told me you can know a lot about a person from the way they treat animals. I believe that's true. She wouldn't even kill insects. If a spider was in her room, she put a glass over it, and carried that lucky bug outside. She even gave that scary bug a name.) Would it be worth fighting a war over? Right or wrong, whoever holds the deadliest weapon will win the war. I wonder what our world would be like today had Native Americans won that war. Since greed and lust for power are common among all of mankind no matter what their religious beliefs are, the outcome might have been the same. Tribal societies fought amongst one another for control, and some made slaves of their captives. We might have inherited a greener planet, but not necessarily a more fair or peaceful one.

In many organized religions, the repression of women was, and is, accepted. Most of us are familiar with the biblical story of creation, wherein Eve was made from Adam's rib to serve as his helpmate. She was weaker than Adam, both mentally and physically, and succumbed to the serpent's blandishments. She broke God's commandment to not eat the "forbidden fruit." Then, as a "sexy" temptress, she encouraged Adam to do the same. Simple disobedience was therefore the "original sin," and the reason it is commonly believed we were born into sin. This inherited stain on our souls suggested the need to be forgiven for even being born, and Eve was to blame for that.

Eve did not go unpunished—Genesis 3:16 says, "I will greatly increase your pains in childbirth; in sorrow you will bring forth children. Your desire will be for your husband and he will rule over you." *Who would write this*, and what caused our ancestors to create religions around it? According to some religious traditions, women must accept the role of passive and maternal, and never appear assertive, outspoken, or provocatively sexy. She might hold a place of honor or even be "put on a pedestal," but obedience to her husband's—or father's—wishes was expected. There were serious consequences when she stepped off that pedestal. Did you know the "Dunking Pool" in Boston was used to publicly dunk women into the water for not obeying their husband? I know these beliefs have lessened over the years in many traditions, but a woman's obedience continues to be the underlying message—and in some, it is still the tradition. If you read between the lines, you will see it somehow gets overlooked that if it weren't for this original sin and the desire to taste fruit from the "Tree of Knowledge of Good and Evil," there would be no hard choices to make, and possibly no one but Adam and Eve on Earth.

After they were cast from the Garden of Eden, Cain was conceived, and life with the knowledge and dynamic of good and evil began. This is not clear and is debated, but there is no recorded evidence of children between Adam and Eve before Cain. Why is that? In either case, it was eating the fruit that gave us the knowledge of good and evil, thus allowing life with a choice, and it was woman who gave birth. Was it the literal truth, a myth, a parable, or man's ideas? The Bible was written and translated through the eyes of a patriarchal society that believed in gods and demons, and punishment by torture that oftentimes included an agonizing death. I sometimes wonder how this account would read had it been a matriarchal society. Might the world be different if the roles were reversed and man ate the fruit and women had the dominant role, or would women be corrupted by wealth and power as well? Had men and women been seen as equals and God's co-creations, they would have worked together to create a more fair and just world. We were meant to be united—not divided. I thank both of my parents equally for bringing me into this world, and we should thank Eve for eating the apple.

As the first Christ-centered church, the Catholic Church played an enormous role in the governing of several countries. A great deal of money and unquestioning allegiance from a sheep-like following were the payoffs. Those who followed a different system of belief were simply jailed, shunned, or worse. Problem solved. You could become one of the sheep or face dire consequences. After all, there could be only one Church. As the Borg in *Star Trek* said, "Resistance is futile. You will be assimilated." Sadly, with that power came massive corruption, and the splits from the one Church began.

The Protestant Reformation began in 1517, when Martin Luther posted his "Ninety-five Theses" on the door of the Castle Church in Wittenberg, Germany. Composed in Latin, Luther's many questions and objections to Church doctrine and devotional practices quickly made the rounds to archbishops and other superiors. The Protestant Reformation survived the years of brutal persecutions, and that opened the door to other Christian religions. The Roman Catholic Church was no longer the only Christian denomination, and now there are many. The Catholic Bible has seven additional books that were omitted from the Protestant Bible. Those books were not accepted as divine inspiration by Luther. Did man add them? I thought everything in the Bible was supposed to be divine. "Catholic vs. Protestant Bibles," by Greg Witherow, is an interesting article as to how and why that happened.

Choosing the wrong church to attend, not being baptized, marrying someone of another faith, and other forbidden behaviors and practices were still frowned upon. I wonder if this is where marrying someone of another color came into play, creating even more separation. In my opinion, keeping a race pure is not a valid pursuit, as we have always been one race—the human race. People began to question the rigidity of those mandates. Nondenominational churches sprang into existence because of the confusion in choosing the right church. The New Life Church, founded in 1984, is one of the first such places of worship, and it's no surprise that it's going strong today. We were told that they did not affiliate with any one denomination, and taught only truths from the Bible, so you would be saved from eternal damnation if you joined them and accepted Jesus Christ as your personal Lord and Savior. It's odd the way many religions profess to base their beliefs on only the Bible, yet their interpretations differ, making each one more righteous than the others. Do you see the irony in that?

In the past it was taught that all religions except the "one true" religion were pagan, and their followers were destined for hell. Today, the way a person defines the one true God tends to vary greatly among those of different "true" religions. A friend once told me that while she was on vacation, she walked into a Buddhist temple and could feel the evil in there. She wasn't born with negative predispositions to "foreign" settings, so did her religion, or the attitudes of fellow churchgoers, teach her that? Seriously!? Buddists are among the most gentle and caring people on the planet. The Crusades of the early Christians, which lasted roughly two hundred years, killed groups of people for not believing what they did. The Church's various brutal Inquisitions also sought to weed out heretics. The Christian religion finally evolved beyond that insanity. But until all religions evolve beyond this, there will be separation and even the sanctioning of wars that authorize killing. It's time to evolve beyond all of this insanity, and wake up to the evil and futility of war.

I found contradictions in the Bible, and the minister I was studying under tried to justify them, but I was never satisfied with his explanations. I now believe the contradictions were the result of man's influence throughout the many different translations. The Old Testament was translated from Hebrew, to Greek, to Latin, and then finally into English. The New Testament went from Greek, to Latin, and then English. That's a lot of languages and belief systems those translations were interpreted through, causing still more confusion. What might have been changed, added, deleted, or lost during those translations, because they couldn't decipher the writings or put their own spin on it?

Within the same religion, sects tend to branch off and form another religion because learned men disagree on their meaning. Are there a number of valid and objective ways of looking at the same passage, or are readers just seeing what they want to see? That was something I was told whenever my interpretation differed from that of my minister—the "learned man." It would be illuminating to have access to all ancient manuscripts before their many translations and alterations, but most didn't survive the arduous journey through time.

The priest who first translated the Bible into English, William Tyndale (1494-1536), was accused of perverting the scriptures. He didn't interpret it the way religious leaders thought he should. He was strangled and burned at the stake—punishment by torture and a harrowing death. Later (to his reported relief in purgatory, where he was sent to contemplate his sin), he was acquitted and given the title, "Father of the English Bible." I guess that would be the consolation prize for all of his hard work and torturous death. No wonder people were afraid to question or speak against these sacralized texts—and some still are.

The King James Version came along in 1611. The Revised Standard Version was published in 1952 and the New Revised Standard Version in 1989, and there are more versions. There are an estimated 6,000 languages in the world today that those versions would need to be translated into in order for everyone to hear and study "the Word" which is prophesied to happen before the end times. It's no surprise there are so many different biblical religions, when interpretations differ so widely. Viewed as a history book by some or as a fascinating compilation of myths and allegories by others, millions more consider the Bible to be the literal truth—the infallible Word of God. I wonder…*What is the literal truth?* How would a person 3000 years ago interpret a solar eclipse or an earthquake and especially the paranormal? For me, while there is much wisdom to be found there, the truths in the Bible are not so black and white.

Years ago I read one version that said when Adam and Eve were banished from the Garden of Eden, there were others out there. That made sense; otherwise, Adam and Eve's children would have had to marry each other for the population to grow. Since Adam and Eve were supposed to have been the first humans, I asked the minister where the others had come from. He told me they were descendants of Satan and therefore they were half demon. God created Adam and Eve, so their descendants were His creation. That begged the question, "What happened to those half-demon people?" The chosen humans married those other humans, and the demonic element was then watered down through the offspring of those marriages. To marry a demon was forbidden, but I thought incest was as well. I was confused. In any case, at the time I believed Satan existed, so I reluctantly accepted his answer. It was more probable that "the other people out there" challenged the story of Adam and Eve, and the "learned man" had to cobble up an explanation.

Most Western religions have taught that upon death, we will be judged and then sent directly to heaven—provided we subscribed to the "right" religious beliefs and lived a reasonably decent life, or asked for forgiveness when we didn't. Otherwise, we could end up in purgatory or be punished for all eternity in hell. The reward for righteousness would be to spend eternity with Him in paradise. I have come to know that there is no creator sitting on a throne, passing out judgments. Do we need a threat hanging over us to be decent people? Would the world be in chaos without religion, or would it be in chaos either way? Just as our judicial system hasn't been able to eliminate crime, the so-called "wrath of God" hasn't, either. The only thing that can, is to know we are one with all of creation, sharing a physical journey together. We are beloved and eternal beings, who were given the power to choose the kind of world we would create—one that embraces love and connection; or one that foments fear and disconnection. The future of this planet will be more peaceful when we realize we have the power to choose good over evil and what the consequence of those choices is.

I had always wondered about beliefs surrounding birth control. Overpopulation of the planet is a very serious problem. How could birth control possibly be a sin? The Bible urges us to "go forth and multiply." The people who couldn't reproduce believed they were being punished for their transgressions, but it was more likely a mandate created by men who needed to ensure a growing population in their church. When the house is full and food is in short supply, it becomes selfish and irresponsible to continue multiplying. Many children need a loving home, so if you want a large family, why not consider adoption? Homeless children should always be considered first. We are polluting our beautiful oceans, cutting down whole forests, and stripping our land of nutrients necessary for growing food that is nourishing. We need to take responsibility for this beautiful green planet that was left in our care, and keep it beautiful and healthy for centuries to come. That is an old mandate, and it needs an update.

Not being baptized, being gay, or committing suicide, I was taught could land a person in hell. Many in these populations have lived their own personal hells here on Earth; or suffered hellish experiences at the hands of righteous people. Why would anyone, especially an "all-loving god," condemn them to a torturous hell for all eternity? Yes, I know there are passages in the Bible that say it is your duty to condemn them. However, there are many more passages that condemn judgment and encourage forgiveness. The creator would not be hypocritical, so which is it? It makes no sense. Maybe the so-called sinners among us came here to teach us to be nonjudgmental, tolerant, and forgiving. When a belief causes more damage than good, it really needs a second look. Imagine the grief it causes so many people when they have to worry if their loved one might be in hell. Or, that their gay child is sinful and must be punished by banishing them from their family and their family's religion. This is unspeakably sad! Why would anyone want to spend eternity with a god who engineered that kind of separation and heartache? It's simply not true, and it breaks my heart.

To recap what many NDE'ers experienced, judgment may be far removed from what we were taught it was. Imagine you've just arrived in a heavenly realm, and immediately you are bathed in unconditional love. That all-consuming love is far greater than any love you had ever felt before. In time, you're filled with the memories of your life on Earth and the joy and pain you brought to others. How can you bask in this love when you know, and can actually feel, the anguish you caused others? For now you know everyone is equally loved and is one family who has eternally loved one another! Many religions teach the importance of forgiveness. How long will you have to wait for that forgiveness to come, or more to the point, what will it take for you to forgive yourself? This is certainly a form of hell—a torment more mental than physical. I learned through reading accounts of NDEs that there is a loving "council" to help guide us through this painful process. I know I will feel remorse for the mistakes I've made and look forward to their insight and love in helping me understand them.

When you search the origins of hell in the Bible, it becomes confusing. In ancient texts, the word Sheol refers to the home of the dead, both good and bad. Mythologist Joseph Campbell said, "Sheol signifies the state of the dead without regard to their happiness or misery." Wikipedia says, *When the Hebrew scriptures were translated into Greek around 200 B.C., the word Hades was substituted for Sheol.* In Greek mythology, Hades was the God of the underworld. Suddenly a place for the dead became Hades, the last stop for evil people that we now know as hell. Was there ever an eternal hell, or did the Greeks filter the translation of the ancient manuscripts through their own mythologies? In any case, the hell we have heard so much about evolved from a neutral place for the dead, to a place for evil people, and finally to a place of eternal torture.

Not all religious dogma posits a place of everlasting torment. It is possible that through the centuries, the tortures of hell were elaborated by religious leaders in an effort to control their followers? Some believe that; others believe it was made more grotesque in order to exact revenge on the people who had harmed them. Early Christians endured years of torture without the rapture they were promised, which was very disheartening. With a torturous hell awaiting their tormentors, they could, at least, shake their fist at them and say, "You'll get yours in the end!"

Some religions and spiritual traditions believe that after death, an astral and/or etheric body stays with you, or you flit around in some other kind of spirit body. Others believe you are reunited with your resurrected physical body when Gabriel blows his horn to announce "Judgment Day" at the end of time. If that's the case, one consigned to hell would feel the physical pain of hellfire. However, if you believe as I do that we are energy, it should give you pause to wonder what kind of pain a body of energy would feel. I rather like the idea of not being confined to my physical body. Don't get me wrong. I've loved my body, and it has served me well. However, when the time comes to leave it, I'll be ready. It seemed to me that man himself had ghostwritten the horrors of hell, and not the creator.

I learned of the end times when I was a child. It was supposed to come "like a thief in the night," but no one knew when. I was told the prophecies were very close to being fulfilled, and the end times were coming soon. Early Christians heard the same thing and were told not to worry, because there would be a rapture in which God's people would be taken directly to heaven just before the end. That terrified me as I considered what a very cruel place the world would be after the end. Would I be taken and someone I loved left behind? I didn't want to be separated from my friends or anyone in my family. Ah, but I needn't have worried! When asked whether the spectacle of their hell-tortured loved ones would sadden those in heaven, Luther replied, "Not in the least." Supposedly, we will only feel joy, so we won't remember them. That's just cold! I could never forget Bre and resent Luther's "comforting" reply! I was told the gates to heaven were narrow and those to hell very wide. Would baptism be enough, or would my sins still be too great? Since God sees all sin as equal, even having bad thoughts was sinful. You could only pray that you had asked for forgiveness everytime and dotted all your "i"s and crossed your "t"s, and everyone you loved had done the same. How sad and cruel it is that we terrify our children like that. Then again, what is ingrained into a child's mind often stays with them throughout their life, and that threat would certainly hold a person in their religion's grasp. Anything or anyone who uses fear to get us to do their bidding feels wrong to me.

I later learned that there may be another chance for me and the people I loved. Purgatory and limbo were midway stations between heaven and hell. This does not appear in the Protestant Bible. It is found in 2 Maccabees 12:46 of the Catholic Bible: "Thus he made atonement for the dead that they might be freed from sin." However, the doctrine of limbo was abolished by the Vatican in April of 2007. It had been described as a place where unbaptized infants (including aborted fetuses), virtuous pagans, and pre-Christian Jews would spend eternity. They would not be punished in limbo, but because of the stain of original sin, they would be eternally deprived of the joy of God's presence. After it was somehow determined that unbaptized babies would not be punished, there was no further need for limbo. Purgatory still remains, so everyone but the hell-bound has a chance to be in "God's presence."

In purgatory one can contemplate his or her life, make amends for sins, and, with God's mercy, ascend into heaven. (In times past, a fee could be paid to have a priest intervene on one's behalf and to have punishment reduced. Today, these "indulgences" are generally granted, but only under certain conditions and upon the recitation of certain prayers, or the performance of good works.) Most religions believe in an afterlife and offer other methods for achieving a spot in it. My religion didn't recognize purgatory, but I wanted to believe in the possibility of another chance for me and my family. Naturally, all of the things I learned as a child flashed through my mind when Bre left. I was desperate to find the answers for myself, and I didn't trust the Bible written and translated by "learned men" to have those answers.

I've talked mainly about Christianity and the King James Version of the Bible because it's what I am most familiar with, but there are of course many other religions that don't use the Bible. I wondered if they had a hell in other traditions, so I did some research. This is not an in-depth explanation of hell for the following four religions, but hell doesn't seem as final in them as it does in Christianity.

Hinduism is a collection of ancient beliefs that grew slowly over thousands of years. It has no one founder, which is uncommon for most religions, and is the oldest religion in the world. Hindues believe in a universal God, Brahman, a part of which, called Atman, is in every soul. Brahman expresses through many individual gods and godesses, who are sometimes worshiped. They also believe in karma and reincarnation. You pass through Bhuva Loka (heaven) if you have been good, or Naraka (hell) when you have been bad. All the while, you prepare to reincarnate. When all bad karma (of thought, word, and deed) has been cleansed, you return to "Source" for the final time and are released from the karmic wheel of rebirth. "Source" is the eternal place of our origin.

Like Hinduism, Buddhism is a peaceful philosophy. You are not condemned if you do not become a Buddhist. They believe that most humans have not yet gained wisdom, but they will through the experiences of multiple incarnations. Buddhist's also believe in karma and reincarnation. Samsara is the seemingly endless *hell* of birth, death, and rebirth, which unenlightened people must endure and learn from before they are liberated. In time, they will reach enlightenment, known as Nirvana, and no longer need to reincarnate.

Islam was established in the year 610 when the prophet Muhammad received the beginnings of what would later become the Quran from the Archangel Gabriel. For them, it is a more accurate interpretation of God's Word. Muslims believe that Islam is the "one" true religion and was the faith of Adam. Therefore, their belief should be accepted over all others. They believe in hell, but it's not eternal. You are released when you make amends for your sins.

The Jewish faith is believed to be the oldest of monotheistic (belief in one god) religions, although, some scholars believe Zoroastrianism is older than Judaism. I had never heard of that one, but it showed me that religious philosophies started years ago—maybe even before the story of Adam and Eve existed. Religions appear to be a blending of several ancient philosophies, as described in *The Power of the Myth*, by Joseph Campbell. The Jewish faith does not believe Jesus was the savior prophesied to come, who would pay the ultimate sacrifice for all earthly sin. Jesus was not a king of wealth and power, which is how the coming savior was described in ancient texts, so that being has not yet appeared. Jews believe hell is a place where you are cleansed of sin before you can ascend into heaven. It's not fun, so repent before you leave this plane and avoid hell altogether.

Jesus was a Hebrew teacher, educated in the Jewish synagogue and authorized to speak from the temple platforms. He spoke of a loving and forgiving Father and not a God to be feared. He spoke against some of the rituals of the time, such as the pilgrimage to Jerusalem to pay tithes. He also caused a great deal of fear in religious leaders, who were the "learned men" of the day, when He taught we could speak directly with God without going through them. We all know how that turned out for him. He didn't teach Christianity—it didn't exist. He taught love, forgiveness, and the personal connection between you and a loving Father. His teachings spread after His death. Christianity became a unified religion some 300 years later when the Council of Nicaea agreed upon what His teachings were and added them to the Bible in the New Testamant. It seems to me that we wouldn't need any religion, and all of this turmoil could have been avoided, if we practiced what Jesus taught—love, forgiveness, and connection.

Many religions put their faith in the whole Bible and some in the Old Testament only. Others include different texts along with the Bible, and there are religions that don't use the Bible at all. Those who believe in science and facts tend to view the Bible and other ancient texts mainly from a historical perspective. It's all good. If you find inspiration and peace in your beliefs and let others find the same in their own beliefs, then there is no reason for fighting. We have been told "God is love," and I believe that is true. Love is universal and unifying. Over time, we will increasingly understand the true nature of who and what the creator is through science. I know I did. It was the daring science of Copernicus that proved Earth was not the center of the universe, but not before scores of scientists/heretics were burned at the stake, tortured, or imprisoned for voicing their doubt. How dare they go against the teachings of sacred texts! One's religion cannot eradicate a proven truth. Thank "God," science survived the persecution and will go on to prove or disprove one idea after another.

Every day, science makes discoveries proving the oneness of everything by demonstrating the connection between all things. That connection is through a world that is unseen. It is the world of energy. Did we come from another dimension, an alien world, evolution, or divine creation? It's all the same to me, as all beginnings appear to have come from one energy. Without the fear of persecution from religious factions, men and women of science have the freedom to look at all possibilities. The creator is far greater than the separate god of each religion and in the end, I believe science will prevail in proving that.

CHAPTER 12

PAST LIVES AND REINCARNATION

*"I'm not afraid of death because I don't believe in it.
It's just getting out of one car and into another."*

— JOHN LENNON —

Reincarnation means that life doesn't end, so you can understand my interest. I learned there were ancient texts that were thrown aside and labeled "pagan" because of their philosophies, and reincarnation was one of them. Is it possible reincarnation caused religious leaders to fear they would lose control, if people believed there was a second chance to get it right? Reincarnation was accepted by early Christians, and some people interpret Jesus' words concerning Elijah in Matthew 17: 11-13 to mean Elijah had come back as John the Baptist. So, even Jesus may have believed it, or personally experienced reincarnation. Most believe reincarnation was opposed and ultimately declared heretical in the fourth century by the Council of Nicaea, while some believe all reference to it was removed from the Bible in 553 A.D. by Byzantine Emperor Justinian. In any case, it was a sin to consider reincarnation a possibility. I had to investigate this issue, even though I knew that believing or not believing wouldn't change how I lived my life.

Reincarnation reappeared in the eleventh century in a Christian sect known as the Cathars, until the "one" church led a crusade to annihilate them. Can you imagine the horror the Cathars experienced and the effect that had on the people living then? It's no wonder there is still fearful reluctance today for a Christian to ponder this possibility. And yet, some religions and systems of philosophy have always embraced reincarnation. Many attach karma (the result of good and bad deeds) to reincarnation and some believe we come back in different forms of life other than human. I can't imagine being a slug, but I'm sure I would learn something from that experience. Coming back in another life form is a bit of a stretch for me, but whatever I choose to believe, it would never cause me to judge another.

Most people don't remember past lives, and it's not important that we do. It is said that the wisdom we gain through living each life stays with the soul throughout eternity, and that is what is important. If we did remember living other lives, we would know we never die, and I wouldn't be writing this book. Many children remember living another life, but generally forget all about it by the time they reach school age, especially if their parents discourage such recollections. Some people hold these memories throughout their lives. The best evidence for reincarnation that I could find comes from the late Dr. Ian Stevenson, who spent forty years investigating the claims of thousands of children around the world. To all but the staunchest of cynics, his findings are convincing.

Years ago, I found myself wondering how one could achieve everything in a single lifetime when the playing field wasn't fair or death came at birth. I was told by the Lutheran minister that

people with severe mental illness were perfect already and didn't
need to learn anything, and the same was true for babies who died
at birth. While that may be true, to me it seemed like a waste of
a beautiful life. A more meaningful purpose is that their presence
and/or suffering carried lessons in love and acceptance for the
parents, caregivers, and others. What about the people who suffer
physical abuse and neglect or wartime trauma, or are born into a
sect society offering only a life of degradation? How would these
lives encourage growth or even offer much choice? What happens
to these people? He said the opportunity to hear and accept "the
Word" will present itself to them ("the Word" is learning about
Jesus and accepting Him as one's savior). Christians believe that
is the purpose of life, so everyone will eventually have a chance
to hear it. But what happens to the people who never heard "the
Word" because it didn't exist in their time? I was told they would
hear it "up there." If I heard it up there, I would know it was the
truth. Down here, I had to accept on faith that it was the truth—
or face the consequence of hell. None of what he was telling me
felt true, and reincarnation was clearly not in the mix. What does
feel true to me is there is more to life than hearing humans' idea
of God's Word. I believe I am an eternal being who is continually evolving, and each life I live has a purpose. The purpose may
vary from teaching to learning, or helping another on his or her
journey. I instinctively know that each life would have a purpose,
whether that life be long and full of experiences or too short to
have experiences.

Would you come back if you believed you could be of service
to the people you left behind? It is said when this happens it is
usually as a sibling, a friend, or another family member. I know
this may sound weird to some, but I used to feel Bre around me.
I almost felt she could hear me and left signs around for me to
find. Signs like finding a note she had written me that pertained

to something I was thinking about, or a picture I thought was lost or that someone had found and given to me at the perfect time. I didn't listen to the words of songs and Bre knew it, but on more than one occasion, a song came on the radio that directly answered a concern I was having. What made me listen? I bought a roll of stamps, and they had vegetables on them. I had never seen stamps with vegetables on them. She was a vegetarian, so I felt she was saying, "Hi." And yes, I still have that roll of stamps. I could go on, but you get the point. If you have lost someone dear to you, you may know what I mean. These are the little signs they send to let us know they're still with us.

Some might say it was more a matter of me looking for signs, and I suppose that became true. I wasn't looking in the beginning because it hadn't ocurred to me to look, but when a jaw-dropper happens, you begin to pay attention. It feels very real when it happens, and is always uplifting. When her son's little sister was born, I lost the feeling of her presence, along with the little signs. I wondered why and felt abandoned, until I studied reincarnation and read about this possibility. I know she didn't want to leave her son, so I can understand her need to come back, especially in close association as his sister. I don't know, but the abandonment and little signs were a noticeable loss in my life.

If you feel something like this has happened in your life, remember that this little person is their own person. They generally have no memory of that other life. They have a new purpose and a new life, and this life is all that is important. It would be unusual for someone to come back so soon, as most will spend some time "at home" before returning. There is a need to heal— especially if their life had been traumatic—and gather strength before coming back. Most lives, including Bre's, usually are in many ways difficult. Basking in the love and acceptance they feel when they are "home" gives them the strength necessary to return—if they choose. Her son's life now has two sisters in it. These three children are as close as any siblings I've seen. I can't help thinking they were meant to help each other in this already challenging life. Some believe we choose the people we share our life with. It seems these three chose well, and their daddy would agree.

It is perhaps more probable that my daughter has not come back, but felt I needed a little more time and space for my healing to continue. When you lose the most important person in your life, healing can move slowly. In fact, your life stops. In either case, it is important to understand that these things happen bcause of love. Whatever journey we are on, sometimes we need a push in order to continue the journey. The dark alley I started down when Bre left, had many fears and challenges for me to overcome as I moved more deeply into it. I think Bre left me alone so I would not stop moving down the alley until I had looked in every crevice.

There are compelling cases for reincarnation, as when child prodigies are born with intellect or talents far beyond the norm. By the time they are old enough to physically express it, astonishing talent in the arts, sciences, and/or music is apparent to the people around them. Others somehow hang on to dramatic memories. *Soul Survivor: The Reincarnation of a World War II Fighter Pilot,* by Bruce and Andrea Leininger, is about their son, who remembers being a pilot in WWII, knows what his name was then, and the name of his plane—even where he was shot down, which was all verified. Another story is *Across Time and Death: A Mother's Search for Her Past Life Children,* by Jenny Cockell. It tells of a mother who remembers her previous family, with memories only the mother could hold—along with validation from her now elderly sons. There are many stories like this that can and have been authenticated. How can they be explained if the recycling of life isn't a possibility?

Some say these memories are stored in our genes and passed down to future generations. That might account for some cases, or some recollections, but you would have to be related in order for memories to pass through genes, and many of those who remember past lives are not. Others believe that memories go into the vast field of energy out there, and our consciousness simply taps into that field. If that's true, then thoughts are things that don't vanish with death. Knowing this phenomenon happens, is the reason we had to come up with different explanations for it. Living other lives is a wonderment, and shouldn't be discarded because science doesn't have an answer for these mysteries. Perhaps the fact that we are eternally advancing is the only answer, and that's very hard for some to accept.

Talk therapy and drugs are the general treatments for patients suffering from various mental illnesses. However, when that doesn't work, some psychiatrists, psychologists, or therapists will try hypnosis to uncover deep memories. It is during these times that a door to another world can open. Some doctors feel inclined to close that door, while others sense the need to open it. If there is a buried memory, whether in this life or a past life, a growing number of doctors are willing to use this approach when it can help their patient.

Many years ago, a client told me she had lived her life feeling fearful all of the time. In an effort to discover the cause, her therapist finally used hypnosis. It seemed that in another lifetime, she had lived in a Nazi concentration camp. With that knowledge, she was able to work through the fears that had monopolized her present life. At the time, I knew nothing about past-life regression and thought there might be another explanation. Today, I would have had a more in-depth conversation about her experience. I love my job, as it has enabled me to meet and talk with so many interesting people.

Allan Botkin is a psychologist who used hypnosis in his prac-tice. His book is titled, *Induced After-Death Communication*. This is one of the first books on the topic that I read, and for me, it offered credible evidence for life after death. Dr. Botkin didn't believe in life beyond death, so past-life regression wasn't a consideration; he simply wanted to help veterans in healing grief and trauma. Years of talk therapy had not helped one of his patients, so he decided to try a form of hypnosis. There are different methods of induction for hypnosis, which was something I hadn't known before. Under hypnosis, the veteran was visited by a child he had become close to inside the war zone. He felt responsible for his inability to protect her during an attack. The child, surrounded by brilliant light, smiled and thanked him for taking care of her and for loving her. She wanted him to know how happy she was and that she loved him. From that moment on, the veteran was able to let go of the guilt, and began to heal.

Dr. Botkin wanted to write it off as a hallucination, but it was very real to the veteran, and the healing result was instantaneous. With patients' consent, he began to use this form of hypnosis on others who weren't responding to talk therapy. The results were the same. The idea that these veterans were actually experiencing contact began to look like a reality. Because it so dramatically helped his patients, Dr. Botkin felt this concept should be examined and no longer pushed aside. His book was written in an effort to encourage more research into this phenomenon, and he also established an institute for these investigations.

Dr. Botkin was not interested in past-life regression or reincarnation, only in healing his patients with trauma in this life. That was also true of other doctors trying to heal patients of seemingly irrational fears, who were then surprised to find their patients in a past-life situation or talking to someone from outside of our reality. The doctors' only choice was to cast it aside, and put it down to imagination or delusion, or gather more information.

Dr. Brian Weiss's seminal book, *Many Lives, Many Masters*, broke major ground in the use of past-life regression. He was able to stop patients between lives, talking to them in their more comfortable spiritual home between incarnations, and follow them into other lives. Their demeanor and intellect changed in each environment, and the information revealed was fascinating. It was the first time I had thought about the possibility that I could be two discrete beings in one—a spiritual and a physical. I didn't like that idea at first. It felt as though I was in a sci-fi movie where an alien had invaded my body. I don't feel that way now, knowing the physical life I am living today is only a facet of the real eternal me. As a child, I remembered hearing things like *listen to your conscience*, or *follow your spirit, or the soul within.* Religion was on the right track because they also understood there was something more to us than a physical body.

A friend told me she thinks of her body as a car. You are attached to that car, even giving it a name. You polish it and give it tune-ups, but eventually the motor stops and you need to leave that car. It served you well while you had it. It took you to places you didn't want to go and places you loved. You'll keep those memories, and, if you choose, get a new car to collect more memories with.

What we learned in Sunday school gave only a hint as to who we are and who the creator is. Yet, church dogma was presented as unassailable fact in the same way that evolution was. There is so much more to learn, and mysteries to be solved, before we have even the slightest understanding of "What's What." We need to eliminate the fear and trepidation of investigating the unexplained and be open to new evidence as it becomes available. Our biggest error is when we're not open to new inquiries and evidence; we get stuck in the old, or ridicule those who find the new evidence. It is only through cooperation that we will find answers.

As investigation into past lives continues to escalate, and many books are sharing the results. The doctors I referenced, and others, found evidence that life never ends. It was not their intention to explore past lives, but because it helped their patients, they felt compelled to share what they'd found, even knowing their credibility would be challenged. Thank you for caring and taking that risk!

Everyone's experience of life is different, and I can't know what your life feels like until I walk in your shoes. We are eternal beings, and eternity is a long time (or non-time), so it's understandable that we would choose to collect a wide range of experiences in the physical realm. My soul will grow in awareness and compassion when I know how you feel though experiencing the things you experienced. I can't do that in one physical lifetime. I know it's not about getting it right the first time around, because there is more than one thing to get right. I am grateful for the opportunity to evolve through the many lives I have already lived and will live in the future.

CHAPTER 13

CREATION, EVOLUTION, OR SOMETHING ELSE

"It's very clear that there is evolution, and it's important. Evolution is here and intelligent design is here, and they're both consistant."

— CHARLES TOWNES —

Did God breathe life into the dirt to create man and then pull a rib from him to create woman, or did He create a universe that allowed for the natural evolution of physical life? Were we planted here by an alien civilization, or is all of creation a random accident of vibrating energy? Creation suggests there is a creator, while evolvement allows for the elimination of a creator, which is why there is so much attention given to this topic. That we are here at all is nothing short of astonishing—a wonderment—and there are too many missing pieces to that puzzle to pass judgment on any idea that presents itself. You may think this is an odd way of looking at creation, but how my temporary, physical body came into being is not important to me.

143

It is the consciousness inside of me that holds my interest. That opens a whole new dialogue of who I am and where I come from.

A naturalist by the name of Lamarck introduced the idea of evolution fifty years before Darwin, but was accused of heresy and scorned by his fellow scientists. What a difference fifty years make! Charles Darwin published his theory of evolution in 1859, but without definitive proof, creation vs. evolution still remains debatable. Evolution proposes that we started as pond scum and began the long process of evolving into the many different species inhabiting the Earth. It was a dog-eat-dog world where the strong and the clever survived. Whoever made it to the top of the food chain would hold dominance over the rest of the world's inhabitants. Even though Darwin's theory justified that mindset, it wasn't anything new. Believing that one holds dominance over others has always been one of man's weaknesses. Interestingly, Darwin's later writings showed he was rethinking his theory because he saw that people and animals who worked together had a better chance of survival.

Chief Seattle (1786-1866) said, "Man did not weave this web of life—he is merely a strand of it. Whatever he does to the web, he does to himself." How did he know the importance of connection so long ago? As I've said before, the world of spirit has been communicating with mankind from the beginning of time. We just had different interpretations for the messages we received. If the human race had not been divided by the fallout of pride and avarice, the world would be thriving today. Working together, we would have developed more amazing technologies and found answers to impossible questions by now. As we evolve and shift into a new awareness, science is recognizing the connection we have with all of nature. The mentality of division and competition will soon be a thing of the past.

Given the vast array of creation stories, I wondered what societies around the world had heard or witnessed that shaped their many different beliefs. I did a little research to get an abbreviated version of other creation stories:

1. Aboriginal: Beliefs vary among the tribes as they do in all groups of people.

   - A Star Baby fell from the sky and started everything. Did they see aliens or a spaceship and called it a Star Baby?

   - Dreamtime as defined by the Aboriginal Art Culture and Tourism Australia: "It is the beginning of knowledge, from which came the laws of existence. For survival these laws must be observed. The Dreaming world was the old time of the Ancestor Beings." Their translation for Ancestor Beings was not in the form of gods or angels, but rather supernatural beings. Some of us rely on prophets and seers to share their divine inspirations, while Aborigines look to messages from Ancestor Beings given to them in dreams. Creatures were created by Ancestor Beings; when I read that people were originally jumbled together with plants or animals which had to be separated and sculpted into humans, that caught my attention. As a hairdresser, I noticed people's hair grew faster in different seasons. I jokingly told them their hair grew faster in the spring, like flowers, or like the animals that grew more fur in the fall. Maybe there is some truth to the myth of human-sculpting after all. Their story suggests that we share a common ancestry with all living beings—including plants and animals. That agrees with what science knows today, and I can't help but wonder if we are of alien descent as well.

2. Christians: Some churches are more rigid than others. Fundamentalist Christians unquestioningly believe in the literal truth of every word in the Bible. The Earth was formed in seven days, and God made Adam from the dust of the Earth and Eve from Adam's rib—end of story. Science says it took

much longer, so some believers simply altered the time frame, maintaining that there are more than twenty-four hours in God's workday. Faced with the theory of evolution, they are prepared, because God would be in control of that evolution. Challenges arise within religions, as science moves forward with new discoveries.

3. Hinduism: Myths about creation differ by tradition, and interestingly, Hindus believe there have been many rebirths of the universe. Some believe Brahma, the creator god, propagated life throughout the universe, while others believe the "golden egg" gave birth to the universe. I wondered if the "golden egg" (also called golden embryo) might symbolize the yolk of an egg where little chicks emerge from. I was taught this is a pagan religion because they believe in many gods. The truth is, Hindus believe in a single divine energy that is the source of everything. And the One can manifest as many gods and goddesses—as it chooses. That sounds like one god to me.

4. Jainism: They believe the universe and soul have always been. There is no beginning, there is no end, and there is no creator. They believe in karma, and that the soul is in control of its destiny. The cycle of rebirth ends when the soul is cleansed of its karma. The Bible says that God has no beginning and no end and has always known us. It follows that if He has always known us, then we too have always existed, just as Jains believe. Science speculates that the universe will implode one day, and, considering eternity, it may have imploded and restarted many times. I believe there is an infinite and living energy-system that exists outside and inside of everything. The wonder of eternity and infinity is beyond our ability to understand, and it seems that every creation story describes an invisible plane that has eternally existed outside of the physical world we know.

5. Buddhism: The Buddha taught that the world has always been, and whether there is a creator was not important to him. The

importance and purpose of life is to cleanse and purify oneself, to grow in spiritual awareness until full enlightenment is realized. Until then, one is subject to karma and rebirth. Through compassion, a Buddhist also strives to reduce the suffering of others, while also encouraging them to reach their full potential. Buddhism is considered a philosophy, not a religion. In my opinion, the difference between philosophy and religion is very slim.

6. Islam: The Muslim creation story is similar to the one in the Old Testament, in that God/Allah created man from mud—not the dust of the earth. Is that because mud is easier to sculpt with? In any case, their symbolic renderings of the story are a bit different and thought to be more scientific. As I said, science is making its way back into all religions, where it has always belonged.

7. Native American: Their beliefs vary between tribes, so I'll touch on a couple.

   • The Maya believed their gods Tepeu and Gucumatz were there in the beginning, and whatever they thought would become a reality. When they thought Earth, there it was. It seems Tepeu and Gucumatz may have introduced the Mayan people to the power of thought long ago.

   • I liked the Lakota Creation Story: There was a world before this one whose inhabitants did not behave themselves, so the Creating Power caused a flood by singing several songs, drowning all life but one. Khangi, the crow, pleaded with the Creator Power to give him a place to rest. From his huge pipe bag the creator took four animals out, instructing them to dive down to the bottom and bring up mud. The turtle succeeded, and the mud was spread on the water. The land was called Turtle Continent in honor of the turtle. The Creating Power then took from his pipe bag all forms of life, promising not to destroy them if they learned to live in harmony.

I know there is so much more to these beautiful religions than my tiny, abbreviated version of their creation stories. I am certainly not a religious scholar, but this research caused me to wonder what similarities the ancients shared. It seemed they all knew there was another realm somewhere out there in the cosmos that has eternally existed. Communication between the two realms has also existed. I believe people experienced similar events and received messages from spirit, but each group put its own spin on it, according to their traditions. Beliefs about the creator and its creations therefore varied amongst societies. The Lakota story is not unlike the biblical story of Noah, and if I did more research, I would likely find many more similarities. There is beauty and truth in all philosophies. I'm sorry if I didn't mention yours, but there are so many religions out there, that I could discuss only a few. Whatever you choose to believe in is right for you, but that doesn't mean it has to be right for everyone. The Lakotas' Creating Power summed up everything for all belief systems when it said, "We must learn to live in harmony with all life forms."

One commonality to every creation story that I zeroed in on, is that we have a purpose in coming here, and will return to another plane after death. That enticed my mind to wander into timelessness, infinity, and eternity. The size of the universe is minuscule when placed inside of infinity. That was mind-boggling, and I got lost in there for a while. The personal and ontological matters we argue over in the physical world seem tiny and ridiculously insignificant in comparison. How and why we are here is a wonderment, not an argument. *Imagine how pivotal it would be to reach above the tiny individual concerns that consume us and embrace our own eternity!* Our temporary "physical" body came into existence through whatever or whoever you want to believe in; then language, math, science, and other means of understanding evolved along with our own awareness. I want to add one more thought: If timelessness, infinity, and eternity have any meaning at all, it is that nothing ever truly ends.

From what we know today, the universe began 13.8 billion years ago with the Big Bang. At 12 billion years, galaxies began forming. Our own galaxy, the Milky Way, has swirling arms that give it the shape of a spiral. I found it interesting that galaxies had to form at precisely the right time and in the exact right way. The ones that do not form these spiraling arms have a very short lifespan, as they lack the ability to form new stars when an explosion occurs. It was supernova explosions that sent the necessary life-giving elements throughout the galaxies. I love thinking that we are full of stardust.

The sun in our galaxie formed 4.5 billion years ago and we are perfectly placed 92.96 million miles from it. Earth's perfect temperature from the sun set the stage for single-celled organisms to develop 3.5 to 2.7 billion years ago, roughly a billion years after Earth formed. These unicellular organisms became multicellular organisms around 600 million years ago. It is surmised that a form of us came along some 66 million years ago. That was long after the extinction of dinosaurs approximately 65 million years ago; unless the story of giant people is true, who some believe lived millions of years before that. That made for an interesting search on my computer, but while the evidence is weak, the jury is still out. You may have heard of Lucy. She lived 3.2 million years ago and is considered by some to be pre-human (protohuman). She walked on two feet, stood four feet tall, and had a small brain capacity. Approximately 200,000 years ago human beings with a big brain mysteriously appeared, and our brain hasn't changed since then. We don't have any archeological evidence showing how we got from Lucy's small brain to the brain we have today. There are many theories out there, including eating cooked food, as to how it happened. As funny as that theory may sound, a theory developes because someone finds a shred of evidence to support it and all things deserve consideration.

In *Human by Design*, Gregg Braden explains human chromosome 2 as the mysterious fusing of two chromosomes, which is believed to be what made the large-brained human possible. It appears as though something was removed from this chromosome, then something was added and fused together again. This doesn't happen in nature and is therfore a rather big mystery. We know we did not evolve directly from the ape, but we came from the same stuff, so we share a common ancestry with them (99% of our DNA is shared with the chimpanzee) and all living things. No matter how you look at how we got here, it all seems impossible. Yet, here we are. We need to find the missing pieces to remove all doubt. It is amazing that archeologists have found and interpreted such ancient evidence of life so far, and exciting to look forward to what they will find in the future.

Some theorize that we were planted here by aliens, or that they assisted in our evolution. Who knows? It's an infinitely big and old universe. Beings with advanced knowledge of traveling through time and space could have been on the cosmic scene long before Earth was habitable. The Earth is around 4.5 billion years old, and given that the universe is 13.7 billion years old, other planets may have formed billions of years before ours did. Regardless of how long everything has been going round and round, it's important to remember that all things are one with the universe. I assume our universal families evolved into compassionate beings, or our story might be different today.

The enormity of this universe is beyond imagining, but it is estimated to be 93 billion light-years in diameter. *One light-year equals a staggering 5.9 trillion miles.* We have not been able to find the edge of the universe, and it may be impossible to find since the universe continuously expands. However, we can use that number today because it is already incomprehensible. Our own Milky Way galaxy is 100,000 light-years across, so the size of our little galaxy is

100,000 x 5.9 trillion miles. And there are an estimated 200-plus billion galaxies in the universe. The universe is still expanding and evolving, so why wouldn't we be evolving apace, along with life on other planets? Maybe we're thinking small when we should be thinking big—really big.

I thought the Earth was large, but its diameter is only 7,900 miles. We went from falling off the edge of the Earth to going around and around it. Now, we may have to change our view of the Earth from being the only habitable planet to it being one of many. We need to stop thinking in prepackaged singularities—me and my planet—and not be afraid or embarrassed to expand our thinking. Words like infinity, or no beginning and no end, suggest countless universes. Okay, maybe that's too big to think about, but there were NDE'ers who were shown many Big Bangs. Was that this universe starting over, or are there other universes and even other dimensions? We must be willing to step out of the box of traditional thinking in order to find answers to the big questions.

Evolution did not eliminate the idea of a conscious creator as some hoped it would. In 1993, a gathering of scientists recognized intelligent design as an explanation for how everything came into being. They did not support the idea of a mystical god, but there was evidence to support an intelligence behind the design of nature. Energy doesn't do much without a thought behind it. Since humans didn't exist in the beginning, some believe the universe started with a thought from an intelligence beyond our own. That is the perennial quandary. Everything in creation happened in perfect order. "Creation has been a perfect dance from the beginning." (*Journey of the Universe*). The amazing little cell, which Dr. Bruce Lipton coined a "little mini me," could not have formed without the perfectly timed sequence of events essential to its genesis.

Genesis 11:1-9, "The Tower of Babel" or "The Tower of Babylon," is the story told by an ancient people attempting to

THE DAY MY WORLD STOPPED

explain how the many different languages came into being, and why God scattered His people all over the world. Since people believed God was a powerful being up in the heavens some- where, they decided to build a tower that would reach there. Why wait when you can build a stairway to heaven? As punish- ment, God confounded their language so they could no longer understand one another and then dispersed them to the four corners of Earth. It was believed the Earth was flat, and it seems they also believed it was a square with corners. Maybe that story is true, but I'd say it's more probable that a potpourri of humans evolved and spread simultaneously around the globe and devel- oped their own form of communication. I had often wondered if we evolved in the same way as all the different birds had. Each one sounds different and has different colors, and no one better than the other, just different. *There are no chosen people; there are just people, unique and beautiful people.* If you choose to think in terms of infinity, as I find fun to do, there would be different people scattered throughout the universe—or in other universes beyond our own.

You may be smiling at me by now and wondering what turnip truck I fell out of. Had I not taken this journey, I would be won- dering the same thing. The ideas I thought were way out there, appear to hold some truth in them.

Has consciousness evolved along with us? Certainly our aware- ness of it has. When did we become conscious? In other words, when did we become aware of our thoughts and ourselves as dis- crete entities? The Bible says we first became conscious when Adam and Eve naughtily partook of the "Tree of Knowledge" and ran for fig leaves to modestly cover their naked bodies. I believe all of creation is an integral part of one infinite conscious energy-sys- tem; so we, and everything else, have always been conscious in one form or another from the beginning.

It's hard to imagine what it was like when we finally became aware of our own consciousness, but it was probably like waking up from a very long dream. Zeroing in on our own individual uniqueness, whether gradually or suddenly, was the human wake-up call. Centuries later, through the discovery of the quantum world, more are beginning to accept the probability of a superconsciousness. This consciousness is fully evolved, and I believe we are evolving into a species that is becoming aware of it and our connection to it.

What about the evolution of science? The moment we started asking questions, science began to evolve. In the beginning, not much attention was given to science; those who delved deeply into the nature of things were considered philosophers. When Copernicus proposed that Earth was not the center of the universe in 1543, scientists became a threat to the very existence of religious leaders and religion itself. For thousands of years, religion reigned supreme; now science was moving to the forefront. Scientists were imprisoned, tortured, or killed in an effort to make them deny what they knew to be true. In 1609 Galileo finally proved this finding mathematically but still faced the Inquisition (an intense questioning and/or torture for the suppression of heresy). Galileo was forced to recant, and spent the rest of his life under house arrest. In order for both to survive, religion eventually shook hands with science, and a division between the two was established. It is this understandable division that to this day prevents science and religion from working together to find the truths. Had they evolved together, the mysteries of creation may have already been solved.

In 1687, Newton proved gravity to be the force that holds things in place. Without gravity, nothing could have happened. In 1905, Einstein published his theory of relativity that forever changed our understanding of time, space, motion, matter, and energy. Not only did he tell us that space has texture like a piece of fabric, he proposed that matter and energy are two aspects of the same thing (E=mc2). The solid world we know is an illusion, as it is just another form of energy. Everything we thought we knew was changing, but this question still remains: Is there an intelligence out there, and/or in here, that is governing all energy? As Einstein said, "Science without religion is lame, religion without science is blind." He wasn't a particularly religious man, but he understood that a connection between the two would benefit both.

Writing has also evolved. The earliest cave paintings are said to date back 64,000 years and are thought to be drawn by Neanderthals. When you do a search through cave paintings, you'll find not only animals, musical instruments, and people, you will see what appear to be aliens and spaceships. I can't imagine what they might have seen that would look like a spaceship or an alien. It's all up for speculation, but there is no way of really knowing. The first sign of written language appears to have been from around 5,300 years ago, in the form of an early hieroglyphics. By the eighth century BCE, or 2,800 years ago, the Greek alphabet, allowing for both vowels and consonants, was established. There were no vowels present in ancient writings before that. This explains why there was some guesswork involved in interpretating these old writings. Written language evolved in an effort to express ourselves and record history, and that hasn't stopped. More new words are added to our lexicon continuously. That hits home with me, as technology has many new words I don't recognize. I needed a translator when getting technical support, and that really slowed me down while learning to use a word processor and publishing this book.

Math has evolved from scratching in the dirt to simple arithmetic to the nearly unfathomable complexities of our day. When it was discovered that the energy of the quantum world acts differently from anything in the physical world, scientists were natually perplexed as to how to investigate or measure it. In the early nineteen hundreds, quantum mechanics evolved. Quantum theory was introduced in 1927, when Werner Heisenberg established his uncertainty principle, giving science a way to measure the random behavior of quanta.

In 2008, the Hadron Collider was completed, enabling scientists to collide protons at close to the speed of light (approximately 670,616,629 mph). Their quest was to find the fundamental particles they are made of. They tell us it will take years for scientists to sift through the debris of those collisions. Prior to the collider, there was no way to break up protons to see what was inside of them. This is so amazing to me, as protons are at the center of an atom that is already too small for our microscopes to see. It is quantum mechanics that allows us to study invisible things. The numbers used in these calculations blows me away, but, in the future, our ability to find and measure invisible things and calculate from a vacuum to infinty may look like we were scratching in the dirt to them.

One discovery from the collision was the Higgs boson ("The God particle"), which was more like a field or a vacuum than an actual particle. It was coined The God particle because it was where all particles appeared to originate. I realize how simple this explanation is, and a physicist would have a much more precise vocabulary to explain how they found and measured it, but I'm not a physicist, and their words are not in my vocabulary. No matter how far you break a particle down, it is still energy. I wondered:... *To what extent can energy be broken down before consciousness is all that is left to measure?* When that happens, we may find the answer we've been seeking for millennia: Is there an intelligence out there, as well as inside of us, that is beyond our understanding?

Knowledge of our own biology has also evolved. In 1953, James Watson and Francis Crick discovered the double helix structure of DNA. I was a little girl, but I remember that day. It was big news! We finally understood how our body knew where to put things

155

during its development. We can now alter the structure of DNA to change the message it is sending. We have done this in small ways and with small things—so far. Imagine the implications of this, and the concern or interest pharmaceutical companies would have in it. It will allow us to alter DNA in a developing fetus to correct birth defects in utero, and eliminate disease by altering the gene it is sitting on using fewer drugs. CRISPR is a new technology that will one day make this procedure easy to do. With this knowledge, are we endanger of playing God? Some think so. I only hope science does not move faster than our own evolvement into more aware and compassionate people.

The Darwinian view is "survival of the fittest." Getting to the top of the heap has spawned a self-absorbed society. "I think, therefore I am," the seminal conclusion of French philosopher René Descartes (1596-1650), promotes the idea that Earth is irrelevant, since it doesn't think. This supposition underlies the destruction of our planet, and along with it, ourselves. Who cares if we cut into the body of Mother Earth, if she is holding a mineral we want? Who cares if we clear-cut the oxygen-producing forests that clean our air, when there is money to be made? Who cares how much garbage we dump into the oceans and landfills? The Earth does not think; therefore, her only purpose is to support the "people at the top." We now know that if we upset the perfect balance of our Earth to the point of no return, she will have no choice but to defend herself, and the "people at the top" will be gone. This planet is very much alive, and its forces far greater than any other. Mother Nature is the one on top. I believe we are evolving into a species that understands we must support the connection all of us have with Mother Earth, with each other, and everything in nature.

Man will evolve in awareness, becoming more conscious and compassionate. Will it be in our lifetime or centuries from now? Evolvement moves slowly, but most important—it never stops.

How quickly we get there is our choice, but all roads will lead there eventually, even if it's through pollution, heartache, and pain. Teach—and model for—our children tolerance, compassion, and connection. A toxic planet can never happen when we understand the connection we have with it. Our children will teach their children, and their children will teach their children, and on it will go until nurturing Mother Earth will be the natural thing to do. In the 1970s most of us had never heard of connection and very little about pollution, but that's not true today, and that is a major step in our evolution.

Looking back through the centuries, you'll see religion has been evolving since its inception. It seems there is an effort being made to fit the biblical teachings that so many have been clinging to into what science is discovering. When people recognize the God they have been defending, and clinging to, as that which simply is and ever has been, it will be the biggest step in evolution for all of mankind.

CHAPTER 14

WHO IS GOD?

"I want to know how God created this world.
I am not interested in this or that phenomenon,
in the spectrum of this or that element. I want
to know His thoughts, the rest are details."

— ALBERT EINSTEIN —

The only place I knew to find God was in religion, yet religion had caused me to doubt His very existence. I needed to know if God existed, and if He did, I felt the answer should jump out at me in the dark alley I was led into. That didn't happen. It was more like my hand was being held as I cautiously walked down that alley; the answer slowly evolved out of the many things I was investigating. It was when I studied the world of energy and consciousness that I realized the image I had of God, was all wrong.

Before Bre was married, the cabin was mine and Bre's unparalleled retreat. She was a very good listener and told me I wasn't—but that I was a very good listener at the cabin. I regret not knowing the things I know today. I would have been a more connected mother, not caught up in the physical world of stress and worry. At the cabin, she had my undivided attention and our conversations were deeper and uninterrupted. I began to know her as an adult, and that's a fun thing for a parent. I am so grateful for the cabin. When I was given the book *Conversations with God* by Neale Walsch, it opened our conversations to God and religion. Neale's view of God was not a biblical "textbook" idea, but it led to an interesting conversation with Bre.

She told me of an experience she had in school. Bre went to a Catholic school through the sixth grade. Not because I wanted her to learn about the Catholic religion, but because it was known to be a good school. She said, "It felt bad when my friends took communion, and I had to sit in the back as though I wasn't good enough."

I never knew that before and felt very sad hearing it.

She replied, "Don't feel bad. I wasn't the only one in the back. I don't think God would have cared if we'd eaten a wafer and drank the juice given by the priest."

Had she been included, they might have converted her. Instead, the exclusion turned her off. Rituals were created and important mainly to energize each man's religion, reinforcing identity and sustaining tradition. Bre didn't feel God needed rituals; His love is freely given, and He has no religious or personal preferences of any kind. As I reflect on that conversation, I wonder how someone in grade school figured out what has taken me a lifetime to understand: *To God, no one is an outcast, and all people are unconditionally loved. It is man who puts conditions on His love.*

Bre and I didn't feel the need to solve the mystery of God at that time. Mostly, because I didn't believe it was a mystery that could be solved. It was just one of those interesting conversations we had at the cabin. My need to know grew with intensity after she left. I feared that God and His heaven were all a fantasy, and Bre would be gone from me forever. I was angry, and felt as though life had no purpose. That was how my journey began, and it led me to Bre and to a creator very different from the one described to me in Sunday school. It was not a god or a supernatural king holding dominance over His domain. *It was a conscious, living system that was the collective energy of all things, and of which each one of us is an integral part.*

Early man believed there was nothing before God's creation. God was fundamentally separate from us, because we knew nothing about energy or connection—only separation. Man caused even more division and discord from God by believing that the God of one's own particular religion told the only true story of who He was. Was He a Jewish God, a Muslim God, a Christian God, the Hindu "Gods," the Native-American's Great Spirit, or another possibility? How about the God of the Baha'i faith—or have you even heard of that one? Joseph Campbell said, "Myth is what we call other people's religion." When we believe that ours is the only true religion, we can feel superior to followers of other faiths. Science clearly shows our universe to be one of entanglements and connections, so at the most fundamental level, everything is connected. It is man who divides and places conditions on God's love. I hope you know there is only one kind of love God knows, and that is unconditional love – the purest form of love.

Our struggling forebears witnessed their share of mysterious and fearsome natural and supernatural phenomena. To explain them, gods, in one form or another, were created. If you heard thunder crashing all around you, would you not also believe someone "up there"—the Thunder god—was furious? It would also appear that in many cases, the fear of gods was used to manipulate people into accepting whatever men in power wanted them to believe. The "one" God was supposed to love and protect us. Yet even He allowed terrible things to happen in order to "test" our faith, or to punish us for having sinned. It's no wonder that over the centuries people began to question the validity of God.

Science was forced to reconsider their stand on a "supernatural" creator when it was discovered that the world of energy responded to human thought. As you've read before, energy doesn't do much without a thought. Was there a superconsciousness that existed before us, and was it in control of all energy? Although the evidence to support that is very strong, it is largely ignored because there is no mathematical formula to prove it. Every road I followed led to vibrational energy, consciousness, and/or connection. I started to see that the creator is all of those things, and we are one with that energy—not separate from it.

Jesus said, "The works that I do shall you do also, and greater works than these." (John 14:12) I believe Jesus understood the power in conscious thought, and He knew we held that same power. Jesus said, "I and the Father are One" (John 10:30), and "Whoever has seen me has seen the Father" (John 14:9). Was He referring to His connection with God, or was He referring to Himself as God in human form? Is it possible to believe that both interpretations are correct? I believe Jesus knew He was at one with an infinite and loving system, just as He knew we were united with it as well. That would also explain why Jesus said we didn't need an intercessor to speak to God; we could speak directly to God ourselves.

I had also been taught that God intimately knew what was in my thoughts. How was that possible, when there were billions of us? "Because He is God" was not an answer I could accept. To me, the logical answer was *connection*. He is not loftily or remotely "up there," and we somehow "down here." He is in everything, and many near-death experiencers felt that connection while they were "there," which was both a very curious and wonderful feeling.

Another question I had asked myself throughout the years was, where did God come from? For us, everything has a beginning and end. Revelation 1:8 says, "I am the Alpha and the Omega," which translates as *I am the beginning and the end*. I found no other answers from NDE'ers or anything else I had read. All I could determine was that He had always been and was not created. We cannot know the meaning or describe the essence of infinity or eternity. Nor can we understand or even get a feel for a place where time and matter do not exist, and where anything one can imagine manifests immediately. NDE'ers say they seem to understand all of this while they are there, as though they've always known it. The loving light they saw seemed to permeate everything, as though it *was* everything, yet it had a separateness. The realm they were in was not like anything they knew, just as the quantum world was not like anything we knew. The world of energy was foreign to us, and was thought to be separate from us. We now know we are not apart from it—we are made of it and awash in it. There was never this world and that world; there is only energy, and science is trying to grasp the hugeness of that.

Does the creator have a name? It seems He has many names: Elohim, Adonai, El, Jehovah, and Allah, to name a few. "Ehyeh-Asher Ehyeh" was how He described Himself to Moses and translates loosely as *I am that I am*. The most frequently used name, YHWH, was given to Moses in Exodus 3:14. Vowels were not used in ancient texts, and it was later translated as Yahweh (Yah-way). We had to take Moses' word for what he saw and heard as there were no witnesses. It was commonly held that to mispronounce His holy name was disrespectful, so only the high priests were allowed to speak it. Considering the translation is somewhat of a guess, I believe the creator is not vested in a name in the same way that we are. The creator is not a mythical god like Zeus or Hera, so if naming Him Charley makes Him more relatable to you, that is the most important.

I don't mean to be disrespectful to anyone who holds dearly to a name they believe to be His true name. A name doesn't explain or describe who the creator is—or anyone for that matter. It's only a means of identification, and just the tip of the iceberg. As we struggle with things that seem important to us, like names, His all-inclusive sound is "I am that I am," and the most important thing to Him is the sharing of love.

In ancient texts the symbol for the creator was neither male nor female. Because our gender pronouns are generally limited to male and female, He was adopted to describe the creator. Even though I know better now, I still use He or God when referring to the creator, as do most of us. Genesis 1:26 says, "Let us make man in our image, after our likeness." That strongly suggests the creator was not alone. I was taught the "us" meant He and His son, Jesus. The world is one of duality, so there could be an argument for both a feminine and masculine god. It might even mean many in one. If we have always been an aspect of one energy, then the "us" in Genesis could actually be us. In other words, we may have had a say in the creation of our physical world. He is beyond anything we can understand in human terms, so we should stop casting stones at each other. I have come to believe that however you choose to know Him—whether as a he, a she, a living system of energy, or Charley—He will love you the same, just as He always has.

Many believe God will judge us in the end, with the majority being dispatched to hell for an eternity of unrelenting torment. If God loves us unconditionally as the Bible indicates in Matthew 5:44-45 or the Parable of the Prodigal Son (Luke 15:11), then what might He be judging? Some might argue that asking Him to forgive us, is the key to receiving His love. In fact, it is guilt that blocks us from feeling His love—a love that is always there.

Are we to fear God or to love God? When I asked that question, it was explained that while God was all-merciful and all-loving,

He was also all-righteous. That sounded contradictory, and in any terms, punishment for all eternity is excessive. A much more reasonable scenario, and one I've come to believe through my study of NDEs, is that we judge ourselves under the guardianship of a loving council for the purpose of relieving the guilt we feel and learning from our experiences instead. We learn nothing from punishment except fear and hopelessness—the opposite of love.

I was taught that God was testing my faith when things were going badly for me. I couldn't accept that God would purposely hurt me like that—man might, but not God. And since He already knows what's in my heart, why would He need to administer a test to see into my already transparent heart? Along with the idea of God testing us, the ancients also believed deformities or the illness they were suffering were punishment for transgressions. They could even result from the sins of a father; in other words, we could be punished for an ancestor's sins. People lived in fear of being punished for one thing or another, and what good did it do?

It was possible we misunderstood the Bible verse John 15:14, "Sin no more, lest a worse thing come unto you." Notice the verse doesn't say God causes bad things; it says sin can cause additional bad things to happen. The truth is, sin carries its own kind of punishment, so He has no need or desire to punish us further. In *The Hidden Power of the Bible,* Ernest Holmes tells us "We are surrounded by a Universal Law, which is entirely impartial, and which returns to the thinker the logical effect of his actions. Man, being a free agent in this law—whether consciously or in ignorance—is continually setting it in motion to some definite end. Therefore it is true, unalterably true, that he must reap as he has sown."

God does not cause bad things to happen! To learn and to grow from the incessant experiences of life is why we choose to come here and the reason this "here" was created. The physical world includes negative energy, created from fear and hate, where bad

165

things can manifest more easily. On the upside, there is hope regarding negative energy—loving thoughts cancel negative energy. The more love we send out, the less negative energy there is. With that knowledge, "we can create heaven on Earth." It's terrifying for many people who are steeped in religious dogma to change their thinking about who and what God is, when the consequence may be to spend eternity in hell. I no longer have that fear, because I believe in unconditional love.

Is there a devil? It's possible that Satan is not an actual being. From what I've read, it seems there is no fear or negative energy in heaven, yet we have a lot of it here. The Bible says God cast Satan out of heaven to dwell on Earth. Was Satan the name given to fear? Without fear, there would be no negative energy, no temptation, and no hard choices to make. *The Devil made me do it!* No, he did not. The temptation arose and you made the choice. Stop making choices through a deceitful and selfish heart. Have you ever considered that the purpose God created the physical world, enabling us to make hard choices, was because we asked Him for it?

Do angels exist? Angels appear 273 times in the Bible, and I believe that is evidence of their existence. So I did a little research, and, as usual, found some variations. Many believe God created angels to watch over us because of the fearful environment we were going into. Some believe we become angels when we die, but I found no evidence to support that. Some believe angels were created before human beings, and others believe they came after. Most believe angels have never lived a physical life while a few believe they have. They seem to have no gender and can appear in any form that the situation requires, including as animals. I often wondered why anything bad could happen when such powerful beings "have our backs." Some say we already had a plan, with a mission or purpose when we came here, and angelic intervention cannot interfere with that plan. People believe they've had angel encounters, and it is possible that some have had one and not been aware of it or wrote it off as something weird and unexplainable. Absent an obvious angelic encounter, it's hard to believe in such a fantastical thing.

Angels remain an exciting mystery to me, but I can't help thinking they are real. Many books have been written on this subject. *Book of Angels,* by Sylvia Browne, offers an interesting interpretation of their individual power and beauty, as does *Invoking the Archangels,* by Sunny Dawn Johnston. I didn't feel the need to do a lot of research into angels because it wasn't central to the journey I was on, but I love that people feel comfortable telling me of their angelic encounters. Imagine what we could learn if we felt safe asking questions and wouldn't be ridiculed for sharing the unexplainable things that happen to us.

The invisible world of energy holds the answer. We are eternal energy beings that are part of one infinite and loving system that was here long before man generated gods, goddesses, and religions to explain the unexplainable, including who and what we are and where we come from.

CHAPTER 15

ENERGY

"A system possesses energy if it has the ability to do work."

— THE PHYSICS HYPERTEXTBOOK —

E nergy is a word that is overused—and no wonder, since absolutely everything is vibrating energy in one form or another. What we see, feel, hear, think, and do is made of energy, uses energy, and emits energy in one form or another. However, I cannot ignore consciousness when explaining energy. Our body is a system that possesses energy, just as defined above, giving it the ability to do work—and our thoughts have a direct effect on energy. Our physical life would be inconsequential without consciousness. When the energy leaves, consciousness leaves with it, and the physical body disintegrates.

We tend to think of energy in the context of how energetic we feel or what it can do for us, like run up a hill, power our car, turn our lights on, or run a hot bath. A physicist thinks of energy in two ways: kinetic and potential. Kinetic is energy in motion and potential is stored energy waiting to be in motion. In other words, it's either doing something or it's waiting to do something. Others may call the two kinds of energy electrical and magnetic—it goes out and it comes back. Energy vibrates at different intensities, and all things can be identified by their own unique frequency. I felt as if I was going every which way when I began to research the definition of energy. That effort in itself defined energy.

Early physicists discovered matter isn't solid when they shot a photon particle through a double slit and it split in two, going through both slots. That was a shock, but further down the road, when they discovered consciousness affected energy, that was mind-blowing. How is that possible and why would it be? It opened a door they hoped to permanently close—an intelligence beyond, and interlaced with our own, was here before us. All of creation would be a hit-or-miss chain of events if energy were not receiving direction from a conscious thought. Consciousness was the Pied Piper that Einstein referred to, and the conscious intelligent mind that Max Planck spoke of.

I began to understand the principle behind practices in energy healing. It made sense that the energy-flow inside my body must move smoothly. If there was a blockage, energy would build up behind it, causing pain and swelling. The energy-flow inside the body was understood centuries ago, but was scoffed at by modern medicine. They didn't see us as energy beings, they saw us as mechanical body-machines. Now that we have more information, this is no longer the case. Practices such as acupuncture, chiropractic, and massage break up energy blocks and are accepted practices today.

Here is something I experienced myself. I didn't know anything about energy at the time of my acupuncture treatment. It was as though a dam broke when she hit the right spot, and all of the pain rushed out of my hand. It takes an experienced acupuncturist to hit the target, but she sure did with me, and I felt it. Strange as it

sounds, the acupuncturist jumped away from me when that happened. She told me she could see energy (auras) around people,
and the energy leaving me was dark. She didn't want it to hit her. I
didn't know you could see energy, let alone that it could be of different colors. The auras around people indicate not only their state
of health or disease but also the kind of mood they are in. Imagine
walking into a room and knowing who to sit next to because you are
drawn to the color of energy emanating from them. That seemed
impossible, but I found myself becoming more and more accepting
of impossible things the deeper I went on this journey.

Bre loved massage and got them regularly. It frustrated her that
I never got them. It was hard for me to relax. When Bre left, Geri,
the massage therapist in the salon, told me she felt Bre was sitting
on the edge of the massage table, dangling her feet, relentlessly
saying, "You have to call Mom!" Of course I complied when she
first asked, and I swear I could feel Bre in the room with us. I could
almost hear her glee. I have seen Geri every month since then.
Even though I don't feel Bre there anymore, I'm sure she's happy
I continue to get them. The interesting thing is, my lower back
has not gone out on me since I started getting a monthly massage.
Thank you, Bre—and Geri.

Bre understood the energy flow inside the body long before I
did. Along with encouraging me to get a massage, she asked me to
go to a yoga class with her. She said it would help keep the energy
flowing evenly throughout my body. Have you ever heard of "Brain
Gym?" I hadn't. It was another class in energy flow she had an
interest in. It uses specific movements to stimulate and change the
energy patterns of the brain, enabling mental and physical healing.
I loved the information from that class. Bre was also curious about
tai chi, and that might have been my next invitation. I loved going
with her on these adventures, and I find myself not wanting to go
without her. I miss her, and her invitations, very much. It would

have been interesting to have talked with her about energy, but I thought energy was one of those New Age buzzwords back then.

I've been a big fan of conventional medicine since surviving breast cancer, but there is much to be said for energy healing. Tibetan monks have known for centuries that the energy of conscious thought together with sound vibrations from their chants has the power to destroy diseased cells through the pounding of vibrational energy. *The Isaiah Effect,* by Gregg Braden, offers a completely different idea: Visualize yourself as healthy, believe it strongly, and you can jump from one reality stream to another with a healthy body on it. I've learned that anything is possible and worth consideration, so why not other dimensions? Mysterious things happen, and miraculous healings are among them. I am confident science will discover that vibrational energy holds the answer to many mysterious phenomena.

As I said, sound emits vibrating energy. It's no secret that music affects our mood, so much so that subliminal messages can be embedded in it—hopefully, to help heal our mind and body and not to create anger. I love the soothing sound of a wind chime, and I have my mom's since she couldn't take it with her to the assisted-living facility. As time goes by, that wind chime will become increasingly special to me. The sound vibration from soundtracks, chants, mantras, musical instruments, singers, gongs, and bells carry different vibrations that penetrate the body. Dr. Anthony Holland, Associate Professor of Music at Skidmore College, along with other scientists, has developed a way to kill cancer cells and other harmful organisms with resonant frequencies. Dr. Holland said, "Imagine a time when children suffering from cancer can sit in a room playing with toys and each other all the while being cured with the bombardment of resident vibrations."

We know the Tacoma Narrows Bridge collapsed because of vibration—high-speed winds matched with the natural frequency of the structure—and crystal shatters when the right tone is hit. Even fire can be extinguished. We need to identify and recreate the many corresponding frequencies in order to use them. Research in the many fields of energy, and how the vibration of energy affects us and this planet, has gained momentum since discovering the quantum world—the world of energy.

The HeartMath Institute, founded in 1991 by Doc Childre, is an organization dedicated to the study of heart energy. Its members consist of scientists, physicians, and other researchers. They hope to bring awareness to the connection between heart and mind, to one another, and to this planet through the study of heart energy. Their mission: "To help people bring their physical, mental, and emotional systems into balanced alignment with their heart's intuitive guidance. This unfolds the path for becoming heart-empowered individuals who choose the way of love, which they demonstrate through compassionate care for the well-being of themselves, others, and the planet Earth."

The heart is the first organ to form in the body—not the brain. It starts as a clump of cells, and then begins beating for no apparent reason and continues to beat for hours after it is removed from the body. In the new field of neurocardiology, scientists discovered a network of nerves in the heart containing 40,000 neurons. This little heart-brain is believed to process information generated by our emotions. When we are under stress or experiencing negative emotion, the energy of the heart becomes erratic. In turn, the neural signals sent from the heart to the brain also become erratic. The vibrational energy of the brain and body are out of sync and open to disease and mental anguish. These same rhythms become smooth and in sync when a volunteer is shown something to appreciate, changing the negative emotion into positive. Remember, positive energy neutralizes negative energy. That energy projects out from the body, and into the energy field that surrounds this planet. Doc Childre said, "One day it could be relevant for us to know that the energy produced by the heart is greater than sixty times that of the brain." I could understand the importance of the HeartMath research. The heart is our lifeline, and it may be the lifeline of the entire universe.

Some believe the brain is the only organ that can process information, including emotions, and that the heart is extraneous. The pain of losing Bre I *physically* felt deep in my heart and not my brain. The question is, did my brain tell my heart to feel that pain, or did my heart already know it?

The energy of the brain is measured using EEG (electroencephalography), MRI (magnetic resonance imaging), and MEG (magnetoencephalography). Human brainwaves have five unique frequencies, from the fastest (gamma approximately 38 to 42 Hz) to the slowest (Delta .5 to 4 Hz). In-between there is beta, alpha, and theta. When the frequencies were given a computerized color, brainwaves became visible, and researchers could recognize patterns indicative of a person's habits, beliefs, and behaviors. Imagine being able to correct a person's bad habits or behaviors permanently, as well as curing mental illness, disease, and pain by changing the energy patterns in the brain. *Becoming Supernatural* and *Evolve Your Brain,* seminal books by Dr. Joe Dispenza, are especially inspiring on this subject. Most affecting is Dr. Joe's own personal story. After his back was broken in several places, he was told he would live the rest of his life in pain and possibly be paralyzed. Using his knowledge of changing brainwave patterns and how the immune system works, he redirected the energy in his body to help the immune system mend his back perfectly without surgery. Today his life is devoted to helping others heal themselves of physical and mental illnesses using focused meditations.

Many researchers in this area have dedicated their time and expertise to finding answers, even at the risk of ridicule. The energy generated by emotion is a promising new frontier we are exploring. However, because related discoveries don't attract large sums of money and don't involve pharmaceuticals, they don't get the media-attention they deserve. Nor do they get research grants, the way drug and medical supply companies do. The bulk of the money for this research comes from concerned people who see the value in the study of energy, and the new technologies that can come from it. In most cases, there are other more remunerative jobs available for these pioneer researchers, but it's not about that. It's about their passion to discover a better way to live for all of us. I want to thank and spotlight these concerned and caring people, because it is their commitment to learning how to use the energy all around us and in us that will take us to a beautiful future.

In Gregg Braden's book, *The Spontaneous Healing of Belief*, he describes how the magnetic field around the Earth spiked when millions of people focused on one event, as during 9/11 or Princess Diana's death. If you are wondering how we find such measurements, there are two satellites that continuously measure the magnetic field around the Earth. It is the magnetic field around this planet that protects us from the sun's destructive rays, so it is closely monitored. The global output of energy from heartfelt emotion had a strong effect on the planet's magnetic field. As I've said, the powerful energy produced by emotion is a force that extends beyond the body. We were born with the ability to generate vibrational energy through the feelings that accompany our thoughts—both positive and negative. When we're aware of the type of vibration our thoughts are projecting, and not letting our emotions run wild, we can consciously change the energy field inside and around us. Some people call this "living with intent."

When Bre left, my heart was broken. I wondered how it kept beating, and I didn't care if it stopped. It just kept beating through all the physical and emotional pain. Had it given out on me, I would not be telling you of the desperate journey I took to find my daughter. Understanding the quantum world and energy, learning of the power we possess through a consciousness that is within us, and all other discoveries that I made along the way offer compelling evidence that show we are more than we think we are. We are eternal energy beings, and we are powerful!

CHAPTER 16

FEAR AND LOVE

"There are only two emotions: love and fear.
From love flows happiness, contentment, peace,
and joy. From fear comes anger, hate, anxiety,
and guilt. They're opposites. When we're in a
place of love, we cannot be in a place of fear."

— ELISABETH KÜBLER-ROSS —

I could have ended this discussion with energy, but things kept coming up that I felt were part of the journey. Being mindful of the only two emotions on this planet, as Dr. Kübler-Ross suggested, is life changing. It enables you to view things through two discrete lenses and then choose between them. If you are feeling hateful, vengeful, angry, anxious, and/or sad, that is fear. So ask yourself, *What am I afraid of that is causing this anguish?* Are you afraid someone will get away with a terrible crime they committed? Are you afraid of losing your power, your possessions, a loved one, your health? Fear spawns negative emotions, making us react without thinking, often involving hasty decisions and fruitless worry. It seems the human condition is to worry—What if this happens, or that? Ask yourself, *If that does indeed happen, how will I handle it?* Most of the time it never happens, but you'll be prepared if it does. When you can identify and analyze your core fear, you will be in control of putting your concerns into perspective.

Bre was a big worrier. I used to tell her to look at the glass as being half full instead of half empty. That didn't help her much. At the time, I didn't know there was only one question to ask: "What are you afraid of?" Had I known that, I could have helped her understand where her worries were coming from—and neutralize them. I regret that, and hope this information will help you and your children live life with less worry.

The deep sadness I felt when I lost Bre was exacerbated by the fear that I would never see her again. I wanted to keep her with me in *this life* because I was afraid that *this life* was all there was. Unknown to me, she had her own agenda and purpose for choosing *this life*, and I didn't know there is more to Bre than *this life*. Nor did I know that there is more to me than *this life*, so losing Bre felt like a permanent loss. Now I know that nothing that happens in *this life* is permanent. Let go of the fear of losing the things you love, because you never do. It is my desire to help you be as sure of that as I am.

Should I worry that I will leave before my time? You probably know someone who believes they wouldn't be here today were it not for a certain circumstance. My friend gave his seat to another person because that man needed the earlier flight, and all people aboard died when that plane went down. I've had some close calls myself and thought, *Wow that was strange!* We ask ourselves, *Why was I spared* or *Why them and not me?* I know my friend was steeped in those questions. Do we choose our time to leave, is it destined for us, or is it simple chance? Life is having the freedom to make choices, so it's possible we choose how long we will remain here—and even how we will die. We're not consciously aware of it, but I sometimes wonder if subconsciously we know because of the strange things that can happen before a person leaves. In my opinion Bre should still be with us, but perhaps there was a plan we were all in agreement to before we came here.

When Bre told me she was going on an African safari by herself, I panicked. Fear can be debilitating, but it did not stop her from doing something she felt she needed to do. Upon her return, she told me how much she loved the people. They had nothing, yet they were happy. She thought everyone should go to Africa so they would appreciate all we have in this country. That was life-changing for her. She also saw a cheetah kill a gazelle. When she realized she was about to witness the killing, she was horrified. She was a vegetarian and loved animals. To her surprise, she was happy for the cheetah, as it meant his survival.

This is a memory of Bre that just popped up. She felt that God shouldn't be the only one to thank for the foods we ate. We should thank the food as well. Bre was heartbroken by the way most animals were treated before they reached the grocery store. I told my sister not to tell Bre that she'd actually heard her plant scream, or she would probably stop eating them as well. Wendy, Bre's other mom, asked her why she didn't eat meat and she said, "It would be like eating my mom." She felt animals had feelings, and friends and family who loved them. Eating meals at Bre's house was always full of wonderful surprises. I miss her meatless dinners, the biscuits and gravy, and her yummy tofu tacos—I miss my Bre.

Thankfully, I wasn't privy to the scary things that happened on that safari. A silverback gorilla charged her when her camera accidentally flashed, causing the guide to push her down a steep embankment—bruised and scratched, but still alive. They drove through a tsetse fly infestation where they had to be enclosed, windows and doors secured, in the stifling truck. Tsetse flies carry trypanosomiasis, known as African sleeping sickness. Their itinerary changed because of a warring faction that had killed and kidnapped the people staying in the campground they were headed to next. A week earlier, she would have been among those people. The new itinerary did not include anything that she and another person wanted to do, so they hitched a ride from a "stranger" to the nearest town with an airport. Just writing about this makes my heart jump. Anyway, they caught the plane the next morning. Her friend returned home, but Bre went on to London. She stayed in a bed and breakfast that had a cat she could cuddle with. She wanted to see a play while she was there, and the Queen walked by her as she stood in the roped-in line. She amazed me! So many bad things could have happened to a young woman traveling alone, but they didn't. I believe we plan our exit before we come here, and the time we leave is not left to chance.

Bre once told me she wanted to see animals in the wild and meet people from other countries. She wanted to experience everything this world had to offer, and she seemed to be in a hurry to do that. I look back on all of her travels and wonder if deep down she had an inner knowing that her time here was limited. She never saw the tigers of India which was on her list, but maybe she has one as her companion over there. I love that visual. It was interesting that when I asked Owen what his favorite animal was, he said it was the tiger.

Her love of animals makes me miss our dog, Liberty, but I know Bre has her, and this is why: I was talking with a friend in the salon when a penny landed at our feet. We wondered where it had come from and decided to make it the salon's lucky penny, so we put it on the windowsill for all to share in the luck. As I turned around, another penny hit the floor, and this time with force. We were stunned!

My friend said, "Cyndi, I saw that, and it came from nowhere!"

I looked at my friend and said, "I know where these pennies are from, and I know who sent them. Liberty is written across the face of a copper penny."

When things like this happen, it's hard to explain. There was nothing on the ceiling and no money in our pockets, and we couldn't say it didn't happen. Bre wanted me to know she had Liberty.

Imagine what the world would be like if we looked at death as an entrance into another realm where all fear was gone—completely gone—and we knew we were unconditionally loved and eternal beings. The brief moment we live on Earth is only an adventure. It is one of experiences, and we feel fear and anxiety because of them, but experiences would feel more like adventures knowing we came for that very purpose. We would welcome aging as the natural flow of life, and death would be a gentle passing instead of a desperate struggle against it. We would have bon voyage parties instead of sad funerals, knowing they haven't gone far. No longer would death be regarded as a crushing loss. Sadness would be buffered, knowing death is a misconception. It took some research, but I finally have that buffer. I know, with certainty, that life is an eternal adventure.

It's fun to think of Bre as on vacation in some exotic place, and in many ways that's true. However, it is the longest vacation she has taken and a phone call would be wonderful. Sadly, the phone service is not good. She drops a note from time to time, and I'm glad I know to pay attention to them when she does. They are easy to miss or ignore when you don't know communication is possible. (In Laura Lynne Jackson's book, *Signs*, she teaches the language of signs. I loved that she referred to signs as a language because it is, and it's how our loved ones communicate with us). I take comfort in knowing that when my job here is done, I will leave my body behind and take that trip myself. My dad, friends, family, pets, and even the brother I never met will be there with Bre. I'm not in a hurry to take that vacation, but in some ways I look forward to the adventure, knowing I will never leave anyone I love behind.

The fear of flying was a big problem for Bre since she loved to travel. Hoping that it would allay some of that fear, she decided she was going to jump out of an airplane. When we were in Arizona visiting her grandparents, she convinced her cousins to go with her. I stayed on the ground, taking pictures. Maybe one way to conquer fear is to challenge the fear, meeting it head-on. A better way might be to look for the cause of the fear and challenge that. If it is death that causes fear, then there is nothing to fear knowing you can never die. If it's pain you fear, that's a different story. However, you don't get through life without it. Permanent injury is also a fear, but you can learn a lot from disabilities; and maybe that was the journey you were meant to be on in this life, so it would have happened anyway.

We would have no hard choices to make in a loving world where fear didn't exist. Earth offers a contrast of both fear and love. I sometimes wonder if death is the source of all fear. Believing life is short, the choices we make become more desperate. What career should I pursue? Should I marry that person? Should I have children? Should I make that move? When you believe this life is all there is, those choices become critical. An unexpected thing happened to me when I realized life never ends—the fear of making choices was gone!

Fear can cause us to make the wrong decision or not make any decision at all. If the decision comes from loving intent and feels good, I believe it is the right decision. At times a decision can feel safe but not particularly good. Is that just fear? When you weigh the pros and cons of a decision, you may find it packed with fearful probabilities. Either way you choose, you'll need to be prepared to deal with the consequences. I lean toward the good-feeling decision, prepared to deal with its consequences, because I believe the outcome over time will be as it should be. When a decision comes from loving intent, it feels good in your heart and is the right decision. Here's something I do: I place my hands over my heart, take a few deep slow breaths, and ask my heart a yes or no question. The answer usually comes immediately. When it doesn't, I assume either decision is the right one. If you think I'm being weird, try it. You might discover it's not as weird as it sounds.

In *What If This Is Heaven,* Anita Moorjani tells of her near-death experience and how she was cured of terminal cancer by replacing fear with love in all things. Ego was an interesting one for her, and I hadn't thought of ego in a loving way either. She had been raised to believe a woman should not have a big ego. Because of her NDE, she learned to embrace her ego. "A healthy ego is a necessary part of who we are. It is the one who is defending you." The problem is, it can become insecure or narcissistic when it is full of fear. It is the one telling us we have to win, because it fears losing means we are a loser. It tells you not to ask that question, because it is afraid you will appear ignorant. It will even devalue another, so you can feel more valuable. It didn't get the memo that said *you have great value, you are loved, you are safe, you are smart, and you can never be a loser.* A healthy ego thinks in terms of connection—*we* instead of *I*.

I learned in business that everyone has to win for it to be a good decision—the salon, the hairdresser, and the customer. An unchecked ego creates a platform for resentment and mistrust, and that's never good in business or personal life. I tried to address my ego first when making decisions by asking if everyone would win with my decision, and not just me. That didn't mean everyone was happy with every decision, but, together, we agreed that the reasons for that decision would benefit all parties in the end.

Nothing about our physical life feels permanent. We fear we will lose our life, the people we love, our health, our things, or we just won't have enough time. The world we come from is a loving and eternal place where nothing ceases to exist and time is non-existent, so the fear of loss is a new and scary feeling for us. As I've said before, in order for us to make choices, we have to know fear. Fear—not hate—is the opposite of love. Hate arises out of fear, so analyze the root of your fear before you react to the hate it engenders. When you know there is nothing you can lose, your choices will become as easy for you as they are for me. The concept is simple but knowing we have nothing to lose is not, because we are conditioned to believe the opposite. It saddened my heart when Bre left all of her precious things behind. That sadness came from my fear that she would never have them again. Those things were never real; they were made of energy like everything else in the physical world. I imagine she can recreate them if she wants to—and much more.

Numerous businessess and nations make money off our fears. Our own political campaigns use fear to win, with each party creating fear in the other. Fear is used to motivate a "yes" or "no" vote on issues that are brought before the people. When I was young, fear and smear campaigns were at a minimum. Now, it seems they are at a maximum because hired professionals are paid to root them out and elevate them. Who gains the wealth or power from fear-mongering? Is it a company, a person, a country, or a religion? This is unsettling, as it is hard to discern when partial or distorted truths are involved, or when events were generated and manipulated to stimulate fear and sway a decision one way or the other. Fear generates negative energy, and lots of it. One day we will more clearly see the damage we are doing to our world by the negative energy created from fear.

People want to live in peace, so why does war still exist? It's a vicious cycle: the fear of losing power, money, and land; the fear of invasion and losing our freedoms; the fear in religious persecution, and the list goes on. Fear tactics are used to incite people to anger, hate, bitterness, and mistrust, causing them to fight someone else's war. Whenever fear is employed, I am suspicious. We are eternal beings, on a brief journey of experiences with nothing to fear because we can't really lose anything. When we embrace this, fear will lose its power and cruelty will end. The countries of the world will use the money they spend on munitions and warfare to build infrastructures and feed the people, ending all oppression. Genocide due to religious or political gain would become inconceivable. This is all within our power, yet we seem incapable of recognizing we have that kind of power. Until then, we have no choice but to defend ourselves against those "very real" fearful things—and the misery continues.

"Fear is the main source of superstition, and one of the main sources of cruelty. To conquer fear is the beginning of wisdom." Bertrand Russell.

A few may disagree, but I believe love is something everyone needs above all else. When love is not felt, we put up walls to protect ourselves from being hurt. Over time the walls increase in size and number, pushing love farther away until we are convinced we don't need it, nor can we give it. Unconditional love—which is very difficult to give or receive in physical life—seems to have been consigned to fairy tale movies. Little children can still love unconditionally because they have not yet put up defenses, and our pets tend to love that way too. Whenever I walked into my home, Liberty came running to let me know how happy she was to see me. It's been noted that dog is God spelled backwards. Knowing what I know of God today, I see that as a good way of looking at the unconditional love Liberty felt for me. She never had a bad day, and she always made my bad day a better day. Imagine being bathed in that kind of love, completely accepted just as you are, in a world where everyone you met loved you and you loved them back. We have forgotten the way we have always been loved because we live in a world where love has conditions, and we have no memory of the world we come from.

Even knowing this, there is one thing I will always fear. That is the painful experiences my loved ones will suffer. The only thing I can offer them is what I've learned on this journey. It helps to remember that nothing that happens here is forever, and there truly is a loving source that eternally fills and sustains them. Originally, my intent was to share this journey with the people I know and love, but was increasingly encouraged to share it with others. That sparked many new fears in me, but I didn't let it stop me because it felt like the right decision.

The description of love in 1 Corinthians 13:4 is beautiful, and I often write it in wedding cards: "Love is patient, love is kind. It does not envy, it does not boast, it is not proud. It does not dishonor others, it is not self-seeking, it is not easily angered, it keeps no record of wrongs. Love does not delight in evil but rejoices with the truth. It always protects, always trusts, always hopes, always perseveres."

The following is a partial list from a photo I saw by Zenera in WP Biographia v3.3.2 that highlights the difference between love and fear.

Love is unconditional—fear is conditional
Love releases—fear obligates
Love is honest—fear is deceitful
Love ignites—fear incites
Love allows—fear dictates
Love energizes—fear saps
Love respects—fear disregards
Love accepts—fear rejects
Love desires—fear needs
Love wants to play—fear needs to control
Love vs. Fear: Which do you feel?

Unconditional love creates an environment where love oozes out of you the way it oozes into you, and whether we know it or not, we crave that love because that's the only love we have known for eternity. That was the love my friend experienced when he had his NDE, and is happy to know he will feel it again.

Bre understood love better than I. When Bre and Ben married, he was stationed in Georgia, so of course she wanted to move there. The problem was she had two rescued cats, and it wouldn't be safe for Max and Molly because of the dangerous critters that lived outside.

Bre asked, "Could you keep them for me, Mom?"

"Max likes me, but Molly doesn't," I said.

"Mom, Molly needs love and you have to force her to let you hold her. Don't you know that when someone resists love, it's because they need love the most?"

Just where did my daughter come from? Molly never warmed up to me during that year, and it kind of hurt my feelings. I think she sensed I was afraid of her, just as she was afraid of me—fear and love. Thankfully, she wasn't afraid of Les and had a happy, safe home while Bre and Ben were gone. After Bre left us, Ben found himself unable to take care of Max, Molly, and Liberty. Les and I adopted them. In time, Molly learned to trust me, letting me pick her up and rub her little head. I finally felt redeemed—and that is what love can do.

CHAPTER 17

Thoughts Become Reality

"A quantum entity's unobserved attributes are not fully real but rather exist in an alternative state of being called 'potentia' until the act of observation promotes some lucky attribute to full reality status."

— WERNER HEISENBERG —

"A man is but the product of his thoughts— what he thinks, he becomes."

— MAHATMA GANDHI —

B re and I, along with the people who worked for me, attended a business seminar years ago. We were instructed to build a board with all of our desires pasted on it, using the pictures and words we cut out of magazines they provided. Some might call this a dream board, or simply setting goals. It doesn't matter what you call it because it's all the same. I didn't keep my board, but I kept Bre's simply because I liked saving her things. She came across it two weeks before she died and later called to tell me that all of the pictures on her board had materialized. She was dumbfounded, as was I. I paid a lot of money for that "business" seminar, but I didn't place any importance on this particular project and believed it was a waste of time.

Was it a coincidence that Bre found her board at that time? I wondered if it was meant to bring me some sort of comfort, knowing she had lived her dreams. In some ways it did, but I would have wanted her dream board extended to include seeing her son have a child of his own. In any case, I believed there was a reason Bre found her dream board when she did and shared what she had discovered with me. I felt there was a purpose for me to understand the concept behind manifesting the things we think about. I didn't know that going down this road was a necessary part of my journey, but I was wrong. We are made in God's image: powerful creators who can create a world of abundance just like He promised. We must learn how to use the beautiful and unselfish gift the creator gave us, and stop wasting it.

I first read about vibrational energy in *The Celestine Prophecy*, by James Redfield. It was 1993, and Bre's first job was with Princess Cruise Lines. She wanted to take me and her grandparents on an Alaskan cruise. That was the book I took along. It was a mystery based on the awakening of humankind and was a New York best seller. The insight I gained from it was that thoughts generate vibrations, which effect not only the person but their surroundings. These vibrations may be viewed as both electrical and magnetic energy—it goes out and comes back. I knew the story was one of fiction, but it gave me pause to wonder.

I remember sitting in the hot tub at the back of the ship discussing the book with Bre and another couple who had read it. She was fascinated by the idea, just as we were. In the 1990s not much information was readily available on the power of thought (though it was in existence), but now there is an abundance. I would love having that conversation with her today.

Dr. Norman Vincent Peale opened one of many doorways into this concept when he wrote his best-selling book in the 1950s, *The Power of Positive Thinking*. Before Peale, another popular sensation was Napolean Hill's *Think and Grow Rich*, written in 1937. The power of thought was a curiosity, and over the years many people got involved. Self-help books such as these, were selling like crazy and "think positive" seminars began blooming. Tony Robbins comes to mind. I referred to them as feel-good seminars. Post seminar, some people could remain upbeat and positive, but most would revert back to their old way of thinking. Because of that, I didn't place a lot of importance on feel-good seminars. The universal Law of Attraction (positive attracts and negative repels) was what they based their overall principals on. In other words, it was based more upon the *law* of nature rather than the *power* within us. People continued the investigation, and a deeper understanding of how it works grew along with what science was discovering in the world of energy. It is the positive and negative vibrational energy born of our emotions that puts the Law of Attraction into action. Remember, I believe emotions come from the heart and not the brain. The brain talks in words, and the heart talks with feelings. Perhaps, this is why the Bible said "God knows what's in our heart"—feelings can't lie. As I've said many times before, there are hidden truths in the Bible.

I had heard people say, "I just gave it to the universe, and it happened." Who or what is the universe? All I can tell you is that something out there responded to my desperate plea, "Where is my Bre?" Finding the book at the cabin made me wonder if Bre had led me to the book, did God, the universe; or was it just a coincidence? I now know there are no coincidences and it didn't matter what I believed, because everything is an integral part of one inifnite energy system that hears all. When a thought is introduced, things begin to happen. I acted on the urge to drive to the cabin, then put in the time and did the research, but in my mind there was no doubt I was being guided. Knowing we get a response, no matter what or whom we believe in, and regardless of whether we're aware of what our contributing thoughts or not are, I realized the importance of understanding this concept further. I wondered what others were learning about the power of thought, and that meant more research.

In 2007 I read *The Field,* by investigative journalist, Lynne McTaggart. I was trying to understand what the field of energy is (the quantum world). She explained it in words I could understand, and I remembered her surprise at learning that consciousness has an effect on energy. I decided to see what she was doing now and checked her website. She was investigating exactly what I was interested in—how the power of thought works. She began her inquiry by working with Dr. Gary Schwartz and other established researchers to give her experiments credibility. In her latest book, *The Power of Eight,* McTaggart shares her discoveries. Using her website to create and monitor "groups of intention," instruction is given to simply focus on one thing to see if together the group could bring about change. Members came from all walks of life and from all over the world—all were welcome to join the study. It didn't seem to matter how many were in the group or what their belief system was, nor if they were experienced meditators—the concept *worked,* regardless of variables. Besides hearing the stories of miraculous healings through intention, McTaggart also discovered something unexpected—their own lives were being healed in all manner of ways they hadn't put their attention on! The universal Law of Attraction was indeed at work here: their good intentions came boomeranging back to them, usually in unexpected ways.

Throughout the years, meditative groups using focused intention, and prayer chains using prayer, have seen crime rates drop, people heal, and war zones experience moments of peace. The Maharishi Effect, in which groups of TM meditators came together to reduce crime in major cities, is proof of that. Some regard these wonderful events as miracles. According to the Free Dictionary, *A miracle is an event that appears inexplicable by the laws of nature and so is held to be supernatural in origin or an act of God.* For some that's hard to swallow, so they call them luck or coincidences and quickly move on to what's "real" in life. Miracles happen when healing thoughts are directed toward a specific outcome. It seems we are built to do this, and, for me, that's biology not supernatural. Intention groups and prayer chains are becoming increasingly popular, and in time I believe the power we possess will be an accepted part of our culture.

Thoughts draw to us the things we put our attention on, and trust is a necessary part of this process. I realized that faith and trust are basically the same thing. Having the faith of a little child, as described in Mathew 18:3, gives strength and purity to prayer, just as trust gives strength and single-minded confidence to our conscious thoughts. I believe prayer was meant to instruct us in the power of thought, but the ancients understood it only in terms of directing requests to their god or gods, and hoping for supernatural intervention. They had no conception of the creative power we were given. Instead, when their prayers weren't answered, they believed He was saying no; they were unworthy; being taught patience or given another lesson of some kind; or their faith in Him wasn't strong enough—and many still hold that mindset.

Over the years, prayer has become a curiosity for many researchers. In *Recovering the Soul*, by Dr. Larry Dossey, I came across an experiment in prayer called Spindrift. In one experiment they used rye seeds; praying for one set and not the other. Consistently, the ones prayed for would yield more than the ones not prayed for. The result was even more dramatic after one group of seeds was stressed with salt water. They discovered that the more prayer given by an experienced practitioner, who knew what to feel while praying, the better the yield would be. Clearly, feelings of love and faith (trust) are important in this process. Along with this, praying that "Thy will be done," as opposed to holding a specific goal for the outcome, made the yields even better. We generally think we know what the goal should be and how to acheive it, but we can't see all of the possibilities. If we get out of our own way and trust the All-Knower to guide us to our goal, we will be led in the best possible direction and receive the best results. "Let go, and let God," is letting your desires be known without giving any particular marching orders.

All scientists agree that thoughts affect energy, yet some won't agree that thoughts affect the physical world of matter. Since all matter is made of the same energy that our thoughts affect, I find that way of thinking hard to understand. The rye seeds in the Spindrift experiment consist of matter that was affected by thought, and there have been many other experiments proving the same thing. For some, it seems the reluctance to accept that we have this kind of power comes from the fear that we are more than an evolutionary accident. That fringes on the possibility that a creator exists. For others, the recognition that we have this power is seen as a prideful sin against God because He is the only one with power. We've just touched the surface, and in order for this kind of reasearch to become mainstream, we must see beyond those fears.

As discussed, the heart and brain emit both electrical and magnetic fields of energy that extend into the world around us. Clearly, there is a reason we are able to do this. The Bible teaches in 1 John 5:14-15, "This is the confidence we have in approaching God: that if we ask anything according to His will, He hears us. Whatever we ask we know that we have what we asked of Him." The ancients were taught that God had all of the power: we had none, and there were conditions for His generosity. Since I believe there are no conditions, it's more probable that sincere, prayerful people unknowingly put their attention on what was wrong in their life then wondered why God was not making things right in their life. Without a clear understanding, many of us inadvertently put our attention on the things we fear and don't want, or on the seeming obstacle that prevents us from getting what we want.

When I asked a medium why Bre had come into this world, she said to teach me unconditional love. At the time, I felt disappointed and angry, wondering what that was supposed to mean. I loved people! I felt that the medium had given me a canned and empty answer. After researching the true meaning of love, I realized that there were indeed conditions to my love. The universe always responds with unconditional love—no exceptions. It doesn't judge whether thoughts are positive or negative or if a person is good or evil; it simply responds to whatever thoughts we send into it. Being able to explain why and how this process works for *everyone*, may be one of the many reasons why it was important to Bre that I learned the true meaning of unconditional love.

As our knowledge in how this process works continues to grow, the thoughts and feelings we must have for manifesting abundance in our lives will become easier to understand and sustain. We are told to write our desires down, as on a dream board, and then visualize our lives with them, and feel the joy that comes with receiving them. We believed we followed all of the instructions, but just as the ancients discovered, it didn't work out the way we thought it should. Feeling disappointed that we didn't get what we wanted, we tossed it aside as someone's fantastical idea. It's hard to fully trust in something that can't be seen, so we often give up too soon or ignore an opportunity that could have been different from what we wanted, but much better. We lost faith and stopped the flow of positive energy coming from us, and thus coming back to us. We fell back into thinking about what we didn't have. Sadly, humankind has been doing the same thing for centuries. We lose faith or we lose trust—the result is the same.

Upon giving up, some people became depressed, feeling again like a victim, a failure, or a sinner who doesn't deserve it. How do you remain upbeat and positive when you believe there is nothing about your life that is positive? You first have to know, you are deserving in the same way that everyone else is. No one is better (or worse) than anyone else, because the universe doesn't make those distinctions. You have nothing to lose by the simple practice of intention. Don't take it so seriously, and don't get stuck in only one outcome. Be a kid again; and let your imagination run wild on your dream board, then go on with your life feeling grateful for the things you already have—with or without the things on your dream board.

Many people have written how-to books on manifesting the heart's desires, so it's interesting to read a few and see what resonates with you. Mike Dooley, author of *Leveraging the Universe: 7 Steps to Engaging Life's Magic,* was one of the presenters in the documentary and best-selling book, *The Secret*, by Rhonda Byrne. His approach is to stay focused on your vision and ignore or "bulldoze" through any negative thoughts swirling around in your head. He also tells us not to wait on the sofa expecting the universe to do its magic. "Do the work, and take proactive steps toward your goals, trusting you are worthy to receive them—or something better." The universe may bring what you think you want or what it knows you really want, whether you're consciously aware of what that is or not.

It's not always easy to bulldoze through feelings of doubt, anger, unworthiness, pessimism, envy, greed, prejudice, etc. These negative thoughts are deeply rooted in fear, and they don't feel good—i.e., we're not happy. We can analyze them and spend years in therapy trying to mend them, or we can choose to ignore them and "bulldoze" through by staying focused on only words of worthiness, hope, acceptance, optimism, excitement, appreciation, joy, enthusiasm, anticipation, and trust. These are the words of love; and we can feel that too—i.e., we're happy. When we replace words of fear with words of love, everything changes.

Sometimes we don't have a clear vision of what we want. In that case, we can let the part of us that sees all possibilities make that decision. Remember, we are a part of something greater. "Thy will be done" means we are letting go and letting something greater take over. It has access to all things and all people that will guide us in the best direction. Of course, we still have to be involved in the process. We must acknowledge the oddities and coincidences when they come our way—whether good or bad—analyze them and decide what or if any action should be taken. It's interesting that we don't need to have any particular desire because the energy of the universe aligns with us and already knows our heartfelt desires. We are unconditionally loved, and that love wants to give us whatever we put our attention on. Let it hear and feel vibrations of appreciation, so that it has a clear vision that you want and are ready for more things to appreciate.

Since negative thoughts are one of the biggest hurdles to overcome in this process, Dr. Dispenza's *Becoming Supernatural* teaches another way to eliminate them. He teaches how to dissolve the junk we carry around with us through targeted meditations. His book is a good place to acquire an understanding, but his workshops take you deeper into the process. We are "supernatural," just as Dr. Joe says. Our brain is amazing; and when we understand how it operates, we can consciously employ it to help heal our minds and bodies while also moving us toward our goals.

I felt guilty that I didn't practice a regimen of meditation, and I had all of the excuses: I didn't have time, I couldn't relax, I couldn't empty my mind, I didn't have the discipline, etc. It seemed when I woke up in the morning the first thing I wanted to do was have my coffee, and the last thing I wanted to do was take time to meditate. The more I learned of the benefits in meditation, the more I realized I needed to find a way to fit it into my life. I no longer feel guilty about this because there are many forms of meditation I can choose from. I don't have to sit stock-still for 20-30 minutes every morning, it can be done in minutes. Research five minute meditations, and you'll find one you like. I can do it while I'm folding clothes or taking a walk in nature; I can use formal breathing exercises while lying in bed, sitting in a chair, or sitting in the lotus position; I can listen to soft music while a voice leads me to the crystal palace, the beautiful ocean, a meadow, or whatever. Meditation is quieting the mind so that we may hear the peaceful voice of spirit within us—a voice we are all familiar with, even though we don't always acknowledge it as such.

Since the benefits of meditation have been proven, it's sad that a few religions still frown upon it. Prayer goes out and awaits an answer from God. Meditation is from within and answers come from within, and that's why some consider it a sin. Don't get hung up on that. Many religions have always embraced meditation because they understood it differently. Unity is a Christain church that embraces meditation, and there are others. It seems that prayer and meditation have always been the same thing but with different interpretations, making one more righteous than the other.

The people who love us that are living on the other side have advised us throughout history. Sometimes from within and sometimes through wise men, prophets, seers, and mediums. Their guidance hasn't stopped; we just don't acknowledge it as such. In *Ask and It Is Given*, by Jerry and Esther Hicks, Abraham, a spirit channeled by Esther, offers profound insights. It is interesting to note that upon asking this spirit his name, he said, "We are many, but you can call us Abraham." *Connection between each other on the other side is normal, separation is abnormal.* I liked this story from Abraham about trust. I condensed it and added a few of my own words (in parentheses) so you wouldn't lose the meaning. According to Abraham, when trust becomes doubt, it not only stops us from reaching our goal, it can cause us to go backward.

Can you get to San Diego from Arizona? You can choose to go by air, by car, or on foot. (By that Abraham means, you have to make an effort to get to San Diego: act on coincidences, do whatever research necessary, show up on time for appointments, etc.). *Some ways are quicker than the others. You face San Diego and begin to move in that direction. As you continue to trust* (a positive vibration), *you would reach San Diego quickly. However, in time, you lose your sense of direction because of doubt* (a negative vibration) *and turn around heading back to Arizona.* (You lost trust because things didn't happen quickly enough; you didn't get what you wanted; you didn't understand that obstacle was put there for a reason.) *When you realize what you have done* (and regain your trust), *you turn around again heading to San Diego. You could conceivably spend the rest of your life going back and forth between doubt and trust and never reach your goal.* (Good things move toward us with trust, but away from us when we doubt).

It can be stressful when we put too much effort into getting this process right—think this, feel that—and desperately wait for the things we want. Abraham teaches that to desperately want something will push it farther away. Desperation is a negative vibration. You know this because it doesn't feel good. Having a desire, knowing it is possible, but not vested in the outcome is positive, and that feels good. Not being vested in the outcome means that when we are asking for something in particular, we should remain open because it may not be what is best for us or what our heart actually desires. When we put our attention on the outcomes we *think* we desire and not on the desperation we feel because we lack them, it clears the pathway for good things to move into our lives—and the outcome will be one your heart desires. I want to express one more time that focusing on words of love gives this process all its power.

Bre didn't know any of this when she followed directions and filled out her dream board at the business seminar we attended. Perhaps her feeling of excitement while she created it stimulated the visual that it had already happened. Knowing that all things are possible, each one of us can stop feeling desperate and make dream-boarding a delightful game. We can then set it aside, feeling grateful that our life is already abundant, with or without the items and situations on the dream board.

It's difficult to remain happy and grateful all of the time, but visualization, sustained by trust works best when we are. The HeartMath Institute is researching ways that will help us regulate the energy field in and around us. For instance: When a person is shown a picture, it changes their energy field. Fun pictures make us feel happy and energized. Pictures of suffering and loss bring our energy down. When I'm down, I look for something that makes me smile, such as: I picture my sweet grandchildren, running to throw their arms around me; I remember the "welcome home" greeting from Liberty; I look outside to see the amazing beauty of this planet; or I notice a bird flying by. I see its colors and hear the sound it makes. I notice its powerful wings, how it glides on the air, and imagine myself flying along with it and seeing the beautiful Earth below. Doing that, I begin to feel grateful and happy again. But then, I ended that sweet vision with, "You pooped on my deck!" In one swell swoop, I had stopped that positive vibration and overlay it with a negative one. I could feel the difference. I therefore chose to be grateful for the poop on my deck by changing my perception of it. I saw it as organic fertilizer for my plants when I hosed it onto them. Sometimes, all we need to do is make a quick about-face and modify our perception of what we're experiencing as bad.

I find it interesting that happy people appear to have a lot of things to be happy about, while unhappy people don't. Which came first, the happy person or the happy things? When something unhappy happens to the happy person, they generally come through that experience differently than the unhappy person. They might see it as a learning experience, a challenge, or harbinger of better things to come. The unhappy person can get stuck there, seeing only bad things happening to them. A person skilled at changing their perception of things is generally a happy person. It's not easy for unhappy people to find a positive reason for the bad things happening to them. They must stop and ask: Is this setback bad, or should I feel grateful that it caused me to reflect on my life, become more compassionate, appreciate my family and friends more, create an organization or develop new laws that can help others, etc.? Is it a gloomy, rainy day, or is the air being cleansed making everything brighter? Is my loved one gone forever, or are they on a wondrous journey that I will one day join them on?

Eloquently expressing this dynamic, Benedictine Monk, Brother David Steindl-Rast urges us to see that "it is not happiness that makes us grateful, but gratefulness that makes us happy." The simple things like being able to see, speak, and hear I used to take for granted. So many others lack these glorious gifts! I am grateful that I can sit by the sea, delighting in its ripples and waves, its colors and moods. I can watch the wildlife, and hear the calls of the gulls. I can take in extraordinary sunsets and ever-changing cloud formations. I am beyond grateful when I hug my grandson and his adorable sisters, and we can tell and hear our stories. The more I thought of, the more I realized how grateful I was. My list grew longer, and yours will too. I'm not saying I don't fall into a pity-party place sometimes. But, I know when I'm doing it, and remind myself of my list. That took work at first, but now it's a habit because I remember the dark hole I fell into when I lost Bre, and the negative energy that surrounded me, which only made a bigger hole for others to fall in with me.

When nothing can be done to change the perception, it is important to find the tiniest thing that can make us feel a tiny bit better, even through our sadness. We can start with acceptance. It's always a better feeling than anger or sadness. Anger and sadness are a prison we can lock ourselves into, where all we feel is despair. Nothing good can get through those prison walls. I could so easily have chosen to sit alone in the darkness, but my desire to find Bre didn't let me stay there long. I would not have found any answers had I not listened to that urge. Please don't give up. Accept what has happened, and let your desires be known. I knew I would never have my daughter back, but I got the next best thing. I know where she is, and I am connected to her through the love we share. In fact, I know this is true of everyone I love.

Originally, the interest in the power of thought grew with our enthusiasm to manifest personal desires, but we learned it can be used for greater things. We can create an abundant world when we live with the intent of sending loving energy, instead of energy that is angry and dark. Sometimes, we feel powerless to change what is going on around us. *Your Erroneous Zones*, by Dr. Wayne Dyer, taught me that I'm never powerless because I can choose how I feel. However I choose to feel, whether happy or angry, is okay. I just need to know that the power is mine to change my feelings. Now when I become aware of the hopeless feelings I am projecting, I remind myself that I am not powerless. I look for people who are helping, or trying to make a difference, and find hope through them. I can embrace feelings of deliverance and hope; or despair and anger. In excess, hopelessness digs a dangerous pit of disheartenment where nothing can change. Now, I know there is always hope, because there is nothing too great for the universe to solve. All it needs is thoughts of compassion and appreciation coming from every direction. You might think that I'm only one person, but I know there are others who acknowledge this, and our numbers are growing.

I understand the reasons we hold angry demonstrations and shout out in frustration, but do they help or hurt us? When you do a search for get-paid-to-protest, you'll see people are paid to attend protests with the purpose of adding fuel to the fire and may not even care what the protest is about. I sometimes wonder what the goal is. Is it to hurt our country or create a better one? Is the purpose to direct attention away from certain issues and keep the focus on one of the manipulators' choosing? Someone is gaining from paid protestors, or there would be no money to pay them. The energy we send is the energy that comes back. When thousands of people come together in peaceful gatherings, focusing on what they want rather than what they don't want, that positive energy does not attract trouble-makers. It attracts the people and things that can bring about the changes we want to see. In my business, I called problems "dirt spots." Instead of complaining about it in the back room, creating a bigger dirt spot, talk to me. Together, we can come up with solutions to wipe that dirt spot away. You may be thinking that anger gets attention faster, but it is often met with more anger or a placating response. Cooperative thoughts will always give us the best chance to attract solutions.

We feed the hungry, find shelter for the homeless, and incarcerate hurtful people, but these problems don't seem to get better, and sometimes they worsen. We know that filling young minds with possibilities, compassion, and self-worth will make a difference, but we will not see the change until the people of that generation become adults. It is reassuring to see many encouraging messages filter into the minds of our children through concerned individuals, childrens' organizations, parents, teachers, media, and in movies today. My mind is filled with hope because I see a time when more people will generate loving energy from knowing how valuable they are and fewer people will be homeless, hungry, or locked away.

I remember telling my mother that my cousin had no money for Christmas. I thought it was wonderful that her church took up a collection, so she would be able to buy gifts for her children. Mom asked what gift she had bought for herself. When I said she bought nothing for herself she replied, "That taught her children she didn't have value. She should have bought a little thing for herself to put under the tree." I was surprised by that reply because Mom is one of the most unselfish women I know. Somewhere along the line, Mom learned the value of self-worth and how important it is to teach children that everyone has value.

Sometimes we become overzealous in our attempt to help others, not noticing when we go overboard to the point of depriving our own family. Are we teaching them that they have less value than the people we are helping? Whenever giving causes pain and resentment, it creates negative energy—the opposite of what we are trying to create. When money and time are in short supply, remember that *thoughts* are a powerful form of action that we can include our friends and families in. The beautiful energy they would create benefits those who are sending it as well as the people it is intended for. I can't say this enough: The more loving energy we send out, the more beautiful this world and our own lives will become. It's a win-win that works for everyone.

We are on the right track, but still experimenting in how all of this energy stuff works and what it means to be creators. Mistakes are inevitable, but that's how we learn. Through practice, we will learn how to trust and use the amazing gift we've been given and shout it out to all who will listen.

If you believe this is all nonsense, then imagine a world where there are mostly negative vibrations. This happens in pockets of the world where the balance has tipped, and little remains but fear and despair. Evil and cruelty run rampant. Now, imagine a world of mainly positive vibrations. It would be amazing! I know big changes can't happen until the people of the world accept and know how to use the creative power entrusted to them. As their number grows, the changes will become undeniable.

How long will it take, or what could happen to transform the world in this way? If you say, "That will never happen," then of course, it will never happen. Let's see a future where this has already happened. People from all walks of life, are uniting and putting their energy together to heal the planet. Just imagine the good that will come from knowing we are part of one loving energy-system that was never disconnected from us. "United we stand, divided we fall," Founding Father John Dickinson. One by one, "we must be the change we wish to see in the world." (Gandhi)

Death comes to all of us, yet losing someone is the one thing that will shake the most positive person. It creates a void in the lives of the people who loved them. I will always have that void, and I accept that. To me, it was a door closing; to Bre, it was a door opening. When that door opens to us, we will realize we never die. We are returning back to where we've come from—we are going home. The "no" we heard was a "yes" to them. I feel such love for my daughter and take comfort in knowing I will see her again. I wish she could have stayed longer so her son could have known her, felt the love she had for him, and received what she could have taught him. For me, and everyone who loved her, there was never going to be the perfect time to see her go. It helps me to know that when I go home, the reunion will be an off-the-chart celebration of "welcome home." It is from that perspective I believe her son has always known her, and at a deeper level knows her still.

For the person leaving, the timing doesn't always feel perfect either. A friend was recently diagnosed with terminal cancer and given six months to live. She told me, "God answered all of my prayers, but one. My affairs are in order and my family is taken care of, but I'm not ready to die."

Having those last tender moments with one's family and friends is a gift of heart opening conversations. The pain that usually accompanies disease shakes everyone's faith. In spite of medication to dull the pain, it will be easier for us to let her go and for her to welcome leaving us. But no matter how it comes, fear and despair surround death because it feels like the end! Alas, it is only the physical body that is coming to an end in order to return us back home—the home we have known for eternity.

I finally understand the assurances given that everyone's prayer, thought, or request is heard and answered. We are part of one energy that has never been biased or deaf; it simply responds to the positive and negative vibrations we send from the heart. The more loving attention we give to gratitude, hope, trust, and compassion, the stronger those signals become. Similarly, the less attention we give to lack, despair, desperation, and hopelessness, the weaker they become. My desires are known through my heartfelt feelings and most inner thoughts, and I know they are being heard when I choose to pray. That listener is the best problem solver there is. And when I pray, I visualize a loving energy coursing through my body, encompassing me and everyone I love.

I hope I have given you some insight into how extraordinary we are, and why we find it easy to cast this very powerful gift aside, and how important it is that we learn to use it. We unintentionally project negative energy because we don't know our power, and we don't trust that there is an even greater power than us that has our back. "Having the *faith* of a little child" or *trusting* creates positive energy, and it opens the way for change to occur.

I'm going to create a dream board. I'll write everything down and act on every coincidence that comes my way. It will include the people I love, as well as myself and the beautiful planet we live on. I will see world leaders and heads of industry working together to heal the planet. I see a world where war and hunger no longer exist, and all of nature is treated with compassion and respect. When I visualize my impossible dream as a reality, I experience complete bliss. At last the people of the world know how powerful they are! I know nothing is inconceivable for the universe to create when I project feelings of love and appreciation. I realize the immense love and power that is all around me and inside of me. I am living this dream.

CHAPTER 18

COINCIDENCE

WRITTEN WITH MY FRIEND, LORRIE LARSEN

"Coincidence is God's way of remaining anonymous."

— ALBERT EINSTEIN —

Words evolve to identify a person, place, or thing. Coincidence, fluke, serendipity, and synchronicity came about to describe the odd things that happen in our lives. Prayer is a biblical word describing how we ask for the things we want, and now we know our thoughts are a form of prayer. Each sends a message into the universe—the world of vibrating energy where strong and persistent thoughts can become reality. Coincidence and strange happenings are energy in action; or as some say, "Coincidence is God talking back to us."

Most of us have had an intuition, an insight, a hunch, a strong feeling, or an inexplicable desire to do something. For me, that was the strong urge to drive to my and Bre's cabin on Mt. Baker when without her, I never wanted to go there again. It could only be *our* place and never just mine alone. I tried so hard to ignore it, but that feeling just wouldn't go away. I finally gave in and drove up there, little knowing that my life would change forever as a result of that trip.

I know I am repeating this, but it was profound for me. It was inside the cabin that I found a book about mediumship that Bre had put two markers in. One was under the chapter titled children, and the other was under loss. I believed those chapters gave my daughter comfort when she had her miscarriage, and, now, she wanted that for me. I can't help thinking that odd things and coincidences will persist until they take you where you need to go no matter how hard you resist. I'm grateful I didn't resist longer because that book launched the journey into finding the answer to my question, "Where is my Bre? And, I was led to even more than I was asking for.

Before I lost Bre, I seemed to go in and out of focus when it came to strange happenings in my life—sometimes responding and sometimes not. After all, how much attention did I want to give to something so benign? I would often say, "Wow, that was weird!" and then go on about my business. I don't do that now. I analyze it and choose a course of action. Sometimes there is no action to take, and that's okay too, because it could just be a sign that my life is going in the right direction, or someone on the other side is saying hi. Remember, they speak to us in the form of signs.

Whether we acknowledge these odd happenings as having a purpose or not, it doesn't stop them from happening to us. For some, fear is attached to that awareness, but there shouldn't be because these phenomena are gifts. Fear dulls and slows everything down, especially our awareness. Becoming aware and acting on the odd things that happen will change your life. You will discover that you were not left alone to stumble blindly through this life without any assistance.

I will tell you of a recent odd happening: We were returning home from a long road trip to take my ninety-year-old mother back to North Dakota to see her brothers. A few hours from home we were following a truck going 45 mph on a long straightaway. As we began to speed up to pass, our RV's motor stopped. We'd had no problem for thousands of miles, and two hundred miles from home the engine dies. As we were coasting to the shoulder, a car rose up from an invisible dip in the road and sailed by. We would have hit it head-on. Some might attribute that to angelic intervention—a definite possibility. Call it what you will. Afterward, the engine started right up, and we drove home with no further problems. You could also believe there is a logical explanation for that to happen and look for an issue with the engine. That could be true, but the timing was perfect because it happened precisely then, and not any of the other times we passed a car.

My friend, Lorrie has tracked the odd things that have happened throughout her life and recorded them in journals. She began to see a pattern in the direction that the coincidences were taking in her life. I loved that she tracked coincidences, which was why I asked her to join me in writing this chapter. The meaning of "coincidence," as defined in Mirriam-Webster, is *The occurance of events that happen at the same time by accident but seem to have connection.* Are they accidental? What follows is Lorrie's story.

"I had known and felt Cyndi's energy for years but never had the chance to really get to know her. After talking with a mutual friend and reading her first book, *When You Think About It* (the book she wrote for her grandson), I realized how much we had in common. I called to meet for lunch and an instant friendship followed. I was surprised to see how many beliefs we shared.

"In 1998, my mom encouraged me to start journaling. Coming from a family of writers, it seemed the natural thing to do. I now had a place to put all of the thoughts that were swirling around in my head. Through this process I was able to piece together a picture. I could look back on my life and see the chance happenings and how they related to future events. Those happenings were sometimes good and sometimes bad. How I chose to react to them was a choice, and I didn't always make the right choice, or ignored them altogether. I began to see that the thoughts I wrote about, and the feelings they generated, created coincidences that were guiding my life. I've learned to pay attention and let them take me wherever they take me.

"I noticed consistent themes in my journals. They were telling me to slow down, live my life with fewer commitments, and to write. I love to help, but it can be overwhelming, especially when I involve myself in too many committees. I abandoned the idea of writing a book since there was a lot involved in that process and my arthritic hand would not allow for the long hours on a computer. When I shared some of my journals with Cyndi, she found I had many detailed accounts of happenings in my life that could meet the definition of "coincidence." She asked if it would be fun for me to write a chapter on coincidence for her book. I knew I was in—all in!

"Was it a coincidence that Cyndi came into my life? I experienced many thoughts that have materialized. Cyndi said the vibration of positive thoughts invites good stuff into our lives and surroundings, while negative thoughts repel them. I must have been sending good vibes because the desire to write was there, but not the ability. The universe saw another way. I am delighted to have this opportunity, in a small way, and am enjoying the mystery as to how it all happened. I will continue to journal, enjoying the journey, while I open my mental vessel to recall a few coincidences to share in this book. Again, was it a coincidence I met Cyndi and she is writing about something I have been thinking about and experiencing for so many years now?

"The chance happenings of people, books, speakers, music, and concepts coming to me in one form or another were often related to what I had been thinking about. I have a passion for thoughts and ideas that either align with mine or elevate and inspire my mind to think more deeply, sometimes causing "aha" moments. Noticing that the odd things that happened in my life affected the directon my life was going in, I learned not to judge them as either good or bad. I knew they were coincidences. If you look back through your own life, I believe you'll see them in yours as well.

"Some believe coincidences are the universe responding to you. That was the concept I took away from reading *The Celestine Prophecy*. This book was given to me after I returned from a trip to San Francisco, where I was hypnotically drawn to some enchanting music. I was certain I was of Peruvian descent as the music, delivered by a band named Kashwa, penetrated my entire soul and being. When I returned from the trip and told my mom about that incident, she was flabbergasted as she too had always felt she was Peruvian. She wondered if perhaps she had been switched in the hospital at birth.

"I learned my cousin felt the same way as well. When I asked her about having children; she said, 'The only way that could happen would be if someone left a Peruvian baby in a basket on my front porch.' It made me wonder if we shared a time together in Peru, somewhere in our past. I so wanted to get a llama and cross the Andes Mountains. Should I have acted on that? I chose to abandon that idea and simply listened to the music I purchased that mentally put me in a peaceful place I was mesmerized by. If traveling to Peru is a necessary part of my journey, I believe that message will continue to pop up.

"Two years after the visit to San Francisco, we returned to Ghirardelli Square where I had first heard the band, Kashwa, and inquired if they were still playing there. After a two-year absence (since I was last there), they were on the schedule for the next night. What a coincidence! I felt so lucky and purchased two more cassette tapes of their music. Who knows, one day I may find myself in the company of that llama in the beautiful Andes.

"*The Agony and the Ecstasy, a Biographical Novel of Michelangelo* by Irving Stone, was given to me while my husband and I were backpacking through Italy. I was immersed in the book and had just finished reading the last page when I was startled to hear loud bells tolling right outside our window. It was the bells from the Duomo, where Michelangelo's *David* had been sculpted. What perfect timing! I knew we had to ready ourselves, walk to the Duomo, and climb the stairs to the top while I imagined a time when Michelangelo walked these same steps.

"Rhonda Byrne's *The Secret* and her innovative gratitude journals were very timely for me, as they were introduced to me when the economy collapsed in 2008, financially devastating many people I knew. I filled two journals myself, in order to better see and appreciate the things in my life that were hard to recognize when life was a struggle. My journals reinforced my own beliefs, and I believed it could also help others. I purchased and gave well over fifty new journals to my friends to fill out. There is so much more to be grateful for than things. The practice of writing them down with thanks and intention became a habit for me, and I now wake up feeling appreciative every day. Good things happen, and continue to happen, since I learned to focus on appreciation. Byrne's gratitude journals came at just the right time, and were great gifts I was able to share.

"My husband and I love to travel, and we have, but I never had the thought of going to Africa until I read a passage in James Michener's *Creatures of the Kingdom*. It was about a man and his dog (a hyena) walking the Serengeti when a stampede of wildebeest and zebras suddenly came right at them. They stood in place as the animals in the rising cloud of dust parted around them, closing back up as they passed by. Call me crazy, but I felt I must witness or have that same experience myself one day. A few days later my husband and I were paired up with a father and his son-in-law for a round of golf. We learned that the father, Jackie, was from Nairobi and owned a safari photography company. We made arrangements through him, and it wasn't long before we too experienced the wildebeest and zebras stampeding around us. Of course, we were safely inside our vehicle as they ran past us, heading for the river.

"After meeting Cyndi, I shared with my mom what she was writing about. She'd asked if Cyndi had read any of Richard Feynman's books. At that time she had not, but was grateful for the suggestion. Mom had started rereading some of his works and thought they aligned with what Cyndi was writing about. Feynman (1918-1988) received a Nobel for his fundamental work in quantum electrodynamics and elementary particles. The big coincidence was that I didn't know Mom had an interest in this subject, but she was reading about it at the same time Cyndi and I were meeting. Many people are exploring these dynamics, and I was happy my mom was among them.

"I especially liked this quote from Richard Feynman: 'It doesn't seem to me that this fantastically marvelous universe, this tremendous range of time and space and different kinds of animals, and all the different planets, and all these atoms with all their motions, and so on, all this complicated thing can merely be a stage so that God can watch human beings struggle for good and evil—which is the view that religion has. The stage is too big for the drama.'

"Quantum physics is a subject I was aware of, but I didn't seem to have the ability to articulate or comprehend it. Then along comes Cyndi on this amazing journey to explain quantum mechanics in a way that I, and others, are able to easily understand. Her words make understanding the quantum world easier, and can help people better comprehend this famous quote from Pierre Teilhard de Chardin: 'We are not human beings having a spiritual experience. We are spirtual beings having a human experience.' Death is not the end, but the beginning of another journey back to the world of energy.

"One of the more significant coincidences began in 2003, when a severe hurricane damaged the hotel in Bermuda where we were to stay. Our trip was diverted to Palm Springs, CA. Bummer, as I really wanted to go to Bermuda and we had already been to Palm Springs. It turned out to be a really good coincidence. After a round of golf and sitting poolside with a bucket of Coronas, we both began questioning, 'How did we get here?' Life is great, and here we are experiencing some much-dreamed-of living. We decided to make someone responsible—in fact, five people. Each had an important influence in our lives. Who and what we become can, in part, be attributed to people we know and the happenings around them.

"I was unfamiliar with one of the names on my husband's list of influencers. He said the man used to live in Palm Springs some 30 years ago. My husband had brought his then wife and son to see him, but after that visit he'd lost touch with him. When we got back to our room I grabbed the phone book, looked up his name, and dialed the number, handing the receiver to my husband. I could hear the exchange.

'Hello, Jim?'

'Who is this?'

'This is Jan, your student from Estancia. You and I ran with the bulls in Pamplona.'

"Jan (pronounced Yawn) proceeded to tell him of the significant role he had played in his life. After a pause from his choked-up emotions, Jim stated that had he known he could make such a difference for someone, perhaps he would have stayed in teaching longer. Jan and Jim have continued to communicate throughout the years.

"In 2008, my mother-in-law passed and left us an inheritance. We had dreamed of having a vacation home one day, and she had encouraged us. We wanted to honor her wishes and thought she would like us to use it that way. It was enough to make a down payment, and the search began in Palm Springs, a place she knew we loved. We wanted to find a place that would call out to us, *This is it!* After a few visits, we still hadn't found it. On the last visit our friend, Jim, asked how the search was going and invited us to his condo for a drink before taking us out for dinner. The realtor had driven Jan and me by Jim's condo complex earlier, and we asked about it. He simply said it wasn't for us, and we left it alone. It was known to be a 'gay building,' and I guess he thought that would make a difference to us.

"Walking up the walkway to enter the secure building and then through the double doors into this well-lit, spacious condo I exclaimed, 'This is it!'

"I jokingly asked Jim, 'Is it for sale?'

"He pointed skyward and said, 'This one isn't, but the one above me is.'

"Entering the condo, we could see that it was everything we could ask for and more. Travertine table, six super-sized sliders, two bedrooms, and furniture that were not only comfortable for reading, but also reclined for that afternoon nap. It was a 70's style home, built in 1977, the same year I graduated. It just called out, *I am the one!* We made an offer and after some minor hurdles, it became ours.

"Between the time when we made the offer and took possession of the condo, an envelope from my sister-in-law arrived. It contained the letters from 1967 that my husband had written to his mom about the journey with his high school teacher, Jim. All the stories my husband had told of his adventures in Europe were documented, and now we had them. What perfect timing! The timing was a coincidence, but I also think Mom wanted to say, 'Hi, I approve.'

"Jim lovingly took the place of both my father and mother-in-law, and we became very good friends as we were both 'wee rascals.' Love, laughter, meals, and travels opened up to us in our amazing new world. We had no problem moving into what was predominately a 'gay building.' I loved all of my new 'girlfriends' especially the Queen, Freddie, who said I was like a sister. Boy, did we ever laugh and giggle on each and every visit in person or over the phone! Also, Freddie had been the one who approved our moving into the Diplomat and was able to convince the sellers to sell to us. Freddie had been very close friends with Dorothy, the gal who passed away, and she had left the condo turn-key.

"She left many of her favorite things (which were my favorite things, too) and placed them exactly where I would have. Many times I would go looking for something, perhaps a lemon juicer, and ask Dorothy where it might be. Miraculously, I would be guided right to where I would have put it. One time I came down from home, where I had just finished reading *The Immigrants*, by Howard Fast. When I arrived, I looked on the bookshelf in the second bedroom and asked Dorothy what she had for me to read. And there it was, *An Independent Woman*, the sequel to *The Immigrants*. Would 'weird' be a good word for that, or a coincidence? Coincidences don't have to be life-changing, but it is confirming to receive a response to my thoughts.

"Here I sit today, in my safe and secure space in Palm Springs, attempting the writing I had wanted to pursue for many years, along with golf, napping, sunshine, reading, and reclining. My life seems to be one good thing after another; even the bad stuff is good, as it helps to create a better measuring stick for the good. My dream is to continue aligning with all the good, positive, loving, evolving, optimistic people who value learning, growing, and behaving in a way that respects the greater whole of the planet. Is it a coincidence that these are so often the people I meet? Everyone on this planet, and perhaps other planets too, is connected via one big energy field and the creator. I believe that, and love and respect myself and all others, regardless of our differences.

"It was appreciation that inspired us to reconnect with Jim, and a coincidence that our perfect vacation getaway was located in the building he had lived in for years. All it takes is a thought and things begin to happen—like writing this chapter. Appreciation has proven to be the catalyst that creates an environment for good things to move toward us. I pay attention and look for coincidences that pertain to the thoughts that continually happen, creating a chain of events that leads me on this journey. My life is one coincidence after another, guiding me from one chapter to the next. Ending this chapter only means the beginning of another."

CHAPTER 19

Raising a
Child with the
Knowledge of Spirit

"The truth is, much of what we have traditionally
believed about babies is false. They are not
simple beings, but complex and ageless—small
creatures with unexpectedly large thoughts."

— THE MIND OF YOUR NEWBORN BABY, —
BY DAVID CHAMBERLAIN

As I walked down that dark alley to find my own child, I learned much about children and human behavior. I was interested in the memories children have, specifically the ones describing where they came from. It is odd that memories like that would occur if our only existence started at birth. We have eternally existed. How many of our children had imaginary friends? No one taught them to create imaginary friends. Bre had two such friends, Mary and Sam. I would listen to her conversations with them, assuming they were imagined because she was an only child who needed a friend. At least, that's what I'd been told. Although I wasn't one of those parents who inform their children that the friends aren't real, I certainly didn't believe they were. We would have little tea parties, and I would even talk to them. Never once did I believe I might actually be talking to someone. Had I been open to seemingly out-there possibilities, I might have asked different questions and received some interesting answers through my daughter, who may have been able to hear and see them.

When Bre left, her son was five months old, and for no apparent reason he would reach for the sky, babble, and laugh as though someone were tickling him. Anyone who saw him doing this believed it had to be Bre playing with her baby. It was so intense that the first few times he did it, we wondered if there was something wrong with him. Sadly, within the first year, it stopped. It's compelling to think of a little baby as a highly evolved spirit, inhabiting a human body. How would we treat our babies if we knew that were true? If they could talk, what would we learn? It must be shocking to transition from free-flowing energy into a tight, restricted body where every movement is an effort, physical pain is unavoidable, and communication is mostly verbal. No wonder so many "fussy babies" are not too happy about it at first. Physical life is an incredible gift, or we would never leave the wondrous world of energy and love.

Bre had a favorite picture she drew from the time she could hold a crayon. She drew it at her dad's house as well. He called my attention to it, wondering if I had noticed she repeatedly drew the same picture. Yes, I had, and she always called it "the attic in the sky." Even though it was gibberish to her father and me, we knew it meant something to her. Each time she drew it, she was in deep thought and excited to show us her picture. I told her how pretty it was, but I never picked up on the deeper meaning it may have held for her. If it weren't for her father, that picture would have been lost and forgotten. He staged an artist interview with her, and had it notarized and framed for me as a Christmas gift. *Thank you for the very thoughtful gift!* She was four years old at the time, and what follows was that interview:

> *On December 12th, 1980, I was commissioned by the artist, Breana McCandlis, to supervise all matting, framing, and publishing of her latest work to eventually be presented on the 25th of December 1980, to her mother Cynthia Mae McCandlis.*
>
> *This multicolor original piece in ink pen depicts the evolutionary progress of humanity. The circular purple and red areas are tomatoes. From the raw purple growing state to the fully ripened red, they symbolize the cultural growth of society. The square shapes with crossbars, the artist states, are cages representing the ever-present darker side to humanity. Significantly, the largest area of the picture is given to a recurring theme in Breana's work...the attic in the sky. When asked if "attic in the sky" was perhaps heaven, the artist's reply was yes. This brilliantly multicolored area represents the hope of the future.*
>
> *Breana has surely tapped the source of her being to create her view of humanity.*

Breana's Attic In the Sky

I'm sorry the picture has faded, making it difficult to see the purple and yellow colors. The red is all that is mostly visible.

Clearly, that interview was enhanced through her father's interpretation. A child's vocabulary is small, but their thoughts are big. "The attic in the sky" were Breana's words. I didn't know if someone had shown something to her, and I didn't find a book with that title when I did a computer search. So, I can't help thinking it was a memory of where she had come from—a place she missed and loved to draw. Gardening was a passion for her, so I'm looking forward to visiting her in her purple and red tomato garden in the sky.

I didn't hold the memory of her picture alive for her, and I'm sorry I didn't know to do that. It was just a picture that hung on our wall. Over time she forgot her "attic in the sky," and so did I. I look back on it now and wonder what would have happened had I kept that memory alive. However, she may have unconsciously held on to some of those memories. When she told me it was time to move out and buy a house of her own, she already knew what she would be looking for. She wanted a small house, and it had to have a spot for a garden.

I wanted her to live in the little apartment in my home forever, so I felt sad that she wanted to move out on her own. I finally accepted she was an adult. Together, we began looking for her perfect house. The tiny house we found had a garden ready for planting and even a hot tub in the backyard. Not that a hot tub was on her list, but it was a plus. Bre was never extravagant. She was independent, responsible, self-reliant, and very good with her money. Although I helped with closing costs, she had saved enough to make the down payment and had a roommate lined up to share expenses. She bought her little dream house, and the first thing she did was plant her garden.

At birth, a child's memories begin to fold back into the depths of their mind and, for the most part, are completely buried by age four. I could see the value in raising children with that forgotten knowledge. I remembered looking down at the little miracle the doctor laid in my arms and knew it was my responsibility to mold this tiny person into a productive adult. Had I known Bre was an eternal being and chose this life because she had an agenda, I would have seen a fully developed being inside her cute little body. Instead, I saw a vulnerable human child with a blank slate that needed molding. I focused on crossing t's, dotting i's, and fitting into what I believed society expected, as though that was the most important thing I could teach her. Had I known what I know now, I would have also taught her she was playing one of the roles in my life, and I was playing one of the roles in hers. In fact, it seems she had the starring role.

While searching for the memories children have, I came across *The Indigo Children*, by Lee Carroll and Jan Tober. These little ones are believed to be the children of the future and what we are evolving into. Most are wise beyond their years, are intuitive and highly sensitive, and may be gifted with evolved talents or paranormal abilities. In the past, many "gifts" were discouraged when viewed as out of the norm. Some gifts were even thought to have come from Satan. Wow, is all I can say to that! When we acknowledge all gifts as normal and not something that must be denied or changed, we will turn a page in our evolution.

When their gifts are viewed as abnormal, some children become depressed or angry; they may even put up walls and withdraw into themselves. In *The Children of Now*, Meg Blackburn Losey, Msc.D., Ph.D., theorizes certain types of autism develop because these special children feel they don't fit in. That brought up a memory of a documentary I had watched about a family with an autistic child—"Son-Rise," which is also the name of the book by the child's father, Barry Neil Kaufman. Barry and his wife Samahria had given up on medical intervention and instead mimicked everything the child did. Between themselves and their friends, all doing shifts with the little boy, Raun, their steady presence and acceptance of his ways eventually worked wonders. If he sat in a corner and stared at the wall, they did the same. If he ran around the room flapping his arms, they did the same. Whatever he did was seen as completely normal, with no effort to change who he was. In time he opened up, graduated from an Ivy League college, and today functions as any healthy adult would. Abnormalities are not abnormal, they are just misunderstood.

To Bre's way of thinking, the things people said and did showed true caring—or did not. In other words things were black or white. Like many of us, she was sensitive to the wrongs people did to one another (and animals) which can only lead to anger, sadness, or depression. The disappointment she sometimes felt in life also came from expecting others to think the same way she did—including me. I didn't know to explain that unlike our eternal home, this temporary home is a world of contrasts, and the motive is not always love. Our differences serve a purpose specific in this life, and that's something we need to understand. In my ignorance and attempt to mold the blank slate I thought babies were, I wonder if I ever made Bre feel like I wanted her to be different from what she was. Accepting children for whoever they are, is healing for them and for you.

It's sad to see the innocence a child is born with fade away. In Dr. Losey's book, a four-year-old boy said, "I remember what it was like to be home. It was a lot different from here. Everything was beautiful. I loved everyone and they loved me back. How come it doesn't feel like that here?" It seemed he remembered another world, and was saddened by the way this world made him feel. His innocence began to fade. I saw this happen with Owen when he was in kindergarten. His friend decided he wanted a different friend and didn't want to be friends with Owen anymore. Owen liked everyone, so he was sad and confused as to why everyone couldn't be friends. When innocence fades, we are fully integrated and are living in the world of fear and no longer have conscious memories of the world of love.

People assured me there is a purpose for everything. Bre left at great sacrifice to her family and friends, so what purpose could it serve? She didn't want to leave her husband, me, her many friends and family—but most of all, her son. From my perspective, he needed her in his life, and so did we. However, there is a "big picture" playing, and we don't know how far into the past or future that picture goes. We wouldn't have Owen if it weren't for Bre; and we wouldn't have his wonderful little sisters if Ben hadn't met Rosey because of Bre. Bre came for many reasons, both for the present and for the future; and when she accomplished what she'd come here to do, it was time to return home. Every child needs to know how important they are in the small picture, but they must understand there is also a "big picture" playing that can't be seen.

I believe the big picture is for physical beings to evolve into compassionate creators, and that we all play a role in getting us to that future. We are empowered, but that idea has taken thousands of years to cultivate and is still not widely accepted. *When every child is reminded of the unconditional love out of which they were created, and how to use the power they were given, everything will change.*

Although we can't always see it, we are evolving. Even the welcoming committee at birth is more compassionate today. It used to be that a swat on the butt forced us to take our first breath and utter our first cry. Now, we are using body massage to coax out that first breath. They both serve the same purpose, but we choose the compassionate method. I wonder what we thought when our first experience of life was a painful (or atleast jarring) smack on the butt. It is an ongoing act of self-preservation that we forget the world we come from as we assimilate into a world where death ever looms, and people can hurt us. Children should be reminded that they are safe because they are eternal energy beings, but until compassion is acquired by all people here, there will be some who cause pain and suffering.

Losing Bre put into perspective all of the things I thought were important. As I said earlier, one thing was stuff. Most of us like stuff, and accumulating more stuff. It gives us pleasure to see and use and display our stuff: the home, the car, the jewelry, the shoes (I love shoes)—lots of stuff. Bre took pride in rescuing old things off a junk pile and making them come to life. I loved that about her. She believed people should recycle more than paper and cans. Walking into my daughter's home that day, it broke my heart to see all the stuff she loved still sitting where she had left it. Stuff is fine to have; even to take pleasure in, but all of it stays here. It's easy to get caught up in the stuff physical life offers and forget we have far more important reasons for being here. We need to put stuff into perspective for our children, as well as ourselves.

I always thought Bre was wise beyond her years, so I believe she came to teach the people around her. She was an unselfish, caring person, who always had your back. Ask any of her friends. She believed in justice and consequence. If a friend borrowed money, she made sure they paid it back, even if they owed it to someone else. It was a mystery to her that so many people didn't understand the consequence of borrowing money: you had to pay it back. She was also not a person who would sit back and let things fester. If it was wrong, it needed to be made right. If there was a misunderstanding, Bre would be on the phone or at your house until you talked it through.

She once told me, "That's why we have the ability to talk, and we need to use it."

The things she said were simple and to the point. Sometimes she was too blunt, but life didn't make sense to her any other way. I had never thought about the gift of communication in that way before. Even knowing this, it's still hard to use it as easily as she did.

Old boyfriends remained friends. She said, "We were friends once, and that shouldn't change just because it didn't work out."

I remember being surprised by that reply, which is why it is so vivid in my mind. She was hurt, yet seemed to have an innate knowing of how senseless that behavior was.

My nephew's wife told me that of all Aaron's family, she was most nervous about meeting Bre. She had been briefed on how protective Bre was, and knew she would be asked a lot of questions. Even Les said he was uncomfortable when he first met her. He felt she stared at him as though she were looking through him. I had to laugh because it was true. She wasn't afraid to ask the questions, and to my surprise, people would answer. Instead of reminding Bre of the forgotten knowledge she was born with, I think she came to remind *me* of what I had forgotten.

I always felt Bre was a gift, but I hadn't thought of her as a predetermined gift. She brought my life frustration and gratitude, joy and sorrow; but most of all, she was always the one in my corner and the one who gave my life meaning. I so miss not having Bre physically with me. I could have told her how special she was and how lucky I was she chose me as her caretaker in this life. Assuming she knew was not the same as hearing it. Be aware that it's never too late to share these thoughts with your children and loved ones. It adds value and joy to their life. Then watch their spirit glow from within. I wish I could have seen that glow in my daughter, but I didn't know anything about these matters before taking this journey. After she left, I did finally tell her how lucky I was that she chose me, but it was too late to see the glow. However, I knew she heard it because I felt my own spirit glow from within. If your loved ones are still with you, do share your gratitude while you can still see their glow.

My mother was born in 1925 and is at the end of her life. Although she has dementia, not a day goes by that she doesn't tell my brother, sister, and me how much she loves us and how proud she is of us. In turn, we have the same opportunity to say it back to her. The realization of death brings out the necessity to say what we haven't said aloud, and highlights the things that are important in life. Mom always made us feel loved, but not in a verbal way. I treasure these closing days with my mom, as I didn't have this opportunity with Bre.

There is a world of difference between guiding and controlling. Many of us like to believe that under the wise, protective umbrella of our control, everyone is safe and all is well—but far from it! Such lives are frustrating to both controller and controlee, as one life is narrowed to the scope of the controller, while the other is diminished by anger and fear. Give those in your charge the guidance they need to be in control of their own destiny. Listen to their ideas and encourage free thought and expression by letting them say what they have to say without fear of ridicule or reprimand.

Don't angrily cut them off or argue back and forth. No one learns anything from that. I loved to hear how Bre thought when she was defending her actions. I was amazed at her inner knowledge, and sometimes she won her case. If she didn't win, I would ask if she thought punishment was warranted for what she had done. Sometimes it was and sometimes it wasn't, but I always let her pick the punishment. Much to my surprise, the punishment Bre picked out for herself was often greater than mine would have been. I frequently buffered it or waived it altogether. Just knowing she understood was punishment enough, as the lesson had already been learned. All we learn from punishment is fear and anger. What's more, to avoid future punishments, many hone their lying skills while also becoming sneaky. But when they pick their own punishment, it is self-inflicted, and they learn more from that than fear could ever teach them. After Bre left, I saw only the things I'd done wrong as a parent, but this was something I felt I did right.

John Lennon said, "Life is what happens to you while you're busy making other plans."

Let's teach our children to be unafraid of going with the flow of life. Life has a way of taking them where they need to go. While it is good for all of us to plan our life, it is also good to be flexible and prepared when plans change. There is a lesson in all situations, wherein lies the opportunity to learn. The ebb and flow of life sometimes seems bad and sometimes good. It keeps changing, beckoning us to change with it. I think that's called being resilient. When we allow and trust in the flow, knowing there is a big picture at play, we and our children will be more accepting of the bad when it occurs. Intellectually accepting this, I still find it extremely hard to apply when applying it to losing Bre. My view of life has changed dramatically, and new doors have opened. But I have a hard time accepting Bre completed her earthly mission, because I can't see the Big Picture. However, I have come to accept my own limited vision and know she will reveal the picture to me when I join her. Sometimes acceptance is the only action a person can take, but it's always better than getting lost in darkness.

In his *Wisdom of the Peaceful Warrior*, Dan Millman uses this fable to explain acceptance and resilience:

Good Luck, Bad Luck

An old man and his son worked a small farm,
with only one horse to pull the plow.
One day, the horse ran away.
"How terrible," sympathized the neighbors. "What bad luck."
"Who knows whether it's bad luck or
good luck," the farmer replied.
A week later, the horse returned from the mountains,
leading five wild mares into the barn.
"What wonderful luck!" said the neighbors.

"Good luck? Bad luck? Who knows?" answered the old man.
The next day, the son, trying to tame one
of the horses, fell and broke his leg.
"How terrible. What bad luck!"
"Bad luck? Good luck?"
The army came to all the farms to take the
young men to war, but the farmer's son was
of no use to them, so he was spared.
Good? Bad?

The farmer didn't see things as good or bad, so he didn't resist. He just accepted the flow knowing a purpose would unfold. It is learning to accept, and not resist, that allows the purpose to unfold more quickly. Acceptance is not passivity or complacency. Complacency is unaware of potential—there is no hope in that. Acceptance knows there is a picture playing and is conscious that it is playing out as it should. Resistance can stop the flow toward the potential outcome altogether. As Carl Jung said, "What you resist not only persists, but will grow in size." Bre was not good at accepting "what is," and going with the flow was to her like doing nothing, so she resisted. Resistance causes worry, anger, hopelessness, and frustration which I sometimes saw in Bre. When you can't change something, go with the flow and allow the potential to unfold in its own way. As I write this chapter, I keep wanting to say, "I wish I had known this."

I don't mean that staying in a dangerous or damaging situation is accepting the flow. Even though accepting abuse can make it more tolerable, that borders on passivity—and ignores one's own self-worth. How many times will the flow repeatedly push someone down, before they stop resisting what it is trying to teach them? They need to stand up, and remember they have value and are essential to the Whole. Eventually, the flow will lead them to that conclusion, but why let it exhaust every avenue before they remember their own self-worth? If a child knows this, the relationships they form throughout life will be more healthy.

A child's imagination is a beautiful and fascinating thing. I've come to believe that the world we come from is a place or state where imagination creates whatever we want. We don't teach children to imagine, so where do they learn it? Don't let them forget their wonderful innate imaginations—explore it with them. It would have been fun and informative to have paid more attention to Bre's creative imagination. I did more of this with Owen and had a lot of fun. We created wild stories, drawing strange creatures and imagining where and what the fish might be up to as we looked out to the sea. Imagination is exhilarating, exciting, and fun. I'm sure it was meant to be used beyond entertainment. If a child knew from birth that he could create whatever he imagined, think how powerful his dream board would be.

Waldorf is a wonderfully liberating school for children. Founder Rudolf Steiner introduced its principles in 1922 at a conference in Oxford. He stressed the role of imagination in learning across all disciplines. Waldorf goes beyond filling children's minds with facts and figures, instead stressing the "ethereal and empathetic" aspects of life. We are heart as well as brain. Bre would have loved this school, as many of the classes are held outside in nature, with frequent festivals and holidays celebrated outdoors as well. Waldorf students and teachers are always up for a celebration! Private schools are expensive, so it is encouraging to see some of these principles being incorporated into our public schools today. Josephine was very proud to have received a Viking hero award for being kind, Owen received one for being helpful to others, and Samantha received one for perseverance. These things were never acknowledged when I was in grade school, yet, in many ways, they are more valuable than the ABC's.

President Roosevelt said, "A nation that destroys its soils destroys itself. Forests are the lungs of the land, purifying the air and giving fresh strength to our people."

Before Les and I could build the house, I had to remove an evergreen tree that stood in the corner. Bre wanted me to build around this ancient, majestic tree. Bre was introduced to the beauty of our environment, and the cruel treatment of the animals we eat through her third-grade schoolteacher. Because of her teacher's influence, she became a vegetarian and an advocate for animal rights and the environment. It would have been impossible to build around that beautiful tree. When the house was finished, I planted five other trees at different locations in the yard just for my Bre and to honor the big evergreen tree.

This planet, and our very existence, are gifts we've been given. We are responsible for the health of our beautiful Earth, and every-thing on it. A child's spirit will sigh with relief when we demonstrate reverence for its beauty. Litter along the roadside, a neglected animal living in filth, a baby's cries that go unanswered—all sadden the spirit. A child quickly buries the truths they were born with and begins to model the ways they are shown.

Babies are hard to resist. Is it just their cuteness, or are we starving for the love oozing from their little bodies? They come into this world with no prejudice, completely trusting, nonjudgmental, and full of love and wonder. As I've said, we came from love, and we need love. When love is not experienced and life is cruel, we bury that need away, becoming afraid to give or receive it. Without our realizing it, fear becomes dominant and can take over our life. Children need to know that no matter what happens, they are eternally and unconditionally loved by a power far greater than any other power—and we need to know that as well.

We should make an effort to teach with love instead of fear. It's no mystery that we often use fear to get what we want, and we use it with our children. Here's an example: "John get out of the street! You'll get hit by a car and hurt very badly, or killed!" Contrast that dire admonition with this much more loving warning: "John, get out of the street! Streets are for cars. If a car hit you, it would be very sad for the driver, for you, and for me." Compassion for other people's feelings comes from knowing love instead of fear. Here's another: "Go to sleep or I'll spank you—or the monster will get you." Why not offer them a choice? "Go to sleep, and we can play with your toys tomorrow, bake cookies, or go visit a friend." Of course you have to follow through and bake the cookies, or not bake the cookies, depending on the choice they make. In my opinion, the following is the worst kind of threat: "Be a good child and do what you're told or God might not let you into heaven." Teaching them to fear God is never good. Losing their electronics for a day is a better choice. They are unconditionally loved, and hell is a contradiction to that love. Teach from love, not fear; and the world will automatically have more love in it.

Bre and I loved to watch Oprah. Her show influenced both of our lives, starting in Bre's childhood. One show invited parents of large families to share ideas on why their children grew up to be successful adults.

One man said, "I never told my children 'no'; I only told them of the possible consequence of each choice they made."

I could hear Bre thinking, "Wow, I've scored!" That struck me as a good way to teach Bre how to take responsibility for her choices. Soon after watching the show, this is what happened:

Bre made a scene in a store because I said no to something she wanted. I remained calm but didn't give in and allowed her to carry on. In the car I explained the consequence of that choice.

"You didn't embarrass me, but you should be embarrassed for yourself. I know you are a nice little girl, but the people in the store saw someone different."

She chose to never do it again. I didn't use the fear of punishment, I explained the consequence of her choice. That was enough punishment. When we teach children personal responsibility, compassion, and consideration, punishment becomes unnecessary.

It was on the same show that I picked up the idea of giving Bre an old checkbook to track her money with. Bre was exceptional at handling money, and I could trace it back to that program. *Money is something to respect and use wisely, not love and spend unconsciously.* Bre learned the difference between what she needed and what she wanted. I told her it was okay to buy things she wanted, but important to know the difference when choosing how to spend her money.

Josephine loves to go out for dinner because there is so much on the menu to choose from. She wants to order all of them, so she can taste each one. I can relate to that. She is such a love, and I want to buy her whatever she wants. The choice is mine. I can teach her that money has no value and wasting food is acceptable, or I can teach her to respect money and that waste is an extravagance.

Our children have concerns, and they worry. When they can't talk to us, it's important to remind them of the loving energy that is all around them and can hear their concerns. Oftentimes they will wake up in the morning feeling better or with a solution to the problem. I was taught God would answer my prayers if they were caring and unselfish. If that were true, there would be no divorce, death, disease, war, or natural disasters, so He got the blame when those unselfish prayers went unanswered. In fact, that is what provoked me to have doubt in God and the power of prayer long ago. As hard as it is to accept, many things that happen are part of the journey we chose, and cannot be changed. In spite of my doubts, I taught Bre to pray to the God I learned of in Sunday school because I didn't know anything different. I sometimes wonder how our lives would have changed, if I'd known then what I know now.

As parents, we are supposed to teach and model right from wrong, giving love and wisdom as we know it. That knowledge was passed down to us by religions, parents, peers, teachers, and experiences, all of which may be biased or misperceived. I was taught to listen to my conscience when making decisions, and I taught Bre the same. But conscience is often clouded with learned ideas and conventional wisdom. Teaching her about the guidance system she was born with – deep heartfelt feelings – would have been a more accurate measuring stick. The heart doesn't have any chatter going on, so it can only *feel* good or bad.

Maybe their conscience is telling them they are right to judge another's lifestyle, belief system, or how that person looks because of something they were taught. Before they do that, they should always ask: Does this judgment make my heart feel good, or is the seemingly good feeling coming from feeling more righteous and powerful? The consequence of feeling more righteous and powerful over others, is separation, and that is never good. All of creation is one big connection, and each person is on their own personal journey. No one can judge that or decide what it should be. Deepak Chopra said, "When you finally see no one in the world is an enemy, only a fellow traveler, all judgments fall aside."

Aristotle said, "Give me the child until he is seven, and I will show you the man." It seems he knew then what we have now scientifically proven to be true. It's a scary thought that throughout history unscrupulous people have used this knowledge for their own selfish gains. Be mindful of the people and organizations you leave your children with. A child's mind does not have enough information to judge whether what is presented to them is true or not, so it stores the assertions of adults as accepted facts. This is how children become adults who are filled with false beliefs. It's hard to unlearn the things we were taught as children, so be aware of what young minds are being filled with.

Ask your child, "Do you like who you are?" Don't be surprised if they look stunned by that question. I tried this with my grandson, and you should have seen the look I got. It makes me laugh to this day. Be prepared to tell them why you like who they are: he is a good listener and is trustworthy; he is kind and a very good brother; he is respectful of other people's feelings and helps his father; he is a good student and loves to learn; he is creative and shares what he has with others; and I love the compassion he has for people and animals. Can you understand how important this question would have been for me to ask Bre? It would have given me the opportunity to tell her "out loud" the qualities I saw in her—and her response to that question would have shown me how I was doing as her parent.

It's impossible to be an effective parent or person, if we don't appreciate who we are. Ask yourself the same question, "Do I like who I am?" It feels strange, doesn't it? That was a difficult question for me because I saw so many ways I'd failed my daughter. But I learned a lot from asking that question. The feelings I generated from disapproving of myself were destructive, descending quickly into sorrow and regret. Slowly, I began to remember the good times and the things I did right with Bre. I am more productive today because I was able to move past the bad and see the good. Forgive yourself for the mistakes you made, because learning from those mistakes may be the reason you came here in the first place. I don't believe we would ever leave our heavenly home if we didn't know we had a really good reason to be here.

Did you know that negative vibrations accompany every lie? If you have ever told a lie you may have experienced the feeling of guilt, and telling a lie that hurts others is the most damaging of lies. In excess, negative vibrations disrupt the flow of energy in the body causing mental anguish, pain, and disease. Children are never liars, and I shudder whenever I hear someone call their child a liar. They learn to lie because of fear, and that carries through into adulthood. Describing to them the havoc that negative vibrations can wreak inside their bodies would serve as a good lie-deterrent. Lies diminish the trust we need to have in one another, and all good relationships start with trust.

Teach those in your care to live in the moment. We have all heard and read about this, but if it isn't taught to us and modeled by adults in our childhood, it's hard to learn when we're older. I don't think I was paying attention to my wonderful mother when she told me to be happy for today. What do parents know, anyway? When we are little, our parents are very smart and everything they say is true, but as we hit our teens they've lost that platform. I didn't live in the present. I worried too much about the future or the past and missed the beautiful flowers that were falling down all around me. It didn't occur to me that the future was going to unfold with or without my worry. You can plan for it, but you can't worry about it—you'll miss the day.

Living in the moment is simply paying attention, and we can teach our children how to do that. It's funny, but here is the first example that comes to my mind: When they brush their teeth, ask them to pay attention to how happy each tooth feels as they brush it. Owen, Jo, and Samantha know I have a fetish about brushing teeth. Bre heard this every day, so it was no surprise that as an adult she shared my same fetish. The mouth and teeth are breeding grounds for disease, so teach them why it is important to brush and floss their teeth. More examples of living in the moment: When you see a butterfly, point out its colorful wings, how it sucks nectar from the beautiful flowers and carries pollen from flower to flower. Join them in looking up at the imagination-sparking forms in the clouds. When Owen was small, we loved to look up at the clouds to see what we could find in them. Ask: What do you see, hear, smell, feel, taste? Whatever it is, appreciate the moment and pay attention to the details. Don't think about the last moment or the next moment, as I often did. Listen to your children as though it's the most important moment—and utterance—of all time and teach them to do the same. *Slow down*, and appreciate what is right in front of you. I often let my mind wander and missed beautiful moments with my daughter. I am now very aware of the beauty in moments, and seize as many as I can. I'm so sorry I missed any moments with my amazing daughter.

As an adult, I was made to feel insecure and not smart. I laugh at that now, but it wasn't funny then. After my divorce, I went into counseling and described my insecurities. The counselor informed me that there were different types of intelligence.

He said, "Tell me, how do you think I'm feeling right now?"

I told him, "You are stressed and in a hurry."

I went on to tell him more of what I thought he was feeling. I was actually right, and he happily said, "Anyone can learn to count, but not many can do what you just did. Never say you're not smart!"

"Everybody is a genius. But if you judge a fish by its ability to climb a tree, it will live its whole life believing that it is stupid." Einstein.

Children need to know that anyone who devalues their self-worth is someone they don't need in their life. They were born because they have value. All they have to do is remember that truth. Post the advice given in the movie, *The Help* on their bedroom wall: "You is smart, you is kind, and you is important." That is so simple and powerful, and when your child knows it is the truth they will be kind and smart, and no one will be able to make them feel unimportant.

Every child wants to make their parents feel proud of them. When a task doesn't meet with your expectations, it probably doesn't meet with theirs, either. They need to know that you are proud of the time, hard work, and care they put into completing the task. They should feel proud of themselves for that as well. Some things they will never be good at, and that's okay. It is doing their best while making the effort, and completing the task that will add value to their already invaluable life. Children can lose pride in themselves and feel less valuable or worthy when they believe they let you down. You will not create a big-headed, arrogant egotist by instilling pride in them. That was something I had been taught to be aware of. Instead, you will inspire them to have confidence in tackling anything that life throws at them. A child becomes arrogant only when they don't see value in other people.

You have no idea how many times I wanted to give up on this book. I was not a professional writer! I was a mom who suffered her greatest loss and wanted to pass the answers I had found on to others. There are many obstacles in publishing a book, including my lack of knowledge in technology, but I know the importance of completing a task. I sometimes felt like Bre was the parent, so I say with a smile, "I hope she recognizes the effort I made and is proud of me for completing this task."

CHAPTER 20

DEFINING SPIRITUALITY

*"I believe in God, but not as one thing,
not as an old man in the sky. I believe that
what people call God is something in all of us."*

— JOHN LENNON —

*"Science is not only compatible with spirituality;
it is a profound source of spirituality."*

— CARL SAGAN —

In Sylvia Browne's book, *The Other Side and Back*, she writes: "It's about the magic and miracles and support from the other side that are always around you, just waiting for you to learn how to notice them. It's about never again feeling alone or help-less or without value." Her book started my journey into the world of energy and finding Bre.

Losing Bre knocked me down, and the journey to find her raised me up into what some might label a spiritualist. I'm not sure I like labels, as labels create the illusion of separation, when I can only see connection. Still, I will explain spiritualism as I see it, though others might define it differently depending on their journey. However, in all cases love is what inspires this movement and pushes it forward. Spiritualists do not subsribe to any one religious philosophy or one way of thinking, so there is never an argument when ideas differ. They are open to all information and continually receive new information from any source that offers it: science, nature, mediums, NDEs, ancient histories, and etc. The search for deeper meaning and finding answers will always be the goal.

I once believed spiritualism was a New Age idea, full of mysticism and flighty people. Now, I know to never judge things through others' viewpoints but to do my own research. I wanted to learn more, but still feeling a little skeptical I asked Les to accompany me to my first Hay House Spiritual Conference, 2006. Some of the authors of the books I was reading were speaking there, and it was sponsored by Oprah. That felt credible to me, and I was happy to see people from all walks of life in attendance who were fellow researchers, seeking just like me.

Les wasn't interested in my research, but he decided to make a vacation out of it. After all, it was held in sunny Arizona. He was fascinated by some of the courses that were offered, and I encouraged him to attend some of them with me. He was impressed to hear scientists speaking on spiritual matters. He didn't expect that. Not that he was all in, but it legitimized the research I had been doing and opened his mind to something new. Knowing that this research was important to me, he gave me all of the space I needed. I am grateful for his continued support, especially considering the fact that passing the information on through my writing consumes most of my time.

I do not attend a weekly religious service because I don't feel the need. I know the spirit inside of me is the real me and not the physical body that was created for me to inhabit. I temporarily left the world of energy and love, to enter the world of matter for the experiences that only physical life can offer. I will then return home with the knowledge I gained from living in a world where fear can and does exist. I believe in the oneness of all things and recognize love as the universal language that I try to live my life by.

Many religions demonstrate an urgency to spread their truth and convert the masses because they believe that God commands this of them, and they will outwardly defend their beliefs to the point of argument, punishment, or even death to demonstrate their obedience and love for Him. That's not love, that's fear. Regardless of our beliefs or the path we choose to follow, if the way is open to love and growth, that makes them good.

I was told God sent me to my parents. I had a good home, but what about the children suffering in bad homes? Should God get the blame for that? No! The creator doesn't send us; we choose to come, and the choice of environment is important for whatever it is we want to learn, teach, or just experience—even when it is cruel. That is as hard for me to say as it is for you to read. An experience in a negative environment is often about learning or teaching. Experiences allow us to internalize and express the true meaning of empathy and love. We couldn't understand pain unless we felt pain. We wouldn't know the beauty and joy of love without having known the lack of love. Grasping the definition of sadness is very different from experiencing sadness. Whatever purpose we have for coming here, we will acheive it. That can happen in a minute or take a lifetime. We predominantly don't know our purpose, so we can get trapped in the good and bad experiences we see and have. Now, I look for a reason or how I can be of service, and avoid the traps.

I had been taught I was born sinful and unworthy of God's love, but to show His love, He sent His son, Jesus, to be sacrificed for me. In freely accepting Jesus as my Lord and Savior, my sins will be forgiven, a spot in heaven will be reserved for me, and the Holy Spirit will be in my heart to help guide me throughout life. I had a hard time accepting that a loving God required sacrifices of any kind, especially that of His own son. *It just didn't feel good.* And when I looked at a baby, I didn't see a sinner, I saw pure love. Trust your heartfelt feelings, they never lie. The ritual of receiving the Holy Spirit into one's heart for guidance is unnecessary because it has always been with you. Remember our built-in guidance system? I call it feelings but some might call it the Holy Spirit. It was like an awakening when I realized the feelings I was born with were guiding me through life, and all I had to do was learn how to hear it.

We spend too much time wondering what the purpose of life is and specifically, what is *my* purpose? We've been conditioned to believe our purpose is about us; but we come from a realm where all we know is love and connection, so our agenda would always include others in it. Maybe, we planned to be here at just the right time to say or do something that affects one person or thousands. The number doesn't matter because each person is of great and equal value. Sadly, mankind often learns through suffering, and some have lovingly chosen to suffer for others in an effort to change behaviors and teach compassion. Jesus spoke of a loving God, forgiveness, love, and compassion, and He certainly suffered to give us that message. When you look back in time, you'll see that many courageous people have done this. That cycle will not end until we finally hear the message they came to give us—love and compassion.

I believe it's true that our world gets back what we give our attention to. As humans, we inadvertently focus on what we don't want which creates negative vibrations. Let's put our attention on the beautiful and inspiring, and get more of that back. Even the Bible has something to say about this. Philippians 4:8 puts it especially well: "Finally, brothers, whatever is true, whatever is noble, whatever is right, whatever is pure, whatever is lovely, whatever is admirable—if anything is excellent or praiseworthy, think on these things."

Bre once told me that one's home should be filled with things that make them feel happy—their little piece of heaven. Her home often smelled of essential oils like eucalyptus and lavender. She had a rainbow-colored hammock she brought home from Amsterdam. She wanted to hang it in her tiny house. I couldn't imagine where she could put that big hammock. She first hung it over her bed, and it looked happy there. She finally found the perfect place in her tiny dining room. It was the first thing you saw when you walked into her home. I must say, it made me smile every time I went over. She was very aware of how things made her feel, so she displayed happy things in her home. I learned a home doesn't have to be beautiful or elaborate, but it should have things in it that make you want to smile.

The meaning of forgiveness has also changed for me. Forgiveness is not about God forgiving me, because there was never a god judging me in the first place. The mistakes I make hurt me and the people around me—not God. It's not unusual to feel guilt for the wrongs we've done, and that results in mental anguish and physical pain. It is guilt that blocks us from feeling God's unconditional love. Again, there are many truths in the Bible and this one is clear—forgiveness is critically important. Whether you feel you need absolution through your priest or direct forgiveness from God or a person you have wronged, it doesn't matter; but, it is essential to dissolve guilt through forgiveness of self and others.

When I lost Bre, my focus was on how I'd failed her as a mother with all of the things I could have said and done differently. Never mind the good things; I saw only where I'd failed her. I wished I could have been one of those wise parents you see in the movies—always with the right thing to say and do. I wasn't; I was just me, and that wasn't good enough. I would cry in the night, asking her to forgive me. *I should have been more present to you throughout your life.* But as the deep and very dark sadness subsided, I began to see more of the good, and the guilt gradually faded. I finally forgave myself, and know that Bre too forgave me long ago. That we have loved each other throughout eternity is the joyous truth that lets in all the light.

Can we forgive the person who has harmed us physically or emotionally—or hurt someone we loved? The book, and later movie, *The Shack* by William P. Young, demonstrates how hard this is to do. When we hold on to anger and resentment, it has a negative effect on us and the people around us—not on the abuser. The abuser continues taking from us, and he has taken enough from us already. Forgiveness does not mean accepting their behavior, it means not giving them any more of our energy. We have no way of knowing what caused them to be the way they are, so ask for help in finding forgiveness and letting go of the harmful energy we carry around inside of us. *We win.* There are so many painful things that happen to us on the journey of life, and forgiveness is one of the most important lessons we can learn. Bitterness and anger bring sadness and depression. I know because I've felt this. *I lost*—temporarily. Please don't lose.

Some, but not all, spiritualists believe we continually evolve throughout many lifetimes, ever expanding through the wisdom we gain. Spontaneous recall and past-life regression suggest that we have indeed lived other lives. I know there are many things (perhaps *everything*) we might want or need to experience, so living many lives seems logical to me. According to an extensive worldwide survey, half of the world's population believes in reincarnation. The rest of the population assumes that one lifetime offers enough opportunity to learn and grow, or they don't believe any of this at all. To me, this is not a topic worth disputing because whether we live one or many, each life should be lived as though it *is* the only one.

A friend told me she feared that her loved one wouldn't be there to greet her if reincarnation was a possibility. In Bob Olson's book, *Answers About the Afterlife*, he offers this viewpoint on reincarnation. Using a medium, he had conversations with spirit and has come to understand that everyone has an oversoul. Each individual life we live, and the knowledge we gain, is held within that one oversoul. From that perspective, it wouldn't need to be the same me reliving life—it could be another "aspect" of me. It was mind-boggling to think that innumerable me's could all be wrapped up into "one" oversoul that is the all-inclusive me; but it also meant that the energy of the person we knew in physical life would still be there to welcome us home. It's wonderful that we no longer fear "the dead" and are finally collecting and examining information from people who live in a world we know very little about. And since there are no sacred texts or dogma in spiritualism, new information such as this may be presented without trepidation.

I loved the details on life-after-death that Olson so clearly presents in his book, validating many aspects about the after-life that I had discovered while on my own journey. His way of looking at reincarnation also gave me another way to describe the creator: It is the oversoul of all oversouls who divided itself into all facets of creation. Given that interpretation "we are one" can be taken literally. As I discovered on this journey, all things are part of one infinite energy-system.

As I've said before, one of my first major realizations on this journey was that stuff doesn't have any real value. Before that, I might have professed disinterest in stuff, but now I know it. Perhaps this is one reason why we often find spiritual masters living in caves, huts, or other simple settings. Their needs are few—if any. Obviously, I am far from being a spiritual master living in a cave, and that would not be my choice. And yet, it is comforting for me to know that without stuff I would still be okay. Stuff is temporary, and we can lose it in a flash. It is the things we learn, and the love we gave and received that last forever; and that's the valuable stuff we will never leave behind. This reminds me so much of my daughter.

Bre loved simple things and bought a tiny house to live in. She would have loved the "tiny houses" made popular on TV. When Ben and Bre married he felt cramped in her tiny house and wanted to buy a big house. By then they had a big dog which wasn't Bre's idea. Bre tried to talk Ben into a tiny dog, but Ben wanted Liberty— a big dog. Bre had never had a dog before and didn't know what to expect, so she bought a book on dog behavior. *She loved that big dog,* and Max and Molly (her cats) tolerated the intrusion of Liberty.

When she called me to come over and meet her she said, "Look, Mom, I can lie on her and she likes it." She was Bre's personal pillow and went everywhere with her. Now the big house made sense to her, as it would fit a big dog better. One of my last and sweetest memories was going to her home to visit, and finding her in her king-sized bed with Liberty, Max, Molly, and baby Owen. She laughed and said, "You should see us with Ben in here."

I sometimes wondered how different Bre's life would have been had she gotten the Volkswagen bus she dreamed of. To her, that would have been the perfect home to live and travel in. Instead she chose a Subaru and a tiny house, and shortly after that her new dream story with Ben began. As I write, there are words that trigger memories I thought were lost, just as "simple settings" which triggered this one. It's important to write them down as they come to me, so I will never forget them and to help you and Owen know his mother better.

I learned that if I fought against the things happening to me, they lingered on or worsened. If I went with them, they would run their course. Knowing an experience is not permanant, since I can't actually lose anything here, has made going with the flow easier to do. I feel liberated, and I'm not afraid to face life's challenges, whatever they might be. It's not that an experience doesn't occasionally throw me for a momentary loop, but then I remind myself that a purpose will unfold from it eventually. I just have to look for the best way to move through it. My life has become a hopeful adventure since discovering the many unexpected things while on the journey to find Bre.

It is great sorrow or catastrophe that impels us to relook at our life. There is no doubt our values will change, as they did for me. We can choose to be sad and angry for years to come or accept what has happened, then try to find a reason to put one foot in front of the other and keep moving on. This is a speck of time in all eternity, and nothing physical was meant to last forever. We are energy that never ends. That knowledge has enabled me to go on without my Bre. I look forward to the time I will see her again and can discuss the things I've learned with her. I was grateful that Ben came to believe these things as well and was able to move through his pain. Life is so much harder when you don't have this knowledge.

I know there is a power all around me, and running through me, that is abundantly different from the God I had known who was separate from me. It was hard, at first, to wrap my head around a formless and infinite energy-system. I knew how to talk to God as a person but not as an infinite energy-system. Now I know that doesn't matter—just start talking. I convey anything that is on my mind. Sometimes my words are angry as I try to make sense of the circumstances around me. Oftentimes, all I say is, "Help me make the most of my life, and thank you for giving me the opportunity to live a physical life and for this beautiful planet. Thank you for my daughter and for the people I love—and most of all, thank you for your unwavering love of us." I can't tell you when or how it happened, but I began to know the perfectly loving intentions it had for me, and the people I loved. As hard as it is for some to believe, *when you start talking, things begin to happen.*

I don't believe hell can exist in a realm where love is all there is. Hell is the projection of fear, and fear lives and thrives only in the physical world. We exist in two states, energy and physical. Energy doesn't feel pain and has nothing it can lose, but our physical body does, and that creates a lot of fear surrounding death and the tortures of hell.¹ I can't help thinking that man used the fear of hell to manipulate people, but for his own selfish reasons—not God's.

Like most people, I was initially afraid to go beyond what I had been taught over the years, and to look at possibilities that were completely foreign—even blasphemous to some. I asked God to change my course if I was going in the wrong direction to find Bre, and was surprised to find myself being guided even deeper into forbidden territory. No! I don't believe God let Satan lead me. He would never be so cruel, and if Satan exists, he would have no power over God. I was led by a conscious and loving energy that had no insecurities and nothing to fear. *When you know all of creation comes forth from unconditional love, you also know we were not created for the purposes of fear and control. In fact, we were given the free will to choose between good and evil. Compassion will fill the world when we choose love which personifies God, over fear which personifies Satan.*

I wanted to find Bre through anything offering facts. I didn't always find a *measurable* fact, but I found such an abundance of evidence that it became fact for me. I know, with certainty, that we do not die. I am, and always have been, and always will be. We are a part of one energy that is an ever-present reality with limitless compassion. Bre is immersed in this loving energy, and one day I will be sitting by that beautiful lake, dangling my feet in the water beside her and all of the animals she so loved.

CHAPTER 21

CONCLUSION

"Religion clings to an outdated God, atheism clings to an outdated God, science clings to an outdated God, all the while proving the existence of a universal consciousness which appears to be an updated God."

—THE FABRIC OF REALITY: —
THE SCIENCE OF PARALLEL UNIVERSES—
AND IT'S IMPLICATIONS BY DAVID DEUTSCH

So much is said in that one little statement by David Deutsch. If we accepted that update, our world would change dramatically. It was easy for me to rule out a world that evolved through happenstance, especially when I studied the intricacies of the universe, our own biology, and the relationship between consciousness and energy. However, I could understand why there was resistance to seeing what I saw. God could be buried once and for all if creation were just a series of lucky coincidings, and life simply blinked out in the end. It's time for a new mindset because the evidence to support an intelligence beyond us is overwhelming. An update is long overdue.

Religion looks to a biased god who has his chosen people, while science is leading us to an unbiased, loving consciousness who has no chosen people. It needs nothing because it has everything, and it chooses everyone and everything.

When I reflect on this journey and see how it started, I am in awe. I was taught the answers were in the Bible, and when in doubt, I should trust the "learned man's" interpretation. The problem was, there were a lot of "learned men" with different viewpoints, which meant no one knew for certain. Consequently, I was completely unprepared for the devastaing loss of my daughter. I believed I was led to a book written by a medium. I knew very little about mediums, the paranormal, or science. The information I gleaned from reading those books caused me to study the field of energy, known as the quantum world. A door to finding proof of eternal life opened while studying the mysterious world of energy. I knew we are made of atoms, but then I learned atoms are made of particles of energy! Einstein said, "Energy cannot be created or destroyed; it can only be changed from one form to another." Bre's physical body reverted back to its energy form. That was the first of many "aha" moments. I knew I was on the right track, but Bre was more than energy.

When you add consciousness to that equation, it raises another question. It's true that particles of energy are the building blocks of the physical world, but without direction, those particles bounce around in a haphazard sort of way. Bre wasn't an accidental happenstance, she was conscious of her surroundings and was aware of her feelings. I realized that energy and consciousness must exist simultaneously because not much happens without the thoughts created from consciousness. They need each other. Energy + Consciousness = Reality (E+C=R), and I'm having that formula put on a T-shirt to be worn by anyone who knows this is true. Bre's energy walked hand in hand with her consciousness into the next realm—another beautiful "aha" moment.

Understanding connection was a big wakeup call for me. Scientists split a photon in two and sent them in opposite directions. Repeatedly, what one did the other responded to in like manner, it was as though they knew what the other was doing no matter how far apart they were or how much time had passed. Science called this phenomenon entanglement—*"Once connected, always connected."* The Big Bang theory is that all matter originates from one tiny dot of energy that exploded. That one dot of energy became what we call the universe, and everything in it was entangled; so when a change occurs in that fabric of energy, it affects the whole fabric. "Do unto others as you would have them do unto you" takes on a larger meaning when we recognize and treasure our interconnections. As Carlo Rovelli wrote in *Seven Brief Lessons on Physics,* "We thought that we existed as unique beings, a race apart from the family of animals and plants, and discovered that we are decendants of the same parents as every living thing around us. We have great-grandparents in common with butterflies and larches."

I remember that "aha" moment vividly. I was sitting in my chair reading *Journey of the Universe,* when suddenly the curtain opened and I heard the applause. The entire universe, and everything in it, was one big ball of connection! This was when I began to think of God as something very different from what I had been taught. "Energy cannot be created," for me, means that energy has always been, just as the Bible said God had always been. The creator is not separate from us, nor does it have a gender; it is a living and infinite energy-system that extends far beyond our universe and has eternally existed, and the physical world came into existence through the thoughts of that one energy.

Because the ancients did not understand connection, energy, or consciousness, their interpretation of "divine" messages suffered accordingly. Like the Crusaders of old, marching off in the wrong direction, many of us today hold on to that same misdirected

THE DAY MY WORLD STOPPED

mindset. The world we come from and this world are not separate; they are different expressions of the same energy. Communication between the two worlds should therefore be viewed as normal—not paranormal. The degree to which the channeled information is wise and useful depends on the messenger's level of awareness and that of the human who is interpreting it. The creator was never a king on high, holding dominance over his domain and passing out judgments on his "little ones." The physical world was designed in a manner that enables us to choose between good and evil. That cannot happen in a world where fear is nonexistent. Creating a world of love and abundance or one of fear and hate, is a choice we were enabled to make. I believe the creative powers we now know we possess were bequeathed to us through the conscious energy we are made of. We truly are "made in His image." Sadly, the inability to recognize and accept divine consciousness both inside and outside of ourselves prevents us from realizing our full potential.

To the layman, this all sounds otherworldly; scientists too felt like they were in increasingly arcane territory the more they discovered about the world of energy. Nothing was as they had believed it to be, and as unnerving as it was for some of them, religion now appeared to have some truth in it after all. Had the ancients been aware that we cannot be separated from something we are a part of (no matter what rules we break), religions would not have developed in the way they did. We will return to the loving energy that allowed us—and itself—to experience living in a physical world. As Dr. Wayne Dyer said, "Like drops in the ocean, we sprinkle out and then we sprinkle back in again."

The ancients believed the cosmos was the home of the gods, so they looked up. Today, many continue to look upward and ever outward through that same old lens. Much of the science community believes there is "something out there" orchestrating energy, but they have an obligation to find a mathematical formula that proves it. Many believe as I do that consciousness is the orchestrator, and it is the connection between the world of energy and the world of form. It is the answer to the unified theory. Reluctance to accept or even entertain this obvious answer is not so much the daunting math as it is the traditional interpretation of the creator. We need an updated understanding.

As we continue to grow in knowledge and love, the freightening notion of separation would become a thing of the past, and bullying or cruelty in any form would be unthinkable. We would work together to cure disease, end world hunger, and homelessness would cease to exist. Technology and science would flourish and be shared among all nations. Working in warm collaboration, human beings would become what they were meant to be—powerful, compassionate creators.

Science should have evolved in conjunction with religious philosophies, but fear of losing control prevented that from happening, causing many half-truths and all-out falsehoods to take root. Ben and I had a conversation about the possibility of science and religion one day uniting. I believed they would, and he believed there was too much fear on both sides for that to ever happen. I could see his point, but it is indeed slowly happening. Scientific understanding changes daily with each new discovery, and religions have made adjustments in accordance with those discoveries as well. It wasn't so long ago that disease and deformities were attributed to God's punishment or the doing of demons, before germs and genes were discovered. Babies, who die before baptism are no longer condemned or banished to limbo; bastard babies are a thing of the past. The religious community no longer rebukes or kills scientists for their discoveries, such as that Earth is not at the center of the universe, or that it is gravity that holds things in place and not God. Science knows evolution is not a complete story, but until they can weed out old superstions, they will step around anything that resembles a god. The Bible says the soul is eternal and science says energy is eternal. How we view that revelation usually hinges on one's religious or scientific orientation—I choose both. When the body is done, our energy transforms and we return to the realm of eternal energy, where unconditional love abounds. Both religion and science realize they don't have all of the answers, but together they could sort through fact and fiction to see the answers have been there all along.

Ben and I may not see them coming together in our lifetime. In fact, transformation of any kind is hard to see when you're in the middle of it. Many scientists acknowledge the existence of an intelligence far exceeding our own. Sermons are changing their focus from fire and brimstone to unity and compassion, with more hopeful and helpful advice. *The Power of I Am* by Joel Osteen, the pastor of Lakewood Church, in Houston, comes to mind. As time marches on, science and religion will resolve their differences and finally be able to see the beautiful complementarity of it all.

Before I leave you, let me restate what I have found to be highly probable:

- Earthly experiences happen simply for the purpose of absorbing knowledge, and they are never permanent even when it seems as though some of them are.

- I have come to believe that we venture back into the physical realm from time to time to experience all that this world has to offer. Our ethereal life is unending, so living other physical lives under different circumstances makes sense to me.

- The creator is not a mythical being of magical or mystical powers. The One Presence that has been eternally "out there" (and in here) is an infinite and loving energy-system.

- We can consciously and unconsciously create with our thoughts, utilizing the same reservoir of energy that all things are a part of. In the future even children will know how to use this ability responsibly.

- Love and trust are the most important feelings to have when creating our vision—the same components necessary for prayers to be answered. Many nuggets of wisdom are buried in ancient texts, and must be reviewed with an updated, scientific mindset.

- Fear is a necessary dynamic in the physical world for two basic reasons. It gives us the ability to choose between good and evil thus giving us an ever increasing awareness. It causes glands to produce adrenaline, providing us the power to run from impending danger, or stick around and fight.

I love the United States and am grateful to be living in a country where free speech and other civil liberties are guarenteed. Sadly, many use fear to control, demean, and manipulate, which creates prejudice, anger, and hate. As I once heard said, "How can you burn the flag of a country that allows you the freedom to burn it in the first place?" In many countries you would be jailed or worse for protesting, and I would be too afraid to write a book that encourages independent thought and action. Think of the lives lost, and the works of literary and artistic beauty that have been destroyed over the years because of fear. It goes without saying that the opposite of love is fear.

Many beautiful people are on their own search, and recommend books to me which I make a point of reading. *Start the Conversation* by Ganga Stone was recommended to me by Jennifer Sasseen, a reporter who wrote a business feature on me and the salon. I chose to gift my successful company to one of my employees in 2016. That was inconceivable to many people, including my accountant. My goals changed after losing Bre, and my focus was on finding her and then helping others see what I saw. I didn't want to sell BreCyn to a stranger. I loved the people I worked with as they became the family that took care of me and the salon during my darkest hours, when it was my job to take care of them. I continued to work two days a week for another four years, allowing me to stay in contact with them and my wonderful clients for just a little longer. Jennifer had read my first book and thought I might find Ganga's book interesting.

I self-published *When You Think About It* in 2015 for Owen, family, and friends. I was encouraged to extend the journey further, going deeper into science and the mystery of it all. I did that in this book and included some of the first book in it, giving you the full journey. I suppose my own journey will never end, as I owe it to Bre and all of us to stay current with the latest findings.

I had lost all faith in God when I lost Bre. Where was He when I needed Him, and where was He when Bre needed Him? I desperately prayed He would help me find someone who could tell me what was happening to my daughter. He didn't hear me. On and off throughout Bre's life, she suffered from disappointment and depression but controlled it with exercise and healthy eating. When Ben was in Iraq her blood pressure skyrocketed, and the military doctor put her on an antidepressant to calm her anxiety. It worked well, so he recommended she stay on it. In time the side effects began, and she asked another doctor to help wean her off of it. He believed the drug was a good one, so he upped her dose and gave her more pills to counteract the side effects. I don't think the doctor knew they were side effects of that drug. Again, she asked him to take her off of the antidepressant when she became pregnant, but he told her not to change anything while pregnant.

After Owen was born, hormones kicked in and things worsened. By the time I found a psychiatrist who understood this drug and what was happening to my now desperate daughter, it was too late. He understood the dangers of the antidepressant she was taking and put her on another drug to help her through the withdrawal. She was already on five drugs. She didn't want to stay in the hospital and leave her baby at home, so he told her to have her doctor monitor this. She had lost faith in doctors, so she didn't ask for the help she should have. The withdrawal was unmerciful, and she decided to help herself by adding an unprescribed drug to the already extensive medications. She wanted to feel normal, and she had already suffered for too long. Accidental overdose was the cause of my beautiful daughter's death. I was shocked and angry at the doctors, the drug companies, myself, and God. How could this have happened to my amazing Bre? It can happen to anyone!

It has been a long walk down that dark alley I entered so long ago, but I found Bre at the end of it, and I learned more than I expected along the way. I have no doubt that I was meant to find the essential story of who and what we are and what the creator is. I believe we leave when we finish what we came here to do, but I still have a difficult time accepting that Bre was done. How we live and how we leave have a purpose that is often hard to see. We come to teach, learn, and assist; and it helps me to know Bre's life never ended.

People often ask how Bre died, and I simply say it was a complication from the medicine she was taking. I was deeply saddened by her senseless death and didn't want to go into detail. I sometimes feel that Bre had nothing to learn but had come to teach the people who loved her. Having read that people plan the basics of their life before they incarnate, I believed she and Owen had this conversation before he came. I am hopeful that you learned something by knowing how she lived—and how she left. All of us are surrounded by an ocean of loving energy, and Bre's energy is all around us. She never really left.

I have decided that this will be the year I bring home all of the Christmas decorations from the cabin. Owen, Jo, and Samantha made ornaments for me in 2016, which made me think of starting a memory tree. I gave ornaments to Bre throughout her life, and now Ben has those. Bre and I made our decorations for the cabin—paper chains and strings of popcorn. Every year we collected more things to add to it. We spent many holidays up there, but never after she left. It was too painful for me, and for Ben.

Bre's wedding theme was a winter wonderland, and I saved those decorations. She wanted to use them to decorate her home for Christmas one day. This year, I will incorporate them in my Christmas tree. The tree will be one of happy memories, both from here and from the cabin. I'm not sure how much longer I will keep the cabin, but I will always have the memories.

I have an update for the last paragraph, and it's a good one. After twelve years, Ben finally felt ready to return to the cabin and asked if we could spend Christmas there this year (2017). I didn't think that would ever happen. It was magical! I put up the tree with all of the cabin decorations, hung stockings, and put presents under the tree. The children played in the snow all day, and we built gingerbread houses in the evening. Then on the way home, a very strange thing happened. Les had put the radio on mute because the reception on the mountain was bad. Then suddenly the radio popped on, and the words, Les's iPod, appeared on the screen. Since that had not happened before and Les had *never* owned an iPod, we were stunned! I suggested we pull over and listen to the song that was playing. The lyrics were something like this: "All I thought I had lost, I have back again—it's a miracle." I think I will keep our Christmas tree at the cabin a little longer.

It's been many years since she left, and I now see that life didn't actually stop when I felt it did. Every day I am grateful for the experience of this difficult life. Owen now has two sisters and together, with their dad, they will support each other throughout their lives. Ben once told me, "When something bad happens, you can't be sure it is the only bad thing that will happen. They will continue to happen, and you have to deal with it." He has certainly seen his share, and so have his children.

I hope that, one day, this book will give Owen a sense of who and where his mom is and that Josephine and Samantha will know the same of their mom—the only mother Owen ever knew. I also aspired to give all of you a true sense of who and what God is. His love for us is unconditional and eternal. We chose to live a very short physical life with its many challenges; and the wisdom we gain is the purpose. Make mindful choices and appreciate all challenges. Knowing that nothing here is forever—except us—makes the hard times less frightening. He gave us the greatest gift of all when He infused us with His consciousness, and we are learning how to use it. He has always been, and will ever be, our constant and loving companion.

ACKNOWLEDGMENTS

To bring a book to publication is a long journey, and one I couldn't do without the support and encouragement of many people.

I first want to thank my daughter, Breana. I know you've been by my side throughout this whole journey. Secondly, if it weren't for my determination to give her son, Owen, the proof he would meet his mother one day, I would never have written any books. Because of the love I share with these two very important people, I had the stamina to do the research and bring that information forward into the light.

Thank you, Les, my long-time friend and supporter, for all of your patience. Even though you would role you eyes from time to time at what I was doing, your encouragement never wavered. Thank you, Lorrie Larsen, for writing the foreward in this book and for cheering me on through the years; and to Debra Farris, for your many ideas and for encouraging me to make a coffee table book out of my "Little Nuggets of Thought." I'm looking forward to that project. I can never thank my sister, Deb Kocher, enough, for the time you've spent in being my beta reader, and for your technical abilities that you continually give to this endeavor. And thank you to all of your friends, who let me practice my first speech on them.

Most importantly, I must thank my mother and father, who gave me their wisdom and the best childhood anyone could have. Thank you to Owen's father, Ben Langan, for standing beside me throughout this heartbreaking journey; Owen's little sisters, Josephine and Samantha, for letting me be another grandmother in your lives; and to all of Breana's friends, who still stay in touch with me; my brother, Garth Allen Mitchell, for your loving prayers; Kate Buckley, for your constant friendship and encouragement; Gene and Wendy Goosman (Jesse and Jolene) for the loving role you each played in mine and Breana's life; Chuck and Ruthie Lee, who let me ramble on about my research, especially, over a glass of wine. Please know how special all of you are to me.

It takes a team! Thank you to my friend, Caryl Conley, for editing all of the support materials in this book. Thank you, Jo-Ann Langseth, for editing both of my books. You make me sound more intelligent than I am. Thank you, Wordzworth Publishing for the beautiful layout and publishing of this book. Thank you, Mark Malastesta, for making this book better, and teaching me how to build a platform of recognition, and encouraging me to publish no matter what obstacles I might face. Thank you, Steve Harrison and group, for providing Jack Canfield a copy of both of my books. He coined me a scout, and the interview with him was an amazing experience! Your follow-up phone calls and support afterward, proves how dedicated you and your team are at helping people achieve their goals. Lastly, thank you, Sibyl Perkins, for designing my beautiful website that every author must have.

I have so many people to thank, I can't list them all. Please know that I didn't forget you, and I want you to know that. I appreciate all of you!

SYNOPSIS

After her daughter passed, the author was lost in grief and wondered if there was any hope of seeing her again. She had lost faith in the Bible long before and questioned if God even exists. However, not knowing where else to turn, she threw her hands in the air and said, "Where is my Breana?" (That's all it took), and she found herself being led on an unexpected and extraordinary journey.

The first leg of the author's journey was the surprising discovery of a book written by a medium that belonged to her daughter. It had two markers in it, one under CHILDREN and the other under LOSS. She instinctively knew she was meant to find that book and began reading other books on the topic of "life after death." She dove into near-death experiences and past life memories—people who claimed to have first-hand knowledge of another realm. Insights from those books led her to energy, and the hard work began.

She wanted to understand what the quantum world of energy is. That led her to the mystery of consciousness and the enigma of God. From there, she studied the physical body's biology in relationship to the energy from which it originates. Looking at evolution vs. creation caused the author to compare creation stories from different religions, along with their versions of heaven and hell. Every path she walked led her to another until she had an abundance of evidence proving not only that we are eternal, but that we are beloved and powerful beings on a mission of discoveries through living a physical life.

Cynthia didn't want people to suffer the way she did. In writing *The Day My World Stopped*, she hopes to remove the many reasons people fear death and to provide the overwhelming scientific evidence substantiating that life is eternal. In addition, she shares the answers she found regarding who and what we really are, why we are here, and where we go when we leave the physical world behind.

Author Biography

Moving through the highs and lows of life, Cynthia had become a mother, hairdresser, and business owner. Life seemed to have a rhythm until, on April 30, 2006, she was plunged into a low from which she believed she would never emerge. She lost her only child, Breana. From that moment on, her mission in life was to find proof of eternal life. After years of study, she felt ready and inspired to share what she had learned with those who suffer from the pain and fear surrounding the loss of a loved one.

Recognizing the commitment involved with writing, publishing, and promulgating a book, Cynthia knew a change would have to be made. In 2016, she chose to gift her successful business to an employee whom she believed would honor the integrity of the salon, its staff, and its many clients. Her "place of business" is now her home in Everett, Washington, where she continues to be devoted to the mission she began so long ago and sharing her findings with others who are looking for an answer to: What happens when we die?

www.cynthiamitchell.com
cyndi@cynthiamitchell.com

Also by this Author
"When You think About It"
Published in 2015,
by Wordzworth Publishing

269

REFERENCES

This is a list of the books I have read over the years. I am sorry, but there are some I have forgotten. I wasn't planning to write a book when I started this research, I was only trying to survive. They are the beliefs of the authors and not necessarily my own. I hoped to gather information from them that would prove life is eternal, and I would see Breana again. Faith simply wasn't enough.

The things you read, hear, see, and experience throughout your life form your beliefs. One thing I have learned in my life is nothing is certain, not even your beliefs. They are always subject to change. New discoveries in science happen every day through new insights into the world of energy. There will never be THE END to discovery.

James Redfield—Celestine Prophecy
   the connection between all things in story form

Gregg Braden—The God Code
   is God coded into our DNA

Hazel Courteney—Divine Intervention
   a near-death experience leaving her with paranormal abilities

Sonya Choquette—Diary of a Psychic

Jan Frazier—When Fear Fall Away
   the release of fear, letting go and letting God

Gary Swartz Ph.D.—The G.O.D. Experiments
   proving God through science

Damien Broderick—Outside the Gates of Science
  is there a connection between quantum theory and paranormal

Dr. Jane Greer—The Afterlife Connection
  communicating with departed loved ones

Brian L. Weiss M.D.—Many Lives Many Masters
  a psychiatrist's experiences with past life patients through
  hypnosis

Betty J. Eadie—Embraced by the Light
  a near-death experience

Robert Brown—We Are Eternal
  medium

Allan L. Botkin Psy.D.—After Death Communication
  a psychiatrist's experience with visitations during patient
  therapy

Concetta Bertoldi—Do Dead People Watch You Shower
  medium

Sylvia Browne—Mother God
  the feminine side to God

Eckhart Tolle—A New Earth
  our attachment to ego and how to break free

Lee Carroll and Jan Tober—Indigo Children
  are these children the beginning of the next human evolution

Sylvia Browne—The Mystical Life of Jesus
  a conspiracy theory of whether Jesus died on the cross

Michael Newton Ph.D.—Destiny of Souls
  life between life using hypnosis

Sylvia Browne—Book of Angels
  the description of angels through her spirit guide

Lynne McTaggart—"The Field
    scientific study of our interconnection through Zero Point
    Field (the energy around each cell)

Sylvia Browne—Astrology Through a Psychics Eyes

Sylvia Browne—Book of Dreams

Bill & Judy Guggenheim—Hello From Heaven
    after-death communication and experiences

Mary T Browne—Life After Death
    psychic view of where we go when we die

Char Margolis—Questions From Earth, Answers From Heaven
    psychic intuitive talks of life, death, and beyond

Judith Orliff M.D.—Second Sight psychiatrist
    and intuitive speaks of discovering your own intuitive gift

Blair Underwood—Before I Got Here interviews with children

Sylvia Browne—Contacting Your Spirit Guide
    everyone has a guide and how to hear them

SQuire Rushnell—When God Winks
    an executive with ABC who led Good Morning America to
    number one and his view of coincidence or synchronicity

Edited by Kent Nerburn—The Wisdom of the Native American
    Native American insights

Kenneth Ring Ph. D.—Lessons From the Light
    what we learn from near-death experiences

Jim B. Tucker M.D.—Life Before Life
    children's memories of previous lives

Sylvia Browne—Secret Societies

Leslie M. Lecron—Self Hypnosis

Sanaya Roman & Duane Packer Ph.D.—Opening To Channel
  connecting with your guide

Chris Dufresne—My Life With Sylvia Browne
  her son's story

Gary Zukav—The Seat of the Soul
  becoming connected to your spirit who guides you,
  learning to pray, and reincarnation

Barbara Marx Hubbard—Conscious Evolution
  the evolutionary path we are on

Carolyn Myss—Entering The Castle
  a journey into your soul, your true story

Dianne Arcangel—Afterlife Encounters
  study of a hospice worker on visitations

Don Piper—90 Minutes in Heaven
  his near-death experience

Sylvia Browne—Conversations With the Other Side

Carolyn Myss—Sacred Contracts
  discovering your purpose and divine potential

Dan Millman—The Life You Were Born to Live

Joseph Campbell—Power of the Myth
  study of myths and how they tie into religion

Sylvia Browne—Secrets and Mysteries of the World

Gordon Smith—The Unbelievable Truth medium

Sylvia Browne—The Nature of Good and Evil

Sylvia Browne—Souls Perfection

Sylvia Browne—God Creation and Tools For Life

Sylvia Browne—Insight

Sylvia Browne—Phenomenon

Sylvia Browne—If You Could See What I See

Sylvia Browne—The Other Side and Back
   The book I was led to read and what started this journey.
   There were two markers in this book, one in children and the
   other in LOSS. Coincidence?

John Edwards—"After Life"
   medium

Bruce Lipton Ph.D.—The Biology of Belief
   cellular biologist explains how cells communicate and how
   our thoughts control life

Allison DuBois—We Are Their Heaven
   why the dead never leave us

Sylvia Browne—Psychic Children

John Edwards—Crossing Over
   medium

Neale Donald Walsch—Conversations With God
   he wrote a series of these books,
   they are his dialogues with God

OSHO—The Book of Understanding
   question everything you've been taught to believe

Gary E. Swartz Ph.D.—The Afterlife Experiments
   the research of an agnostic into the proof of God
   and his amazing experience

P.M.H. Atwater, L.H.D.—Beyond the Indigo Children
   the new generation of children being born

Joel Martin & Patricia Romanowski—We Don't Die
   interviews with George Anderson, a psychic medium

Gordon Smith—Spirit Messenger"
   a barber/hairdresser by profession,
   tells of his experience as a medium

Allison DuBois—Don't Kiss Them Goodbye
   her story as a medium, she is also the person
   who inspired the NBC series "Medium"

Janis Amatuzio M.D.—Beyond Knowing
   a forensic pathologist on the conversations
   she had with family members of the deceased

Sylvia Browne—Lesson for Life

SQuire Rushnell—When God Winks at You
   there are no coincidences

Rhonda Byrne—The Secret
   the universe brings what you believe you already have

Sylvia Browne—Blessings from the Other Side

Sylvia Browne—Father God
   masculine side of God

Meg Blackburn Losey—Children of the Now
   are they misunderstood children of the future

Sylvia Browne—Adventures of a Psychic

Sylvia Browne—Prophecy

Colette Baron-Reid—Remember the Future
   discovering and developing you own intuitive gift

Sylvia Browne—Visits from the Afterlife

Lee Strobel—The Case for Christ
   a detective gathers evidence for Christ

James Van Praagh—Heaven and Earth

Echo Bodine—The Gift
  learn to recognize your psychic gift

Sinclair Browning—Feathers Brush My Heart
  stories of mothers connecting to their daughters after death

Jerry Sittser—A Grace Disguised
  his personal struggle to find light in all the darkness after
  losing his mother, daughter and wife in auto accident

Kathy Cordova—Let Go Let Miracles Happen:
  The Art of Spiritual Surrender
  a three-step process to experience the peace of surrender in
  any situation-learn to swim with the current of life

Arron Mitchell—Death of an Ordinary Life
  a mystery novel of a spiritual journey to forgiveness-
  Aaron is a gifted psychologist and also my nephew

Marianne Williamson—The Age of Miracles
  a spiritual look at aging gracefully

Kim Sheridan—Animals and the Afterlife
  If you love and respect animals, as I do,
  this is an uplifting book to read.

Neale Walsch—Happier Than God

Elizabeth Gilbert—Eat Pray Love
  finding herself and God

Sylvia Browne—End of Days
  future predictions

Michael Books—13 Things That Don't Make Sense
  scientific mysteries

Alberto Villoldo Ph.D.—Mending the Past and
  Healing the Future With Soul Retrieval
  a medical anthropologist who came to be a shaman and why

Byron Katie—Loving What Is
   living without fear and the four questions to ask yourself

Bill Bryson—A Short History of Nearly Everything

Dan Millman—The Laws of the Spirit
   bullet point laws of spirit

Dan Millman—Wisdom of the Peaceful Warrior,
   companion to Way of the Peaceful Warrior
   spiritual insights into living a peaceful life in story form

Rosemary Brown—Immortal by My Side
   medium

Max Lucado—Fearless
   Christian view of sin

Tara Singh—Nothing Real Can Be Threatened
   a philosophy

Bruce Lipton Ph.D. and Steve Bhaerman—Spontaneous
   Evolution our positive future based in science
   and with his usual humor

Deepak Chopra—How to Know God

Colin Wilson—Afterlife
   a journalist documents evidence of another life after death

Paulo Coelho—The Alchemist
   a novel of the treasure within

Betty Eadie—Embraced by the Light
   an afterlife experience

Sylvia Browne—Accepting the Psychic Torch

Brian Greene—The Elegant Universe
   how the universe and life began from
   what science knows today

Trudy Harris RN—Glimpses of Heaven: True Stories of Hope and Peace at the End of Life's Journey

Joan Wester Anderson—Guardian Angels: True Stories of Answered Prayer

Todd Burpo & family—Heaven is for Real: A Little Boy's Astounding Story of His Trip to Heaven near-death experience

Mary Evelyn Tucker—Journey of the Universe how we fit into the 14-billion-year history of the universe, weaving science and wisdom of the ages

James Van Praagh—Looking Beyond medium

James Van Praagh—Unfinished Business medium

Joan Wester Anderson—Where Miracles Happen stories of modern-day miracles and how God still makes himself known to us today

Michael Singer—The Untethered Soul the voice in your head who continually talks to you should be given a name and a hat to wear

Julia Assante Ph.D., M.D. and Larry Dossey—The Last Frontier: Exploring the Afterlife and Transforming Our Fear of Death an anthropologist presents evidence of life after death

Eben Alexander III M.D.—Proof of Heaven an unbelieving neurosurgeon has a near-death experience which changes him forever

Maggie Callanan and Pat Kelley—Final Gifts experiences of hospice nurses

Joel S. Goldsmith—The Thunder of Silence
being one with God-the hidden meaning of
"sermon on the mount"

Elsa Barker—Letters from the Afterlife
medium

Esther and Jerry Hicks—The Vortex
the law of attraction

Esther and Jerry Hicks—The Astonishing Power of Emotion
the role emotion plays in the laws of attraction

Esther and Jerry Hicks—Ask and It is Given

Fred A. Wolf—Taking the Quantum Leap: The New Physics
for Nonscientists traces the history of physics and our
relationship to the cosmos

Fred A. Wolf—Dr. Quantum's Little Book of Big Ideas
where science meets spirit

Nick Herbert—Quantum Reality: Beyond the New Physics
an introduction to physics-the scientific and philosophical
controversy

Sandra Anne Taylor—Quantum Success:
The Astounding Science of Wealth
a formula for success and an abundant life

Tara Singh—Nothing Real Can Be Threatened:
Exploring a Course in Miracles
a philosophy

Larry Dossey M.D.—Recovering the Soul
how to pray, etc. "thy will be done"-
quantum physics-non-local and local realities

Steve Volk—Fringe-ology: How I Tried to Explain Away the
Unexplainable-And Couldn't
a journalist's journey into the unknown

Anthony Borgia—"Life in the World Unseen"
medium who claims to channel Monsignor
Robert Hugh Benson speaking from the afterlife

Fred Alan Wolf—Mind Into Matter:
A New Alchemy of Science and Spirit
thought provoking look at consciousness

Susan Blackmore—Dying to Live
a near-death experience who later became a skeptic

Ernest Holmes—The Hidden Power of the Bible
a deeper look at scripture through a scientific mind

Gregg Braden—The Divine Matrix
an aerospace computer systems designer and
geologist tell of our connection and role we
have in the quantum stuff that rules us.

Brian Weiss M.D.—Only Love is Real
Pastlife regression

Louise Hay—You Can Heal Your Life
the mental patterns that create physical illness

Lynne McTaggart—The Intention Experiment
the effect your thoughts have on things

Neale Walsch—Home With God
a conversation with God

Tom Brown, Jr.—The Quest
a man's search for peace and insight

Dan Millman—The Journey of Socrates
a novel in spiritual advice

John Edwards—After Life
 medium

Jeff Guidry—An Eagle Named Freedom
 a beautiful story of love and healing

Dan Millman—Sacred Journey of the Peaceful Warrior
 spiritual novel of peace and understanding

Wm. Paul Young—The Shack
 a welcome look at God and eternity written in story form

John Lerma M.D.—Into the Light
 stories of extraordinary experiences by a hospice doctor

Joseph McMoneagle—Memoirs of a Psychic Spy
 the life of a remote viewer and his work
 with the U.S. government

Caroline Myss Ph.D.—The Creation of Health
 the effect emotion has on health

Randy Alcorn—Heaven
 a biblical evaluation of Heaven with the use of scripture

Alan Cohen—Handle With Prayer
 how to pray

Alan Cohen—Wisdom of the Heart
 insights

Douglas Ell—Counting to God
 proof of God from an MIT mathematician and lawyer

Tobin Hart Ph.D.—The Secret Spiritual World of Children

Gerald G. Jampolsky, MD—Love is Letting Go of Fear

Pam Grout—E Squared
 experiments proving power of thought

Patricia Pears—Opening Heaven's Door
   stories of life, death and what comes after

Theresa Caputo—There's More to Life Than This
   medium

Emanuel Swedenborg—A Swedenborg Sampler
   theologian and philosopher 1688-1772

Hope R. Reynolds—What Is Heaven

April Crawford—In The Afterlife

Pamela Heath and Jon Klimo—Handbook to the Afterlife

Dennis and Nolene Prince—-Nine Days In Heaven
   a rewrite of the original book Scenes Beyond The Grave

Diana Stuart—Journey To The Other Side
   a near-death experience

Rod Pennington and Jeffery A. Martin—The Fourth Awakening
   mystery novel with an interesting analogy
   of man's evolution in Chapter 15

Diana E. Ruiz—Heal Your Life With Water
   Self-worth

Dr. Wayne W. Dyer—Your Erroneous Zones
   the power you have to choose how you feel

Dr. Wayne W. Dyer—The Power of Intention

Dr. Mary C. Neal—To Heaven and Back: A Doctor's
   Extraordinary Account of Her Death,
   Heaven, Angels, and Life

Ed Gaulden—"Heaven Is: A Visit to Heaven"

Dr. Eben Alexander—The Map of Heaven: How Science,
   Religion, and Ordinary People are Proving the Afterlife

Lorilee Craker and Marvin Besteman—My Journey To Heaven and How It Changed My life

Andrea and Bruce Leininger—The Reincarnation of a World War II Fighter Pilot

David Deutsch—The Fabric of Reality: Parallel Universes and Its Implications

Janis Heaphy Durham—The Hand on the Mirror: A True Story of Life Beyond Death

Francis Collins—The Language of God:
A Scientist Presents Evidence for Belief
bridging the gap between science and God

Paul Ferrini—Love Without Conditions

Dr. Wayne Dyer—Memories of Heaven
children interviews

Carole J. Morton—Entering Your Own Heart
self-healing

John Assaraf—The Answer
Grow Any Business, Achieve Financial Success,
and Live an Extraordinary Life

Duncan Maclean—Conscious Universe
a fictitious love story that covers thousands of years

Max Velmans—Understanding Consciousness

Deepak Chopra—The Future of God

Amit Goswami, Ph.D.—The Quantum Doctor

Sam Kean—The Disappearing Spoon
understanding chemistry

Richard Feynman—Six Easy Pieces
physicist and professor

Larry Dossey, Jean Houston, and Ervin Laszlo—What is Consciousness

Matthew McKay Ph.D.—Seeking Jordan:
How I Learned about Death and the Invisible Universe communication through remote writing with his son

Richard Feynman—Surely Your Joking, Mr. Feynman
a physicist and professor

Steve McIntosh—The Presence of the Infinite: The Spiritual Experience of Beauty, Truth, and Goodness

Paul Kalanithi—When Breath Becomes Air
an auto-biography of a neurosurgeon diagnosed with stage IV lung cancer and his search for the meaning of life.

John Holland—The Spirit Whisperer: Chronicles of a Medium

Patrick Mathews—Forever With You: Inspiring Messages of Healing and Wisdom from your Loved Ones in the Afterlife

Sam Harris—Waking Up: A Guide to Spirituality Without Religion

Don Miguel Ruiz—The Four Agreements: A Practical Guide to Personal Freedom

Patrick and Kathleen Matthews—Everlasting Love: Finding Comfort Through Communication with Your Beloved Spirit

Helen Greaves—Testimony of Light: An Extraordinary Message of Life After Death

Julia Assante Ph.D.—The Last Frontier: Exploring the Afterlife and Transforming Our Fear of Death

Maggie Callanan and Patricia Kelley—Final Gifts: Understanding Special Awareness

Gabrielle Bernstein—The Universe Has Your Back

Gregg Braden—The Isaiah Effect
the lost science of prayer

John Holland—Bridging Two Realms
medium

Wm. Paul Young—Lies We Believe About God

Cynthia Sue Larson—Quantum Jumps
we live in an interconnected holographic multi-universe

Mary R. and H. Ronald Hulnick, Ph. D.'s—
Remembering the Light
soul centered living

Kim Russo—The Happy Medium

Jeffrey A. Marks—The Afterlife Interviews (volume I and II)
a medium asked 52 questions of spirit

Bob Olson—Answers About the Afterlife
A private investigator's 15 year research

Gregg Braden—Human by Design
evolution and the energy of the heart

Joe Dispenza—Becoming Supernatural
how to use the power within us

Lynne McTaggart—The Power of Eight
how to form groups of intention to
create change and heal our bodies

Mike Dooley—Leveraging the Universe
7 steps to engaging the universe

Anita Moorjani—What If This Is Heaven
How cultural myths prevent us from
experiencing Heaven on Earth
A near-death experience

Whitley and Anne Strieber—The Afterlife Revolution
    an after-death communication

Joe Dispenza—Evolve Your Brain
    how the brain works and how to change it

Michael A. Singer—The Surrender Experiment
    personal journey of letting go

Laura Lynne Jackson—Signs: The Secret Language of the
    Universe

Larry Dossey, M.D.—One Mind
    one mind, one consciousness, and why it matters

CPSIA information can be obtained
at www.ICGtesting.com
Printed in the USA
FSHW022121211020
74992FS